"The lens of kinship with refugees that Mark and Luke G
to be revolutionary. This book will change and deepe
biblical ethic for welcoming refugees, and I highly recommend it."
Jarrod McKenna, host of the *InVerse Podcast* and co-initiator of the #LoveMakesAWay
movement

"This volume offers a unique synthesis of biblical theology, political science, and missional practice. In the face of the 'wicked problems' of forced migration, the maintenance of academic boundaries is manifestly unhelpful, but rarely have we seen such a detailed integration of all the key issues. The Glanville brothers offer us an inspiring model of both intellectual and practical engagement, and their book will become essential reading for all who are concerned with the plight of refugees and asylum seekers in an age of displacement."
Mark G. Brett, Whitley College, author of *Political Trauma and Healing: Biblical Ethics for a Postcolonial World*

"What would it mean if, rather than just providing support and protection for people experiencing displacement, we actually lived life with them? In this important book, Mark and Luke Glanville provide an answer to this question through the biblical concept of kinship. Building on existing work in political theory, theology of hospitality, and our responses to people on the move, Glanville and Glanville suggest that the Scriptures call us to enfold displaced people as kindred, in relationships where both the host and the hosted bless and receive blessing. This framework has the potential to radically disrupt existing approaches to refugees and protection in both scholarship and practice, as they demonstrate through their engagement with key biblical texts and day-to-day institutions and processes. It's a radical disruption that is desperately needed in these dark and challenging times for the politics of migration and politics in general."
Erin Wilson, associate professor of politics and religion at the University of Groningen

"*Refuge Reimagined* provokes urgent conversation on the importance of responding to and welcoming refugees like family. Glanville and Glanville summon Christians to welcome those forcibly displaced through the face-to-face recognition that they are, in fact, our global brothers and sisters and must be welcomed as such. *Refuge Reimagined* powerfully reminds us that when we embrace the opportunity to welcome the most vulnerable and uphold their dignity, we discover the fullness of our being in God. The book is both a powerhouse of sound biblical exegesis and a perceptive modern-day analysis that compassionately and rightly calls us to listen to God and learn from our biblical ancestors and contemporary practitioners. It inspires reflection on our base impulses that too easily lead to inaction or polarized entrenchment, positions our imaginations and communities for welcome, and prompts action on the profound truth that in the end, refugees are, indeed, the you and me of another place and family."
Loren Balisky, cofounder of the Kinbrace Community Society

MARK R. GLANVILLE

and LUKE GLANVILLE

REFUGE

REIMAGINED

BIBLICAL KINSHIP
IN GLOBAL POLITICS

Foreword by MATTHEW SOERENS

IVP
Academic

An imprint of InterVarsity Press
Downers Grove, Illinois

InterVarsity Press
P.O. Box 1400, Downers Grove, IL 60515-1426
ivpress.com
email@ivpress.com

InterVarsity Press® is the book-publishing division of InterVarsity Christian Fellowship/USA®, a movement of students and faculty active on campus at hundreds of universities, colleges, and schools of nursing in the United States of America, and a member movement of the International Fellowship of Evangelical Students. For information about local and regional activities, visit intervarsity.org.

Cover design and image composite: David Fassett
Interior design: Daniel van Loon
Images: gold textured background: © Katsumi Murouchi / Moment Collection / Getty Images
  cardstock texture: © Zakharova_Natalia / iStock / Getty Images Plus
  grey bird wing: © Grafissimo / E+ / Getty Images
  illustration of the earth from space: © SCIEPRO/SCIENCE PHOTO LIBRARY / Getty Images

ISBN 978-0-8308-5381-6 (print)
ISBN 978-0-8308-5382-3 (digital)

Printed in the United States of America ∞

InterVarsity Press is committed to ecological stewardship and to the conservation of natural resources in all our operations. This book was printed using sustainably sourced paper.

Library of Congress Cataloging-in-Publication Data
A catalog record for this book is available from the Library of Congress.

| P | 25 | 24 | 23 | 22 | 21 | 20 | 19 | 18 | 17 | 16 | 15 | 14 | 13 | 12 | 11 | 10 | 9 | 8 | 7 | 6 | 5 | 4 | 3 | 2 |
| Y | 41 | 40 | 39 | 38 | 37 | 36 | 35 | 34 | 33 | 32 | 31 | 30 | 29 | 28 | 27 | 26 | 25 | 24 | 23 | 22 | 21 |

For Mum

CONTENTS

FOREWORD

MATTHEW SOERENS

HOSPITALITY IS A MISUNDERSTOOD VIRTUE. At least in contemporary English, we tend to speak of hospitality as having friends over for a particularly extravagant meal, or making sure a guest room is clean for visiting relatives. Others might think of hospitality primarily in the context of an *industry*: hotels, restaurants, cruise ships and theme parks.

But when the Apostle Paul commands the people of God to "practice hospitality" (Rom 12:13) and insists that leaders in the church must be "hospitable" (1 Tim 3:2, Titus 1:8), he was not talking about showing attentiveness to one's friends, family or customers, but rather to *strangers*. *Philoxenia*—literally, the love of strangers—is precisely the opposite of xenophobia, the fear of strangers.

So it is entirely appropriate that Christians of various traditions (including myself) have applied the various biblical commands to "welcome the stranger" to contemporary debates around refugees and immigration.

Hospitality is certainly an important first step. But as theologian Soong-Chan Rah observes, "We need to move from hostility, to hospitality, and then to household . . . to becoming family." When we welcome strangers well, they do not remain strangers: we quickly recognize them as neighbors and ultimately embrace them as a part of *us*.

Christians—especially those of us who do not share Jesus' Jewish ancestry—have a greater reason than anyone to embrace others as a part of our family. Ephesians 2 describes how Gentile believers were once "separate from Christ, excluded from citizenship in Israel and foreigners to the covenants of the promise, without hope and without God in the world" (Eph 2:12). But through Christ's death and resurrection, we have been naturalized into God's kingdom and adopted into his family: "fellow citizens with God's people and also members of his household" (Eph 2:19). Having been sanctified by God's grace, Jesus "is not ashamed to call [us] brothers and sisters" (Heb 2:11).

Having been welcomed in by God's grace, we are called to welcome others—not merely as guests but as *family*.

Indeed, as Mark and Luke Glanville argue persuasively, that has been God's design throughout the Scriptures, from the Pentateuch—where Yahweh instructs his people to integrate the vulnerable stranger in vivid detail—to the Gospels, where Jesus consistently cares for those on the margins of society and explicitly redefines family to include those beyond those sharing a biological connection.

Interwoven throughout this biblical exegesis are practical, contemporary examples of the church in various parts of the world embracing refugees and other immigrants as kin. Many of these stories come from the community of Kinbrace in Vancouver, where for decades Canadian Christians have been welcoming refugee claimants (what Americans would call asylum seekers) and providing housing, practical support and—most importantly—love.

From there, Mark and Luke ask how these biblical principles could and should be applied not just to individuals or congregations but to states, building a case for public policies that integrate a much greater number of refugees. In the midst of a season when my country, the United States, has dramatically retreated from its historic leadership role in refugee resettlement, with various other countries following its lead, the world's refugees—some of the most vulnerable people on our globe—desperately need the church to influence public policy, pointing to a better way.

At its best, the church already knows how to do this. In the Spanish-speaking congregation where my family and I worship—where most of our congregation has come from Mexico or Central America, and we're the minority as native-English-speaking, US-born non-Latinos—I'm always warmly greeted as *hermano*. At first, I suspected this was just a convenient way to obscure that someone had forgotten my name, but in time it became clear that I was fully embraced as a part of this family. We're kin, and we take every opportunity possible to sit down for a shared meal.

It grieves me that, too often, Christians have seen refugees and other immigrants as a potential threat, heeding often-inaccurate rumors rather than the consistent commands of Scripture. Having been embraced by those with life experiences very different than my own, I want to extend that same embrace to others, which I am convinced presents a vital opportunity for the church to join God in his mission. I pray that this carefully considered book will point the way forward.

ACKNOWLEDGMENTS

CHRIST SAID THAT IN welcoming the stranger we welcome Christ himself (Mt 25:35–40). So, we want to thank those newcomers who have been Christ to us, welcoming *us* into their lives, shaping our minds, and allowing us to share some of their stories with you, especially Sahel and her daughter and Raúl Gatica.

Friends who work and advocate in solidarity with refugees have deeply shaped this book. In these pages you will meet many of the staff and volunteers at Kinbrace Community Society. From Kinbrace we thank in particular Loren Balisky, Anika Barlow, Emily Parsons Dickau, Fran Gallo, and Adriana Zepeda. Emily and Anika gave us feedback on the full manuscript of the book. Other advocates have allowed us to share their stories and insights. We are indebted to Jarrod McKenna, Mary Kaech, Ebony Birchall, Jim Mullins, and Adam Estle. Your faith and life are inspiring.

Writing on kinship should rightly be shared with others, so a highlight of our journey was an international gathering of scholars, advocates, and activists at Australian National University in Canberra, Australia, in August 2018. Together we workshopped several draft chapters of the book, and participants presented papers on their own work done in solidarity with refugees. We are deeply grateful for the insights and ongoing work of the participants: Loren Balisky, Ebony Birchall, Mark Brett, Danny Carroll, Ben Day, George Glanville, Erin Goheen Glanville, Carly Gordyn, Cecilia Jacob, Jarrod McKenna, Alana Moore, Byron Smith, Mark Stephens, and Erin Wilson. Their critical feedback deeply formed our thinking and writing.

We are indebted also to Cian O'Driscoll and Liane Hartnett, who provided detailed and thoughtful comments on several draft chapters; Phil Orchard and Bina D'Costa, who intervened at crucial moments to help clarify our thinking; Ben Day, again, who time and time again offered examples and metaphors and other means of expression that helped land an idea or improve an argument; and Doug Loney, who graciously put his editing powers to work on the draft manuscript. We are thankful again to Erin Goheen Glanville, who accompanied us throughout the writing process, opening to us the insights of critical refugee studies.

Our thanks, too, to Anna Gissing and the supportive and talented team at InterVarsity Press.

This book is dedicated to our mother, June Glanville. Mum died as we were writing this book. Christ's healing presence was the gift mum's life offered; she embodied Christ's love with every person she encountered. If even traces of mum's kindness are found in these pages, this book will have accomplished enough.

ABBREVIATIONS

ABS	Archaeology and Biblical Studies
AIL	Ancient Israel and Its Literature
ARA	*Annual Review of Anthropology*
BTB	*Biblical Theology Bulletin*
BZABR	Beihefte zur Zeitschrift für altorientalische und biblische Rechtsgeschichte
BZAW	Beihefte zur Zeitschrift für die alttestamentliche Wissenschaft
CBQ	*Catholic Biblical Quarterly*
ConBNT	Coniectanea Biblica: New Testament Series
EIA	*Ethics & International Affairs*
EJIR	*European Journal of International Relations*
EJPT	*European Journal of Political Theory*
FAT	Forschungen zum Alten Testament
FRLANT	Forschungen zur Religion und Literatur des Alten und Neuen Testaments
IBMR	*International Bulletin of Mission Research*
IDP	Internally Displaced People
IJRL	*International Journal of Refugee Law*
Int	*Interpretation: A Journal of Bible and Theology*
IO	*International Organization*
IR	international relations
ISQ	*International Studies Quarterly*
JBL	*Journal of Biblical Literature*
JRefS	*Journal of Refugee Studies*
JSHJ	*Journal for the Study of the Historical Jesus*
JSOT	*Journal for the Study of the Old Testament*
JSOTSup	JSOT Supplement Series
NSBT	New Studies in Biblical Theology
NTS	*New Testament Studies*
OLA	Orientalia Lovaniensia Analecta

OTL	Old Testament Library
PNAS	*Proceedings of the National Academy of Sciences of the United States of America*
Providence	*Providence: A Journal of Christianity and American Foreign Policy*
SAHL	Studies in the Archaeology and History of the Levant
SBL	Society of Biblical Literature
SCE	*Studies in Christian Ethics*
SJT	*Scottish Journal of Theology*
SNTSMS	Society for New Testament Studies Monograph Series
TDNT	*Theological Dictionary of the New Testament.* Edited by Gerhard Kittel and Gerhard Friedrich. Translated by Geoffrey W. Bromily. 10 vols. Grand Rapids, MI: Eerdmans, 1964–1976.
TDOT	*Theological Dictionary of the Old Testament.* Edited by G. Johannes Botterweck, Helmer Ringgren, and Heinz-Josef Fabry. Translated by John T. Willis et al. 16 vols. Grand Rapids, MI: Eerdmans, 1974–2018.
UNHCR	United Nations High Commissioner for Refugees
VT	*Vetus Testamentum*
ZABR	*Zeitschrift für altorientalische und biblische Rechtsgeschichte*
ZAW	*Zeitschrift für die alttestamentliche Wissenschaft*

Introduction

KINSHIP WITH REFUGEES

ON THE MORNING THEY LEFT HOME, Naza tried to appear unhurried to her two young daughters. They were, after all, going on holiday to America to see old family friends. This was true, at least in part, as Naza's husband Ardil had continually reminded her in the weeks leading up to this day. Threats had been mounting after Naza, a freelance journalist, had posted an article on her blog criticizing the recent election. They had decided that Naza would go ahead with the children and Ardil would stay behind to sell the house. Within a few weeks, with the money from the sale, he would repay the debt for three one-way tickets to JFK and finance his own ticket. *Inshallah*.

Upon arrival in New York, Naza and her daughters took a taxi to a nearby motel. The driver, hearing their story, advised Naza to speak with an immigration lawyer as soon as possible. The next day Naza located a lawyer's office. The receptionist apologized, saying that the next available lawyer could meet with her in two weeks. "I can't pay for two more weeks in a motel," Naza confided to an Iraqi couple sitting next to her in the waiting room. They relayed to her what their own lawyer had told them: that the political mood in the United States was making it hard for refugees, and Canada might listen more carefully to the details of her story. "Go to Canada," they said. And so the journey continued.

Five days and multiple bus transfers later, they were standing at the US-Canada border, staring up at a huge white monument that read, "Children of a common mother." "Just walk across," Naza thought to herself.

Quickly they were picked up by the Royal Canadian Mounted Police and whisked away to an office where Naza was questioned without her children. That night they were dropped off at a women's shelter in the city center. They were given three bunks, but needed just one: Naza slept with one arm around each child. A few days passed, until one of the staff at the shelter asked Naza more questions and told her to pack her bags. Someone was coming to get her. She had no choice but to trust.

They arrived at a place called Kinbrace. The front door opened into what looked like a big family eating together. There were joyful shrieks of children and a big pot on the stove. Naza thought she smelled Kurdish rice. The sound of a woman speaking her mother tongue confirmed it. She felt safe. And hungry.

Naza and her daughters lived within the Kinbrace community for their first four months in Canada. The girls started school, and Naza enrolled in English classes with the hope of finding a job in journalism like she'd had at home. She started cooking the weekly community dinner, always with an eye on the door for another mother and two kids who might walk in seeking shelter.

Eighteen months after their arrival in Canada they were finally granted refugee protection by the Canadian government. That was a special day; their friends at Kinbrace had a party waiting for them after six exhausting hours of questions regarding their case.

Despite her joy and profound relief, Naza still waits with her daughters in their new home just outside Vancouver. It will be at least another year until they hold the permanent residence documents that will allow Ardil to be reunited with his wife and daughters.[1]

This is a book about people like Naza and her family, forced to flee their countries of origin and welcomed into new communities, and about the hope for others in situations like theirs, that they too may find welcome, safety, and home. It is a book about communities such as Kinbrace that embrace and enfold displaced people as kin and about the hope that other communities— church communities, national communities, even the global community— might do the same. It is a book to encourage communities to express love for the stranger and repentance for harms done to strangers, to make themselves vulnerable for the sake of the vulnerable, and to accept responsibilities and

---

[1]This story was told to us by Anika Barlow, lead host at Kinbrace Community Society.

embrace opportunities in response to a global crisis of forced displacement that is worsening every year.

THE SCOPE OF SUFFERING AND OUR RESPONSE

Not all displaced people find refuge. Not all communities provide welcome. Think of Alan Kurdi, the three-year-old Syrian boy in the red T-shirt who, on September 2, 2015, drowned while seeking passage across the Mediterranean to Europe. His lifeless body was found washed up on a Turkish beach. Think of Tasmin, the thirteen-year-old Rohingya girl who had become separated from her family while fleeing ethnic cleansing in Myanmar, then snatched by people traffickers, and sold into forced labor in Bangladesh.[2] Think of Jasson and Alex, two unaccompanied teenagers fleeing violence in Honduras, impeded by bureaucratic hurdles from applying for asylum promptly in the United States and lacking the funds to pay people smugglers to facilitate undocumented entry, murdered while waiting in Tijuana, Mexico.[3] Think of Omid Masoumali, a young Iranian refugee placed by the Australian government in indefinite detention offshore in Nauru. Having been informed that he would remain on the island for another ten years, Omid set himself on fire and died.[4] Think of Laura, twenty-three, fleeing domestic violence in Mexico but pressured by US officials into agreeing to "voluntary return,"[5] and Acevedo, twenty, fleeing gang violence in El Salvador, whose application for asylum in the United States was rejected.[6] Both were killed upon returning home. And think of the millions of people around the world who have been forced to flee their homes and now wait in refugee camps or urban destitution in "countries of first asylum" that are often unstable and impoverished, with little hope of resolution to their displacement.[7]

The numbers are staggering. The office of the United Nations High Commissioner for Refugees (UNHCR) tells us that, as of the end of 2019, 79.5 million people around the world have been forcibly displaced from their homes due to persecution, conflict, violence, human rights violations, or

---

[2]Siobhan Heanue, "Rohingya Girls Targeted by Child Traffickers at Bangladesh Border Crossings," *ABC News*, February 7, 2018.

[3]Wendy Fry, "Honduran Teenagers Killed in Tijuana Remembered as Respectful, Helpful Friends," *Los Angeles Times*, January 7, 2019.

[4]Michael Edwards and Peter Lloyd, "Omid Masoumali Set Himself on Fire After UNHCR Told Him He Would Remain on Nauru, Asylum Seekers Say," *ABC News*, May 2, 2016.

[5]Sarah Stillman, "When Deportation Is a Death Sentence," *New Yorker*, January 15, 2018.

[6]Kevin Sieff, "When Death Awaits Deported Asylum Seekers," *Washington Post*, December 26, 2018.

[7]A "country of first asylum" is the first country to which a displaced person has fled and found a degree of temporary protection.

events that have seriously disturbed public order. That's more than the entire population of either the United Kingdom or France, more than the combined populations of Canada and Australia. More than thirty million of them are children under eighteen years of age.[8]

Of these 79.5 million displaced people, 45.7 million are "internally displaced," meaning they remain in their countries of origin. Slightly more than four million have fled their countries of origin and are waiting for a decision on an application for asylum. A further 3.6 million are Venezuelans who have fled their country in recent years. UNHCR at present describes them not as refugees but as "Venezuelans displaced abroad." The remaining 26 million have fled their countries and been recognized as refugees. The majority of refugees come from only a small number of countries. More than half of Syria's population has been displaced by the brutal civil war that has raged since 2011: 6.6 million Syrians are internally displaced and a further 6.6 million are refugees displaced beyond Syria's borders. Millions more have fled intractable violence in Afghanistan (2.7 million), civil war in South Sudan (2.2 million), and ethnic cleansing in Myanmar (1.1 million).[9]

Displacement for most is long lasting. More than three-quarters of the world's refugees have been displaced for more than five years.[10] And things are getting worse as climate change is amplifying the frequency and severity of armed conflicts, food and water scarcity, and other drivers of displacement.[11]

While many people in the West feel overwhelmed by large numbers of people approaching or crossing their national borders in search of refuge, the vast majority of refugees—85 percent—are hosted by countries in developing regions beyond the West—countries that are neighbors to war, conflict, and persecution.[12] Turkey hosts 3.6 million refugees. Colombia hosts 1.8 million. Pakistan and Uganda each host 1.4 million. One in every six people in Aruba

---

[8]United Nations High Commissioner for Refugees (UNHCR), *Global Trends: Forced Displacement in 2019*, June 18, 2020, 2, https://www.unhcr.org/en-au/statistics/unhcrstats/5ee200e37/unhcr-global-trends-2019.html.

[9]UNHCR, *Global Trends: Forced Displacement in 2019*, 2-3, 8.

[10]UNHCR, *Global Trends: Forced Displacement in 2019*, 24.

[11]Guy J. Abel, Michael Brottrager, Jesus Crespo Cuaresma, and Raya Muttarak, "Climate, Conflict and Forced Migration," *Global Environmental Change* 54 (January 2019): 239-49. In 2018, 181 countries voted in favor of a Global Compact on Refugees that, among many things, acknowledged that "climate, environmental degradation and natural disasters increasingly interact with the drivers of refugee movements." UNHCR, *Global Compact on Refugees, A/73/12 (Part II)*, September 1, 2018, 2, www.unhcr.org/gcr/GCR_English.pdf. The only countries that voted against the compact were the United States and Hungary. We discuss the compact further in chap. 10.

[12]This discussion draws on Luke Glanville, "Hypocritical Inhospitality: The Global Refugee Crisis in the Light of History," *Ethics & International Affairs* 33, no. 4 (2020): 3-12. Used with permission.

is a "Venezuelan displaced abroad." One in every seven people in Lebanon is a refugee. Certainly, some Western countries welcome tens of thousands of refugees each year and provide protection to hundreds of thousands of asylum claimants. But the combined efforts of developed countries provide home to only a small fraction of the world's forcibly displaced people. Only 107,800 refugees—less than half of 1 percent of the global refugee population—were welcomed and resettled into new countries and communities in 2019.[13]

Western countries have far greater capacity to provide safety and sustenance than many developing countries currently hosting millions of refugees. But these more affluent countries not only refuse to welcome larger numbers of displaced people; they spend billions of dollars each year containing displaced people in developing countries, deterring asylum-seeking people from approaching their territories, and detaining for long periods those who manage to claim asylum in the hope that they may simply give up, return to their countries of origin, or seek new homes elsewhere. And things are getting worse. Resurgent nationalism sees many people in the West hardening their attitudes toward displaced foreigners, while growing mistrust and antagonism among the world's most powerful states hampers efforts to develop international solutions.

Western Christians tended in past decades to be sympathetic to the plight of forcibly displaced people, but they too have hardened their hearts in recent years. Indeed, certain groups of Western Christians now tend to be less sympathetic toward refugees than their fellow citizens. A study by the Pew Research Center in 2018 found that only 51 percent of Americans say that the United States has "a responsibility to accept refugees into the country." This low percentage is concerning enough. But consider that the same study found that only 25 percent of white evangelical Protestants say that the United States has such a responsibility—a lower percentage than any other group categorized in the study. While some white evangelical Protestants said they did not know the answer to the question, a full 68 percent were willing to say that the United States does not have a responsibility to accept refugees. Agreeing were 50 percent of white mainline Protestants, 28 percent of black Protestants, and 45 percent of Catholics.[14]

Whatever concern Christians may have for the plight of displaced foreigners, these concerns are, for many, trumped by concerns for the security of their

[13]UNHCR, *Global Trends: Forced Displacement in 2019*, 2-3.
[14]Hannah Hartig, "Republicans Turn More Negative Toward Refugees as Number Admitted to U.S. Plummets," *Fact Tank: News in the Numbers* (blog), Pew Research Center, May 24, 2018.

own families, the economic well-being of their own communities, the culture and values of their own nation. These are legitimate concerns. But the way we frame them, the weight we give them, and the implications we draw for our responsibilities toward refugees and other displaced people are too often mis-shaped by problematic theologies, partisan politics, and misinformation.

THE NEED FOR THIS BOOK

We write this book because we feel an urgent need for a biblically grounded Christian perspective on our present global crisis of forced displacement and an outline of how this biblical ethic might be applied faithfully and creatively at the levels of the church, the nation, and the globe. This is a big task, requiring an argument with many moving parts. But there are good reasons for attempting to tackle these many parts in a single book.

We have found that *biblical* arguments for compassionate welcome of strangers are often met with rebuttals: But you misunderstand politics. It is all very well for individuals to be open-hearted and open-handed toward strangers, but you have not grappled sufficiently with the conceptual limits, the large-scale practicalities, and the sheer imprudence of applying this to countries and their governments.

In a recent book offering a Christian perspective on American immigration policy, for example, Mark Amstutz laments that individual Christians and churches too often offer recommendations for public policy that "emphasize biblical morality, but . . . contain little political science."[15] They draw proposals from biblical teachings about the love of neighbor and the welcome of strangers, but they fail to appreciate the constraints faced by government officials seeking to devise just policies, he claims. They fail in particular to grapple with the realities of global politics, the nature of sovereign statehood, the meaning of citizenship, and the necessary limits to the rights of outsiders.[16]

Likewise, *political* arguments offered by Christians for a more compassionate approach to refugees are often met with different rebuttals: But you misunderstand the Bible. You're bringing political ideology to your reading of Scripture. Biblical injunctions to welcome the stranger are not as straightforward as you think.

In a book on "the immigration crisis," James Hoffmeier argues that Israel was called to care only for the sojourner who entered their lands "legally," and

[15]Mark R. Amstutz, *Just Immigration: American Policy in Christian Perspective* (Grand Rapids, MI: Eerdmans, 2017), 225.
[16]Amstutz, *Just Immigration*, 224-25.

Romans 13:1-7 makes clear that the responsibility of the state is "to enforce its laws and provide for its citizens."[17] Hoffmeier's argument has had great influence, having been discussed in a Bible study run by Capitol Ministries for members of the US Congress in 2016 and repeated in a memo on "the Bible and the wall," written by Capitol Ministries at the request of members of the White House Cabinet Member Bible study in 2019.[18]

Such efforts to soften the urgent and radical implications of the biblical call to welcome the stranger are, in our view, problematic. But to appreciate and articulate why requires engagement with a variety of fields of scholarship: biblical, missional, and political theology as well as history, political theory, and international relations. Amstutz is right to note the need to think hard about how biblical injunctions to show compassion for the stranger should be applied collectively, particularly in a world of sovereign nation states, even if, as we will argue, the conclusions that he draws are unjustifiably restrictive. Hoffmeier is right to note the need to wrestle with the meanings of words used to describe non-Israelites in the Bible and the implications of Romans 13 for the governance of citizens and foreigners, even if, as we will show, his interpretations are profoundly mistaken.

We write this book as brothers with complementary expertise across the scholarly fields mentioned above. Mark is an Old Testament scholar (formerly an urban missional pastor) who has published on historical and ethical issues regarding displacement as addressed in the Pentateuch.[19] Luke is a scholar of international relations who has spent the past decade researching past and present understandings of the responsibilities of states to care for the well-being of people both within and beyond their borders, with a particular focus on the care of people at risk of mass atrocities.[20] We have been delighted to discover that our varied research interests have enabled us to engage in this book with a wide range of questions commonly asked by Christians grappling with refugee issues. We offer what we hope is a faithful,

---

[17]James K. Hoffmeier, *The Immigration Crisis: Immigrants, Aliens, and the Bible* (Wheaton, IL: Crossway, 2009), 71-73, 151.

[18]Ralph Drollinger, "What the Bible Says About Our Illegal Immigration Problem," *Members Bible Study, U.S. Capitol*, Capitol Ministries, September 26, 2016, http://capmin.org/wp-content/uploads /2016/09/Illegal-Immigration-9.26.16.pdf; and idem, "The Bible and the Wall," *Ministry Updates*, Capitol Ministries, January 26, 2019, https://capmin.org/the-bible-and-the-wall/.

[19]See for example Mark R. Glanville, *Adopting the Stranger as Kindred in Deuteronomy*, AIL 33 (Atlanta: SBL Press, 2018).

[20]See for example Luke Glanville, *Sharing Responsibility: The History and Future of Protection from Atrocities* (Princeton, NJ: Princeton University Press, 2021).

empathetic, imaginative, and attractive vision of a way through our present crisis of displacement. We pray the book will go some way toward equipping Christians to understand that the biblical model for communities is one in which people will relentlessly and joyfully enfold the vulnerable, the marginalized, and the displaced, and to comprehend how this model can be applied in practice in church communities, national communities, and even the global community.

INTRODUCING A BIBLICAL ETHIC OF KINSHIP

Those advocating for greater compassion and generosity toward refugees and other migrants in recent years have grounded their arguments in a variety of theories, concepts, and traditions. Some recommend a commitment to human dignity and human rights.[21] Others urge the recognition and performance of human responsibilities.[22] Some endorse a posture of hospitality.[23] Others call for the provision of sanctuary.[24] Each of these approaches is biblical and valuable. We might worry that the notion of human rights fails to clarify who in particular should ensure these rights are protected. We might worry that the attribution of responsibilities to potential protectors in theory is insufficient to motivate action in practice. We might worry that the idea of hospitality diminishes refugees by portraying them as people who are always in the position of receiving. And we might worry that sanctuary provides only an impermanent resolution to the ongoing problem of displacement. But, in the hands of clear thinkers, each of these approaches has proved capable of sustaining profound insights into how individuals and communities ought to engage with displaced people.

In this book, however, we offer a new approach, one that is arguably both more demanding for Western nations and more transformative: a biblical ethic of kinship.[25] The deep narrative structure of Scripture, we argue, urges

[21]Mark G. Brett, *Political Trauma and Healing: Biblical Ethics for a Postcolonial World* (Grand Rapids, MI: Eerdmans, 2016), 163-78.
[22]Tisha M. Rajendra, *Migrants and Citizens: Justice and Responsibility in the Ethics of Immigration* (Grand Rapids, MI: Eerdmans, 2017).
[23]Matthew Kaemingk, *Christian Hospitality and Muslim Immigration in an Age of Fear* (Grand Rapids, MI: Eerdmans, 2018).
[24]Luke Bretherton, *Christianity and Contemporary Politics* (Oxford: Wiley-Blackwell, 2010), 126-74.
[25]For a powerful Christian study of US immigration issues, which is likewise grounded in the theme of kinship but does not devote much space to retrieving this ethic from Scripture, see Kristin E. Heyer, *Kinship Across Borders: A Christian Ethic of Immigration* (Washington, DC: Georgetown University Press, 2012).

the people of God to embrace and enfold refugees and other displaced people as kin. This call to kinship is a pattern of thought that runs from the beginning to the end of the biblical story. God's people are urged again and again to extend kinship to those who are marginalized, to welcome into the protective center of the community those who are without clan, without family, and without home.

We begin the book by retrieving carefully this ethic of kinship from Scripture. We then proceed to explore how such an ethic might be embodied within church, national, and global communities today. Recognition and acceptance of the biblical call to kinship with displaced people, we suggest, has the potential to generate profound change within each of these communities, prompting us to repent of our own participation in the exclusion, marginalization, and harm of vulnerable people, leading us to embrace our own vulnerabilities as we enfold the vulnerable and helping us to joyfully grasp new opportunities for mutual transformation.

WHAT IS KINSHIP?

Kin comes to modern English from an Anglo-Saxon word that means simply "family."[26] Kinship is our sense of family feeling, the ties of commitment that structure our individual identities and our belonging to others. It addresses basic questions of relationship: To whom are we obligated? From whom may we expect support? "To the extent they lead common lives," cultural anthropologist Marshall Sahlins suggests, kin relations "partake of each other's sufferings and joys, sharing one another's experiences even as they take responsibility for and feel the effects of each other's acts."[27] In the language of the Yolngu people, a people indigenous to Australia, the word for *selfish*, *gurrutumiriw*, means "acting as if one has no kin."[28]

We can be tempted to think of kinship quite narrowly as a blood tie, a connection that is natural and unchangeable. But kinship is not only biological, and it does not remain static. Kinship is often constructed socially. Think of marriage. Think of adoption. We speak of an intimate friend as a "brother from another mother" or a "sister from another mister." We conceive of bands of brothers in war—brothers in arms. We construct

---

[26]For a similar discussion of kinship, see Mark R. Glanville, "'Festive Kinship': Solidarity, Responsibility, and Identity Formation in Deuteronomy," *JSOT* 44 (2019): 133-52, at 133-38.

[27]Marshall Sahlins, *What Kinship Is . . . and Is Not* (Chicago: University of Chicago Press, 2013), 28.

[28]Richard Flanagan, "The World Is Being Undone Before Us. If We Do Not Reimagine Australia, We Will Be Undone Too," *Guardian*, August 5, 2018.

sisterhoods across a variety of contexts—from religious orders to traveling pants! These ties, these kin relationships, can be felt just as strongly and held just as dearly as ties of blood, and in many instances more strongly and more dearly.[29]

After decades spent observing and reflecting on kin relationships, Sahlins concludes that kinship is simply "mutuality of being." Kinsfolk, he suggests, are "persons who belong to one another, who are parts of one another, who are co-present in each other, whose lives are joined and interdependent."[30] While blood ties are frequently the source of kinship, anthropologists such as Sahlins tell of kinship relations produced also by shared meals, shared habitation, shared memories, and shared suffering. And they emphasize that the use of *kinship* as a descriptor for nonblood relationships should not be thought of as merely metaphorical or symbolic. Even the label "fictive kinship," commonly offered to distinguish a social construction from supposedly "real kinship," may be too weak. Constructed forms of kinship can be found enjoying equal status or even taking priority over biological forms often enough that they ought to be considered no less real.[31]

We commonly speak in terms of kin relationships not only when describing relations between individuals or within small groups and communities but also when we talk about nations. We speak of the motherland or the fatherland. We remember our founding fathers. If we are not citizens by birth, we become so via "naturalization."[32] Again, such kinship tends to be socially constructed. While some may conceive of their nation in biological and naturalized terms—appealing to ties of blood and soil—in reality, as Benedict Anderson famously observed, nations are "imagined communities."[33] "We have made Italy, now we have to make Italians," Massimo d'Azeglio admitted upon Italy's unification

---

[29]"Suppose two men, one a relative of yours and one not, had something you needed, which would you go to?" an ethnographer asked a Fijian. "I would go to my relative of course," the Fijian replied. "If he didn't give it to me, and the other man did, I would know that the other man was really my relative." As told in Sahlins, *What Kinship Is*, 62-63. See also Janet Carsten, *After Kinship* (Cambridge: Cambridge University Press, 2004).

[30]Sahlins, *What Kinship Is*, ix, 21.

[31]Sahlins goes so far as to say that "kinship categories are not representations or metaphorical extensions of birth relations; if anything, birth is a metaphor of kinship relations." Sahlins, *What Kinship Is*, ix.

[32]Carsten, *After Kinship*, 154, discussing David M. Schneider, "Kinship, Nationality, and Religion in American Culture: Towards a Definition of Kinship," in *Symbolic Anthropology: A Reader in the Study of Symbols and Meanings*, ed. Janet L. Dolgin, David S. Kemnitzer, and David M. Schneider (New York: Columbia University Press, 1977), 63-71.

[33]Benedict Anderson, *Imagined Communities: Reflections on the Origin and Spread of Nationalism* (London: Verso, 1983).

in 1861.[34] And political leaders have expended enormous energy and resources across generations "making" Italians, "making" Britons, "making" Americans, and so on—cultivating national kinship.[35]

Ties between fellow nationals are typically thinner and less intimate than those between family members or close companions. The vast majority of members of a national community will never even meet each other. Appeals to kinship at the level of the nation may thus often take a more symbolic or meta-phorical form. But we still commonly observe a certain "mutuality of being" as members of a nation feel that they are in some sense joined together. They belong to each other; they are parts of each other and also parts of the whole. And this feeling of mutuality can be extraordinarily powerful, leading people frequently to lay down their lives in wars fought for their country and their compatriots.[36]

Of course, even as it produces solidarity and mutual care for those within the group, kinship can prove exclusionary, generating and validating extraor-dinary harms done to those outside the group. The past and present horrors of nationalist xenophobia, whereby neighbors are made alien and foreigners are rendered inhuman, attest to that. But it doesn't have to be that way. Kinship is "susceptible to continuous transformations and adaptations," anthropologist Janet Carsten concludes, and so it can expand to enfold outsiders.[37] We see this happen within families, worshiping communities, and even nations. When Canadian Prime Minister Justin Trudeau personally welcomed a planeload of Syrian refugees to Canada in 2015—the first of more than twenty-five thousand that would arrive over the next few months—he made a point of inviting them into the Canadian "family." Three years later, one of those Syrians, Basel Al-zoubi, who had arrived with his wife and three children, reflected on both the grief and joy of transformed kinship: "My Syria and my country is like my mom, in my soul and in my heart. I never forget for a second. Canada is my kids' home, their mother, because they will grow up here."[38]

---

[34]Quoted in F. J Hobsbawm, *Nations and Nationalism Since 1780: Programme, Myth, Reality*, 1st ed. (Cambridge: Cambridge University Press, 1990), 44.

[35]Linda Colley, *Britons: Forging the Nation 1707-1837*, rev. 3rd ed. (London: Yale University Press, 2009); Hobsbawm, *Nations and Nationalism*; and Desmond King, *Making Americans: Immigration, Race, and the Origins of Diverse Democracy* (Cambridge, MA: Harvard University Press, 2000).

[36]Carsten, *After Kinship*, 153-62. Jørgen Johansen observes that members of Maori tribal groups identify themselves with their group to the extent that they use the first-person pronoun, *I*, to refer to the group as a whole as well as its collective history—leading Johansen to describe it as the "kinship I." See the discussion in Sahlins, *What Kinship Is*, 35-37.

[37]Carsten, *After Kinship*, 154.

[38]Kathleen Harris, "'I Will Be Born Again': First Wave of Syrian Refugees Set to Become Canadian Citizens," *CBC News*, December 11, 2018.

People use the motif of kinship even to talk about global relations. Again, sometimes this can be used to justify the exclusion and exploitation of outsiders. Think of how Europeans deployed the notion of a "family of civilized nations" in the nineteenth century, to articulate their mutual bonds and shared rights and responsibilities but also to validate the exclusion of "uncivilized" nations beyond Europe and to help justify the conquest and colonization of non-European peoples.[39] But, again, kinship doesn't have to be constructed in such exclusive ways. Reflecting on the ten-year anniversary of the 1994 Rwandan genocide, UN Secretary-General Kofi Annan urged the international community to move "from dehumanization and toward a stronger sense of global kinship," according to which we accept that everyone on earth is "fully worthy of our interest, sympathy, and acceptance."[40] Martin Luther King Jr. articulated a similar idea in a powerful 1967 speech condemning the Vietnam War. Invoking the notion of the "brotherhood of man," he urged his American listeners to remember that all are called "to be a son of the living God," to recognize Vietnamese peasants therefore as brothers, and to "transform the jangling discords of our world into a beautiful symphony of brotherhood."[41] While such a global vision may, like national visions, lack the thickness and intimacy of close interpersonal relationships, it still evokes a real and genuine "mutuality of being."

KINSHIP AS A BIBLICAL ETHIC

Kinship was a vital part of the social worlds of both the Old and New Testaments. The cultures within which Scripture emerged were Middle Eastern communal cultures in which kinship networks were reflected in daily activities, patterns of residence, economic cooperation, and political organization.[42] In the Old Testament we find that genealogical ties are emphasized (Deut 29:10-12). An individual is commonly identified as "the child X, of the clan Y, of the tribe of Z, of the people of Israel."[43] People are expected to

[39]Luke Glanville, *Sovereignty and the Responsibility to Protect: A New History* (Chicago: University of Chicago Press, 2014), 100-131.

[40]Kofi Annan, "Rwanda Genocide 'Must Always Leave Us with a Sense of Bitter Regret and Abiding Sorrow,' Says Secretary-General to New York Memorial Conference," *Meetings Coverage and Press Releases*, SG/SM/9223-AFR/870-HQ/631, United Nations, March 26, 2004.

[41]Martin Luther King Jr., *A Call to Conscience: The Landmark Speeches of Dr. Martin Luther King, Jr.*, ed. Clayborne Carson and Kris Shepard (New York: Warner Books, 2001), 145, 149, 164.

[42]J. David Schloen, *The House of the Father as Fact and Symbol: Patrimonialism in Ugarit and the Ancient Near East*, SAHL 2 (Winona Lake, IN: Eisenbrauns, 2001), 70 and citations.

[43]Ronald S. Hendel, *Remembering Abraham: Culture, Memory, and History in the Hebrew Bible* (Oxford: Oxford University Press, 2005), 34.

submit to the elders and the paterfamilias (Deut 21:18-21). The sins of the fathers are said to fall upon the children until the third and fourth generation (Ex 34:7). Frank Moore Cross concludes, "The social organization of West Semitic tribal groups was grounded in kinship. Kinship relations defined the rights and obligations, the duties, status, and privileges of tribal members, and kinship terminology provided the only language for expressing legal, political, and religious institutions."[44] In the New Testament we see again the importance given to genealogy (Mt 1:1-17) and a presumption that people will ordinarily submit to their parents (Mk 10:29) and provide mourning rites and burial for their deceased kin (Mt 8:21). The centrality of kinship to the social world is visible also in the ways that Jesus challenges these presumptions and forms new kin relationships, as for example when he declares, "whoever does the will of God is my brother and sister and mother" (Mk 3:35).

Given the centrality of kinship to the social worlds of both testaments, it is vital that we pay attention to how the biblical authors treat the concept. Such a context-sensitive approach is not only faithful to the text; it also brings to light a radical and exciting response to the plight of the marginalized throughout Scripture that might otherwise remain invisible to those of us in the West, who ordinarily give little thought to kinship. We will see that God's people are called again and again across Scripture to extend kinship to those on the margins, those without community, the dispossessed, the dishonored, and the displaced.

Given the centrality of kinship to the legal, political, and religious life of the communities of both testaments, this is a vital ethic indeed. It is not only how God's people are called to behave; it is constitutive of what it means to be God's people. As we recognize that God's people are called to be a light to the nations, we can begin to comprehend this biblical ethic of kinship as God's design and desire for all communities—not only worshiping communities but also national communities, and even the global community.

THE STORY OF KINBRACE

Kinship is a creative act. Carsten reflects on the creativity that people invest in nourishing new kinship. "I take it as fundamental that creativity is not only central to kinship conceived in its broadest sense, but that for most people

---

[44]Frank Moore Cross, *From Epic to Canon: History and Literature in Ancient Israel* (Baltimore: Johns Hopkins University Press, 1998), 4.

kinship constitutes one of the most important arenas for their creative energy." Kinship, she observes, "is, among other things, an area of life in which people invest their emotions, their creative energy and their new imaginings."[45] The creativity that communities can invest in enfolding displaced people is of particular interest for this book. In the chapters that follow, we will observe the tremendous creativity of the biblical authors as they urge their communities to pursue kinship with those who are vulnerable and marginalized.

We will also return often to stories from "Kinbrace," a community based in Vancouver, Canada, that creatively pursues kinship with refugees. Birthed in 1998 by Grandview Church—the church in which Mark pastored for seven years—Kinbrace Community Society has been providing housing and support for refugee claimants for over twenty years. Throughout the book, we will hear from people who went through their refugee claim process while living at Kinbrace. We will also hear from the Kinbrace staff, some of whom have refugee experience of their own. It is our hope that hearing from the Kinbrace community will keep this book practical and personal, even as we dive into some of the complexities of Scripture, missional theology, and political theory. Most importantly, the Kinbrace story may give you hope as you read. It might inspire in you some creative responses to be cultivated within your own communities.

A brief introduction to Kinbrace here will help us to paint a picture of what the practice of kinship with the displaced can look like.

For many years, Grandview Church has shared a vision of being attentive to and living alongside vulnerable people, of being alive in its neighborhood. Two members of the church, Tama and Loren Balisky, grew up in Africa and have long been aware of and concerned for the plight of displaced. Tama and Loren realized that many refugee claimants in Vancouver were living on the streets, bouncing between homeless shelters. In 1998, a hundred-year-old house was purchased close to the church. The house had already been roughly renovated into seven apartments. The Baliskys moved into the house, and the life of Kinbrace began! Some years later, in 2005, Kinbrace was able to purchase the house next door, and today these two houses, with their joint yards, form a common space for the Kinbrace community. Over the years, this space has been home to 550 refugee claimants, as well as to many others who have lived there in solidarity with them.

---

[45]Carsten, *After Kinship*, 9.

At the heart of Kinbrace is the practice of living together. Sharing weekly community meals was a practice from day one, and it continues to this day. Along with the food, grief and loss are often shared, as refugees speak of family separation, of being unable to travel back to their countries of origin, and of the deaths of family members back home. But there is also a deep joy around the table in the discovery of new community, their common journey, and shared life.

Kinbrace cultivates kinship with and among displaced people, enfolding newcomers on the basis that "refugees are the you and me of another place," as Loren says. Perhaps you may already be thinking, How might the creative example of Kinbrace stir the imagination of my church as it contemplates what it might do in solidarity with displaced people? Or, How might recognition of a biblical call to kinship help me and my local community challenge the prevailing national rhetoric of fear and antagonism toward refugees and enable us to model and advocate for generosity, welcome, and love for the stranger? Or even, How have I personally been enfolded into kinship by others, and how might I do the same for strangers in need?

Kinbrace's Five Core Values

The Kinbrace community shares five core values (see https://kinbrace .ca), which nourish its ongoing daily activity and inform its operational policies. When we first set out to write this book, we adopted these five core values as our guide, and they have served us well as they help define in practical ways the biblical ethic of kinship that we find in Scripture. The five core values, as Kinbrace expresses them, are

Welcome. We are in solidarity: bearing witness to exile, we live with refugee claimants.

Trust We are a community: affirming dignity, we commit to the best in one another.

Mutual Transformation. We are diverse: striving to listen well, we learn and grow.

Celebration. We are grateful: amidst joy and sorrow, we discover hope.

Prayer. We are sojourners: held by grace, we journey into the mystery and love of God.

A Biblical Ethic for the Church,
the Nation, and the World

We develop the argument of this book in four parts. Part one, The Bible, traces how God's people are called throughout the biblical story to enfold as kin those who are marginalized from community, without land and without family. In calling Israel, in sending the Messiah, and in forming the church, God is reconciling humanity not only to himself but also to one another, as kin. Kinship is a theme, we suggest, that the church must rediscover if we are to have a truly biblical vision for displaced people. Our use of biblical material is selective, in order to attain depth, focusing on Deuteronomy in chapter two, a small number of other Old Testament books in chapter three, and the Synoptic Gospels in chapter four. The motif of feasting unifies this biblical discussion. Throughout the biblical story, meals are important opportunities for outsiders to be enfolded as kin. Inclusive festivity, where God's people feast together on divine supply, is an evocative image for the joy of kinship with displaced people that we highlight and celebrate in this opening part of the book.

Part two, The Church, examines in a single chapter—chapter five—how this biblical ethic of kinship might shape the mission of the church today. It provides a transition point for the book, drawing on the biblical theology presented in part one to articulate practical and creative ways that worshiping communities can seek to enfold displaced people as kin and contemplating how the church might model and advocate for just and compassionate responses to forced displacement. We explore ways of cultivating a spirit of thanksgiving and generosity in worshiping communities, encouraging them to share the "feast" with displaced people while also sharing in their grief.

Part three, The Nation, shifts the focus from worshiping communities to political communities. Chapter six examines God's desire for national communities, highlighting the call to justice, including justice for the stranger, and suggesting that borders and boundaries should be regulated only with the purpose of serving this vision. We acknowledge the value of national identities. Yet we emphasize that, insofar as these identities do not drive us to embrace vulnerable outsiders as kin, we should work to develop new narratives of ourselves and our collective purposes. Chapter seven wrestles with common arguments that downplay the obligation of political communities to welcome strangers, from appeals to Romans 13 and the prerogatives of sovereign authority to claims about the justice of prioritizing one's own people. Consideration of these arguments actually amplifies our appreciation of the mandate to enfold displaced people as kin as they help us perceive how we have so often contributed to their past and present suffering. Kinship with refugees is not only an opportunity to be seized but also a practice of repentance. Chapter eight then works through some practical implications. We take seriously fears surrounding national security, economics, and culture. We lament, however, that these fears are often manipulated and overstated to justify practices of exclusion that do great harm to strangers. Nations can reimagine themselves, we explain, letting go of fears and nurturing compassion for displaced people. And they can "lock in" this compassion, in a sense, via policies and procedures grounded in love and trust rather than fear and antagonism toward those whom they might enfold as kin.

Acknowledging that no single country can fully address the global refugee crisis on its own, we shift the level of analysis once more in part four, The World, to explore the possibility and opportunity for a cooperative global response that might ensure the provision of safety, welcome, and home to our global kin. Chapter nine wrestles with a dominant approach to thinking about global affairs, Christian realism, which insists that it is right for countries to behave selfishly in a dangerous and unpredictable world. We argue that we can and should discard realism's fear-based ethic and pursue instead a renewed vision for international relations, grounded in a biblical ethic of global kinship with the vulnerable. Chapter ten then strives to imagine a practicable, creative, and comprehensive response to our present crisis of displacement. Among numerous tangible suggestions, we propose that, given the enormity of the crisis and the contribution we in the West have made to it, countries ought at minimum to cooperate immediately to increase global resettlement numbers ten times over. We explain how we arrive at this figure. As radical and idealistic as it may sound, we contend that we must pursue it. Anything less, we suggest, constitutes a grave moral failure of the global community.

The book concludes with a reminder that, as worshiping communities embody Christ's radical welcome, we live as a foretaste of the kingdom of God, a sign to our nations of the joy that may be found in extending kinship to the stranger. The church, moreover, has a profound opportunity to invite national and global communities to reimagine themselves, to risk and rejoice in the transformation that occurs when communities embrace the displaced. The challenge before us is, above all, a spiritual one. The biblical call to embrace the displaced as kin displays the beauty of Christ and of what Christ is busy doing in his world. Despite the appeal of this ethic, the movements that are required—from fear to trust, antagonism to welcome, restrained charity to mutual transformation—constitute nothing less than spiritual renewal, as we are shaped by Scripture and by the Spirit of Christ. The challenge, therefore, must drive us to individual and communal prayer, to discernment of God's will for our lives in regard to our kin, and to action.

Too Political? Too Idealistic?

But perhaps we've already lost you. Perhaps you're thinking this is all sounding too political. Doesn't the biblical call to love thy neighbor and welcome the stranger only apply to individual Christians and the church? Is it really applicable to sovereign nation-states? Should it really inform how countries develop their policies toward refugees domestically and how they cooperate with other countries globally? Such concerns are often expressed. We address these questions in more detail over the course of the book, and especially in chapter six. For now, we simply suggest that the mission of God has in its scope the whole world, for through Scripture we discern God's desire for human community, and we thereby discern what the Spirit is longing to restore, and is busy restoring, in the world.

Mission is the encounter with the world of a community gathered by Christ to be caught up in the Father's reconciling purpose for all of Creation. Our hope is that the church might grab hold of the opportunity to model and prophetically advocate for a just and compassionate national and global response to displacement as it participates, by the power of the Spirit, in God's mission.

Alternatively, perhaps you're thinking this is all sounding too idealistic. We have heard this critique more than once while writing this book. Can we really hope for communities to radically change how they engage with displaced people beyond their borders? Wouldn't it be better to lower our sights and seek more realistic, incremental change—perhaps a firmer commitment to funding the work of UNHCR and other humanitarian agencies that assist and protect displaced people in developing countries, a softening of political rhetoric that dehumanizes asylum seekers, and a marginal increase in the refugee intakes of Western countries that is generous, but not radically so? We acknowledge that, certainly, there can be a time and a place for seeking to nudge reluctant communities and their leaders toward more compassionate rhetoric and more generous policies—a time and a place for negotiation, for compromise, and for accepting marginal gains in the direction of justice. But that is not the task of this book. The task of the book is to examine, as best we can, God's vision for how communities should engage with dispossessed, dishonored, and displaced outsiders and to explore, as best we can, how this vision might ideally shape the responses of church, national, and global communities toward displaced people today. It *is* idealistic, in the sense that God's desire for human society is so much more beautiful than the present reality. Only once we comprehend the ideal can we know what, by the power of the Spirit, we ought to strive for.

And this is where the multidisciplinary nature of our book comes in. We grapple with the complex realities of church communities, the sovereign state, and the global order in this book. And yet our appreciation of the complexity of the global refugee crisis, and the real impediments to transformational change within church, national, and global communities, while helping to guide our claims, does not dictate a more limited moral vision or a more restricted set of policy recommendations—for it is Scripture also that guides us. We hope and argue for more than merely the pragmatic pursuit of marginal gains. We are convinced that the radical ethic of kinship with the displaced that we retrieve from Scripture and whose implementation we urge today is feasible, even if challenging. We are also convinced that it is a better, richer, more joyful ethic for community, even if a fearful world says otherwise. But its realization will take creativity and courage, prayer and spiritual renewal, and God's hand.

Our friend, Jarrod McKenna, who lives in community with refugees in Australia and engages in creative activism on behalf of the vulnerable, put it beautifully, when we asked him about his hope for change:

> I don't expect my activism can possibly change policy, society or the government. Yet being faithful to Christ's reign sets us free from the confines of what the Powers dictate as possible. The empathetic, imaginative, creative business of living God's love opens in prayer the space where God's impossible can come to pass.

Final Clarifications

Before we proceed, let us clarify three terms that are central to this discussion.

Refugee. In this book we speak of refugees. But we also speak of asylum seekers, the internally displaced, and other displaced persons. Who exactly are we talking about? We have in mind a wide range of people: anyone forced to flee his or her home to seek safety or sustenance elsewhere. The 1951 Refugee Convention and the 1967 Protocol that augments it define a refugee quite narrowly, as someone forced to flee her or his country due to "a well-founded fear of being persecuted for reasons of race, religion, nationality, membership of a particular social group or political opinion."[46] But this definition is a product of a particular historical and political context. Persecution is just one reason that people flee their homes, particularly today. "Environmental disturbance, including that due to climate change; generalized violence, whether because of war or drug- and gang-related violence; and food and water insecurity—these have all been identified among the 'new drivers' of displacement," refugee scholars Alexander Betts and Paul Collier tell us.[47] A common thread connecting these drivers of displacement is the growing phenomenon of state fragility and state collapse in developing regions of the world. Unable to secure their basic human needs in unstable and impoverished countries of origin, many people who have an opportunity to flee choose to do so. Scholars helpfully describe this phenomenon in terms of "survival migration" or "distress migration."[48] Some are recognized as refugees in accordance with the Refugee Convention's definition, but not all. It is this broad range of displaced people that we have in mind.

A distinction is often made between people who are displaced and forced to move in order to survive and people who choose to leave their countries of origin in search of a better life, improved work opportunities, improved education for their children, and so on. This distinction may be morally relevant in the abstract. But we should recognize that, when dealing with reality, the distinction is frequently blurred. Refugee scholar Jørgen Carling helps us understand:

> The "two kinds of people" argument is . . . undermined by the drawn-out trajectories of many current migrants. A Nigerian arriving in Italy might have left Nigeria for reasons other than a fear of persecution, but ended up fleeing extreme danger in Libya. Conversely, a Syrian might have crossed into Jordan and found safety from the war, but been prompted by the bleak prospects of indeterminate camp life to make the onward journey to Europe.[49]

---

[46]UNHCR, *Convention and Protocol Relating to the Status of Refugees*, https://www.unhcr.org/en-au /3b66c2aa10 (the quotation is from Article 1.a.2 of the Convention).

[47]Alexander Betts and Paul Collier, *Refuge: Rethinking Refugee Policy in a Changing World* (Oxford: Oxford University Press, 2017), 43-44.

[48]Alexander Betts, *Survival Migration: Failed Governance and the Crisis of Displacement* (Ithaca, NY: Cornell University Press, 2013); and Jacqueline Bhabha, "When Water Is Safer Than Land: Addressing Distress Migration," *Harvard Magazine*, January-February 2016.

[49]Jørgen Carling, "Refugees Are Also Migrants. All Migrants Matter," *Border Criminologies* (blog guest post), September 3, 2015, www.law.ox.ac.uk/research-subject-groups/centre-criminology /centreborder-criminologies/blog/2015/09/refugees-are-also. See also Erin K. Wilson and Luca Mavelli, "The Refugee Crisis and Religion: Beyond Conceptual and Physical Boundaries," in *The*

Consider the 4.5 million Venezuelans who have fled increasing rates of poverty, corruption, organized crime, and political instability in recent years.[50] Should our response really be contingent on the extent to which the mixed and messy causes of their displacement correspond to abstracted legal criteria? So while we focus in this book on forcibly displaced persons, we don't consider it our task to draw a clear distinction between "legitimate" and "illegitimate" claims for asylum, and indeed we worry when our leaders draw such distinctions with the aim of avoiding the obligation to welcome vulnerable people—such as US Attorney General Jeff Sessions declaring domestic abuse and gang violence to be illegitimate grounds for asylum, or Australian Prime Minister Tony Abbott declaring that refugees who move on from the first country that they flee to are no longer refugees but economic migrants.[51]

Crisis. We speak in this book of crisis: a global refugee crisis, a survival migration crisis, a crisis of forced displacement. *Crisis* is a dangerous word. It directs our attention in particular ways. Mishandled or manipulated, it can pervert our understanding of what really matters. How sad it is that Europeans only began to speak of the long-standing and enormous problem of forced displacement in the Middle East and Africa in terms of a refugee crisis when Europe received a large influx of displaced people from those regions in 2015. And how worrying it is that we commonly frame it as a "European refugee crisis," as if it is Europe that is in crisis rather than our longstanding global crisis of mass displacement.[52] Likewise, how concerning it is that US officials and commentators frame the mass movement of asylum seekers from Central America today primarily in terms of a border crisis, when numbers of illegal crossings of the US-Mexico border, while substantial, are lower than they were twenty years ago,[53] and when the greater crisis is surely

---

Refugee Crisis and Religion: Secularism, Security and Hospitality in Question, ed. Luca Mavelli and Erin K. Wilson (London: Rowman & Littlefield, 2017), 1-22; and "Gabriel," with Vicki Squire, "Sharing Stories," in Mavelli and Wilson, *Refugee Crisis and Religion*, 109-18.

[50]UNHCR variously categorizes these people as refugees (93,300), asylum seekers (794,500), and "Venezuelans displaced abroad" (3.6 million). UNHCR, *Global Trends: Forced Displacement in 2019*, 3.

[51]Katie Benner and Caitlin Dickerson, "Sessions Says Domestic and Gang Violence Are Not Grounds for Asylum," *New York Times*, June 11, 2018; and Tony Abbott, "Transcript: Tony Abbott's Controversial Speech at the Margaret Thatcher Lecture," *Sydney Morning Herald*, October 28, 2015.

[52]More generally, Chimni notes that Western countries have historically perceived large-scale migration as a crisis when the people seeking to enter their territories are not fellow Westerners but people from the Global South. B. S. Chimni, "The Geopolitics of Refugee Studies: A View from the South," *JRefS* 11, no. 4 (1998): 350-74.

[53]Caitlin Dickerson, "Border at 'Breaking Point' as More Than 76,000 Unauthorized Migrants Cross in a Month," *New York Times*, March 5, 2019. Updated figures can be found at https://www.cbp.gov/newsroom/stats/sw-border-migration.

the increasing displacement in and from Guatemala, Honduras, El Salvador, and elsewhere—a crisis that is only made worse by the United States' efforts to prevent or deter families from these countries seeking asylum (efforts that we discuss in chap. 10). And yet, even in speaking of a displacement crisis we need to always keep in mind that this is the story of individual people and families, people with dreams, skills, ingenuity, creativity, and bravery—people just like us. We use the language of crisis in this book, as risky as this is, because we want to highlight the enormity of the global issue of forced displacement. But we seek constantly to keep in mind that it is this displacement that is the crisis, not the fact that we are presented with a need—indeed, a wonderful opportunity—to respond.[54]

The West. We use another problematic term in this book: "the West." This term is not only imprecise, but it risks implying the superiority of the West over the "non-West" as well as encouraging generalizations about both the West and the rest.[55] Nevertheless, the term seems the best label for the countries whose opportunity to offer kinship to displaced people we focus on in the book: the United States, Canada, Australia, and the countries of Western Europe. It is worth noting the historical ties of these countries to colonialism. Some are former centers of empire. Others were established by such centers as white settler colonies. The European colonial project involved not only the migration of tens of millions of Europeans to colonies beyond Europe but also the displacement and slaughter of massive numbers of indigenous peoples and the extraction of natural and human resources back to Europe, bequeathing historical injustices and facilitating the establishment of global inequalities that remain with us today.[56] We believe that this history, and the echoes of this history that we continue to see in global rules and practices, must be taken into account when considering the repentant and self-sacrificial kinship that Western countries might "owe" to displaced people today. We explore this further in later chapters.

But for now, let us turn to part one, where we retrieve the scriptural call to kinship with the displaced.

---

[54]On how countries "securitize" the suffering of others, giving it their attention but focusing on the implications for their own security rather than the needs of the vulnerable, see Barry Buzan, Ole Wæver, and Jaap de Wilde, *Security: A New Framework for Analysis* (Boulder, CO: Lynne Rienner, 1998); and Anne Hammerstadt, "The Securitization of Forced Migration," in *The Oxford Handbook of Refugee and Forced Migration Studies*, ed. Elena Fiddian-Qasmiyeh, Gil Loescher, Katy Long, and Nando Sigona (Oxford: Oxford University Press, 2014), 265-77.

[55]Lucy Mayblin, *Asylum After Empire: Colonial Legacies in the Politics of Asylum Seeking* (London: Rowman & Littlefield, 2017), 8-9.

[56]For a powerful recent argument along these lines, see E. Tendayi Achiume, "Migration as Decolonization," *Stanford Law Review* 71, no. 6 (2019): 1509-74.

PART ONE

THE BIBLE

1

KINSHIP WITH THE STRANGER

IMAGINE THE CIRCUMSTANCES of a family of three generations that has fled their own village because of war, in this case nearly a millennia before Christ. Jonathan and Abital, their children, and Abital's mother—all those from the family who miraculously survived the conflict—have struggled for miles along a hilly trail to find sanctuary. One circumstance is in their favor: the time when kings go to war is also the time of the spring harvest, and they have some hope at least of finding a little food to eat. After seeking work in a number of settlements along their path, they come at last to one where Abital and her mother are invited to help with the herds that roam within the village walls; there may be other work for them here as well. The father at the head of the family is, in time, invited to join with some laborers who are harvesting grain nearby. Perhaps the family finds shelter under a disused, ramshackle mud-brick roof, one of just seven buildings making up this settlement. Or perhaps (and what joy and relief this would have been!) one of the family households makes room under their *own* roof for the newcomers, and they crowd in.

Here is shelter, and food, a respite from violence—even the blessing of companionship. But is it as good as it seems? This family is desperate and has nowhere to turn. For the present, there are no other options and no one advocating for them. Will these outsiders receive their pay, their daily allotment of grain? And what happens in the future, after the harvest? Will they be homeless again, to endure the searing heat of the summer months without shelter? Will they be forced to beg for food, or borrow to purchase it, and so become indebted and enslaved like so many others in their situation?

THE STRANGER IN THE BOOK OF DEUTERONOMY

In this chapter we examine Deuteronomy's urgings of the Old Testament people of God to embrace the "stranger" as kin.[1] Deuteronomy's concern to protect the stranger, the fatherless, and the widow is well known (e.g., Deut 24:19-22). But by the sheer number of the book's references to the first member of this triad, *the stranger* (the noun appears twenty-two times), it seems that widespread displacement was a particularly pressing social concern of that place and time. In ancient times people who had been displaced, wrenched by war or other crises and hardships from their lands and kinship groupings, were in real danger of exposure and starvation. Such people were often obliged to offer themselves as the cheapest of cheap labor simply in order to survive. They were often exploited and abused. A Babylonian proverb reflects this reality: "A resident alien in another city is a slave."[2]

For these most vulnerable strangers, the only real hope for a future was the prospect of adoption into a new kinship grouping: "The landless and their families needed to be integrated into the clans."[3] Renowned Old Testament scholar Nadav Na'aman puts it well:

> Traditional society in Judah was based on family solidarity, on the leadership of the elders and notables, and its economy rested primarily on land. Integrating into such a traditional society was a major hurdle for displaced people who had been torn from their own former family structures, and had neither land nor means of production to provide them with self-sufficient subsistence.[4]

---

[1]A more thorough treatment of this topic is found in Mark R. Glanville, *Adopting the Stranger as Kindred in Deuteronomy*, AIL 33 (Atlanta: SBL Press, 2018); and Mark R. Glanville, "The *Gēr* (Stranger) in Deuteronomy: Family for the Displaced," *JBL* 137, no. 3 (2018): 599-623. See also Mark R. Glanville, "'Festive Kinship': Solidarity, Responsibility, and Identity Formation in Deuteronomy," *JSOT* 44, no. 1 (2019): 3-18. See the first two references for a full bibliography of the scholarship on the stranger in Deuteronomy. Awabdy has also provided a recent study of the stranger in Deuteronomy. Mark Awabdy, *Immigrants and Innovative Law: Deuteronomy's Theological and Social Vision for the "gr,"* FAT 2.67 (Tübingen: Mohr Siebeck, 2014).

[2]Raymond Westbrook, "Slave and Master in Ancient Near Eastern Law," in *Law from the Tigris to the Tiber: The Writings of Raymond Westbrook*, vol. 1, *The Shared Tradition*, ed. Bruce Wells and Rachel Magdalene (Winona Lake, IN: Eisenbrauns, 2009), 161-215, at 178n7.

[3]Eckart Otto, "ša'ar," in *TDOT*, 14:359-405, at 380.

[4]Nadav Na'aman, "Sojourners and Levites in the Kingdom of Judah in the Seventh Century BCE," *ZABR* 14 (2008): 237-79, at 276-77.

Israel's very identity as a nation is invoked in what is perhaps the most famous of Deuteronomy's edicts on this matter: "You shall also love the stranger, for *you were strangers* in the land of Egypt" (Deut 10:19 NRSV).

As we read these texts, we must keep in mind that Deuteronomy is about a *community*, a people called into being as a nation and formed by Yahweh himself, which is now (as Deuteronomy is being communicated to this people for the first time) in the process of being renewed and re-formed by God. Deuteronomy is a covenant charter for the people of Yahweh (e.g., Deut 29:9-14; 31:9-13).[5] The community shaped by this text is to be different from others of the ancient Near East. In particular, it is to stand for *justice*, in stark contrast to the oppression the people had endured as strangers in Egypt. The renewed community is to celebrate the life and joy of the one true God in communion with one another, utterly separating themselves from the idolatry of the surrounding nations. Deuteronomy's laws in regard to the stranger can be understood only in the context of the life of the community it serves. Every person within this new community is to experience the freshness, the genuineness, the grace that flourishes when people are knit together as sisters and brothers through the redeeming acts and the loving rule of God.[6]

Some readers will already be thinking, but what about Deuteronomy's commands to destroy the Canaanites? Surely there is nothing welcoming about that! Well, if this thought is yours, wait for the next chapter, where we will explore the meaning of the Old Testament texts (including some from Deuteronomy) that seem to urge the exclusion—even the elimination—of "outsiders."

WHO WAS THE STRANGER?

Before we explore Deuteronomy's response to the stranger further, it is important to establish precisely who it is we're talking about.[7] "Stranger" translates the Hebrew word *gēr*. In Deuteronomy, the dependency of this person is always in evidence: in their labor within the household and the settlement (Deut 5:14; 24:14), in their inclusion within the triad of the vulnerable ("the

---

[5]S. Dean McBride Jr., "Polity of the Covenant People: The Book of Deuteronomy," *Int* 41, no. 3 (1987): 229-44, at 237.

[6]See further Mark R. Glanville, "A Missional Reading of Deuteronomy," in *Reading the Bible Missionally*, ed. Michael W. Goheen (Grand Rapids, MI: Eerdmans, 2016), 124-50.

[7]There are two other generic terms for "outsiders" in Deuteronomy, apart from the term *gēr*: גֵּר, *nokrî*, and זָר, *zār*. These are not vulnerable figures, and they are not being incorporated into the community, so they will not concern us here. A discussion of these terms is found in M. Glanville, *Adopting the Stranger*, chap. 6.

stranger, the fatherless, the widow," e.g., Deut 16:11, 14), and in the laws that
dictate that the community should provide means for their sustenance (Deut
14:28-29; 26:12-15).[8]

Like Abital and Jonathan in the story above, the stranger in Deuteronomy
is dependent, landless, and on the lowest stratum of the social ladder.[9] Such
strangers have left kinship ties and land and now live where they have no
blood relations nearby. They are now without the security and privileges that
family ties and place of birth once provided. They are in social limbo for,
although technically they are free (not enslaved), they lack those things that
lend status and security: land, a means of subsistence, and meaningful social
connection. Since there are no family members to come to the defense of
such strangers, they are easily victimized and oppressed; they can all too
easily fall into debt; they may be reduced at last to slavery.

Where does the stranger come from? Scholars suggest that a stranger in Deuteronomy could have been a displaced person from the kingdom of Judah (the
Southern Kingdom); a refugee from Israel (the Northern Kingdom), displaced
by the Assyrian invasion; or a foreigner from a kingdom other than either Judah
or the Northern Kingdom. Or perhaps there were strangers from each.[10]

There is evidence that at least some of the strangers referenced in Deuteronomy were foreigners (see Deut 14:21; Deut 28:43). However, as we consider
the situation of these dependent strangers in Old Testament society, it is a
mistake to think about their ethnicity only in terms of national categories, as
either Israelite or non-Israelite. Such distinctions may be normal today. I may
hold a passport identifying me as belonging to a certain country and will be
obliged to present that passport for permission to travel from one country to
another. My *nationality* is constantly in view. But in a clan-oriented society
such as that of the Old Testament, personal identity is rather more complex.
It is not as simple as distinguishing between Israelite and non-Israelite, as a
person from a different tribe or even the next settlement is an outsider.[11] As

---

[8]The common translation, "resident alien," fails to take into account the dependence of the *gēr* in
Deuteronomy. This translation seems to be influenced by the usage of *gēr* in Leviticus, wrongly
assuming that this term means the same thing in Leviticus and Deuteronomy. (It is not uncommon
for a particular word to have a different meaning across the various traditions of the Pentateuch.)
[9]Na'aman, "Sojourners and Levites," 258.
[10]See M. Glanville, *Adopting the Stranger*, chap. 7, for a full explanation and assessment of these views.
[11]Walter J. Houston, *Contending for Justice: Ideologies and Theologies of Social Justice in the Old Testament* (London: T&T Clark, 2006), 108. Deuteronomy most often speaks of strangers not in relation
to *national* identity (in the sense of "a stranger *to Israel*") but in relation to the household or the
clan (e.g., Deut 16:11, 14). Thus, for example, the phrase "the stranger within your gates" carries the
sense of "the one who comes from outside your clan but who is, at present, living within it."

a member of a communal society, I might very well think of any natural-born member of my household and my clan as an insider, and thus think of *all* others as outsiders.

Consequently, the stranger in Deuteronomy is any vulnerable person from outside the core family: an outsider in relation to the clan and the household within which he or she now dwells. Some of these strangers would have come from another nation, but others might have come merely from the clan group over the hill, so to speak.[12] However far they have come, these strangers have been separated from their land and their kin and no longer know the protection that family and patrimony (land inheritance) provide. An old Italian term for *orphan* comes to mind: *esposito*, "exposed." The Deuteronomic "stranger" is exposed to all manner of ill.

Deuteronomy's vision for the stranger. The book of Deuteronomy has a three-part structure—it's shaped like a doughnut. The first and third sections (Deut 1–11 and 27–34) provide the covenantal and narrative framework within which stands the "law corpus" (Deut 12–26). These laws at the center (of the doughnut) are intended to shape the people into a community radically different from all the other ancient Near Eastern nations that surround them. Thus, many aspects of Israel's communal life are dealt with in the law corpus, including social law, judicial procedures, and feasting texts. And within this body of laws, Deuteronomy makes special provision for the welfare of the stranger.

THE SOCIAL LAW'S CONCERN FOR DEPENDENT STRANGERS: RESPONSIBILITY AND SOLIDARITY

Hireling law. Many of the law types in Deuteronomy provide for strangers such as the family that we imagined in the chapter's opening; the social laws in particular are meant to restrain a creditor's ability to accumulate indentured workers and slaves.[13] Our discussion probes the implicit cultural meaning of the social laws of Deuteronomy, that which the original audience would have taken as the obvious sense of the text.[14]

---

[12] See M. Glanville, *Adopting the Stranger*, 138-42. The concern of Deuteronomy's framework (Deut 1–11, 27–34) to include the stranger within the covenant community is not due, necessarily, to the foreignness of the stranger. Rather, severance from kinship and from land brings the displaced person's standing in the assembly into question. See further M. Glanville, *Adopting the Stranger*, chap. 6.

[13] A similar discussion of the hireling and the gleaning laws is found in M. Glanville, "'Festive Kinship,'" 146-48.

[14] For a general discussion of the law corpus, Deuteronomy 12–26, see Frank Crüsemann, *The Torah: Theology and Social History of Old Testament Law*, trans. Allan W. Mahnke (Minneapolis: Fortress, 1996).

From Deuteronomy's social laws, two are particularly relevant to our consideration of the stranger: (1) regarding hired laborers and (2) regarding the harvest:

> Do not oppress a needy and destitute hired laborer, whether one of your brothers-sisters,[15] or your stranger who is in your land and within your gates. You shall give them their wage in their day, before night comes upon them, for they are poor, they are always in dire need of it. Otherwise they will call out against you to Yahweh and you will incur guilt. (Deut 24:14-15 author's translation)

This hireling law is in two parts: a general prohibition against oppressing a day laborer, followed by the specific direction to pay a day laborer on the day of his or her work. A hireling was among an ancient Near Eastern society's poorest (Job 7:1; 14:6). The term "brother-sister" is designed to arouse a sense of kinship solidarity and responsibility, as if to say: "treat your brothers as *brothers!*" But the phrase that follows, "whether one of your brothers-sisters or your stranger," goes further, to enfold *the stranger* within Deuteronomy's brother-sister ethic. In regard to justice and compassion, then, the displaced person is to be held as equal to the brother or sister.

Gleaning laws.

> Supposing that you reap your harvest in your field and you accidently leave behind a sheaf in the field, do not return to get it. It shall be for the stranger, the fatherless, and the widow, in order that Yahweh your God may bless you in all the work of your hands. (Deut 24:19 author's translation)

Establishing an olive orchard or a vineyard took considerable time and expense, and landowners were understandably careful to make the most of what the land produced for them. But during Israel's harvest, Deuteronomy forbids the landed farmer to go back over the field, vineyard, or olive grove a second time to gather the residue (Deut 24:19-21). Instead, the remnants of the harvest are to be left for the poor or displaced.[16] The stipulation that these most vulnerable people should share in the fruit of the land demonstrates that they are to be treated as participants in the community, co-recipients of Yahweh's gifts (Deut 24:20, 21).

Cultural meaning of the social laws.
At the very least, these social laws communicate a certain responsibility toward vulnerable people. Yet, for whom did ancient Israelite people have responsibility?[17]

---

[15]"Brothers-sisters": both men and women could work as hired laborers.

[16]Indeed, there are nine occurrences of a phrase within this section of law that use the preposition *for* (in the sense of "intended for") in describing the remnants of the harvest: "it is *for* the stranger."

[17]See a similar discussion in M. Glanville, "'Festive Kinship,'" 147-48.

The warmth of the climate didn't always translate into a warmth of welcome. Culturally, ancient Israelites acknowledged no responsibility toward outsiders. In fact, outsiders were viewed with suspicion, often as a threat; in many cultures local to Israel, outsiders could be harmed or even killed with impunity.[18] Consider, for example, the violent aggression toward Lot and his guests (Gen 19). The men of Sodom exclaim of Lot: "This fellow came to sojourn, and he has become the judge" (Gen 19:9 ESV). The paradox within the phrase itself is that a stranger with no legal privileges would assume for himself the role of judge. Within the narrative, Lot's helplessness before the mob illustrates how a person without kinship connection may have no legal recourse.[19] Practical expression of solidarity from one's immediate kinsfolk could generally be relied upon (Deut 22:29; cf. Deut 5:16; 21:18-21). But clearly there were no guarantees for vulnerable strangers.

In light of this oftentimes antagonistic attitude toward outsiders, we need to shift our understanding of social law away from questions of "mere" poverty alleviation, the way social law is commonly interpreted, toward questions of responsibility and solidarity. The issue of solidarity is explicit in the requirement of the hireling law that brothers-sisters be treated as *brothers-sisters*, and (remarkably) that strangers too should be treated as brothers-sisters (Deut 24:14-15). Solidarity is also behind the gleaning laws (Deut 24:19-22), which may be viewed as rules that governed the sharing of possessions with kinsfolk. Kinship is experienced in such sharing in innumerable texts in the Old Testament, as, for example, in Abraham and Lot's sharing of livestock and land (Gen 13:8-9; cf. 20:14; 21:25-30; Ex 19:5-6; Deut 33:1-29). Set within this cultural context, the gleaning laws encourage a sense of kinship solidarity with vulnerable people, urging upon those who have much a willingness to share the harvest with those who have little.

Evidently, these social laws respond to the question, For whom do we have responsibility? Whom must we protect? Whom must we enfold and incorporate? These laws, in other words, were heard and experienced across the field of kinship: they are Scripture's answer to the question, Who is my kin? The social problems addressed by these laws were *kinship* problems: the

---

[18]David D. Gilmore argues that a general suspicion of and aggression toward outsiders characterized the pan-Mediterranean area. David D. Gilmore, "Anthropology of the Mediterranean Area," *ARA* 11 (1982): 175-205, at 178-79.

[19]There are also examples from Scripture of the Israelites' reluctance to fulfill their social responsibilities even toward disadvantaged *insiders*. In the narrative of Zelophehad's daughters, for example, clansmen were unwilling to preserve the name and patrimony of a deceased relative (Num 27, 36; see also Deut 1:16-17; Ruth 4:5-6).

stranger, the fatherless, and the widow needed a clan that would take responsibility for them, extending subsistence, protection, and a sense of belonging.
Deuteronomy's social laws required Yahweh's people to act as kinsfolk to
those who had been without the protection of kinship.

When the author of Deuteronomy was renewing the community under
Yahweh's rule, he did so in culturally recognizable ways. The human phenomenon of *kinship*, where identity, responsibility, subsistence—life itself—
could be found, was the background upon which the social laws were set out:
foreground figures painted against a cultural landscape that was assumed and
understood by all. So we see here the working out in ancient Israelite society
of the concept introduced in chapter one, that kinship, across time and place,
is not static but is continuously being reconfigured for new circumstances.

THE STRANGER IN THE LAW OF JUDICIAL PROCEDURE: PROTECTION AND PARTICIPATION

Another group of laws in Deuteronomy's system of protection and inclusion
for the dependent stranger has to do with just legal processes, often called the
laws of judicial procedure. Returning to our imaginary displaced family, let's
consider what might happen when an employer gives the food to the family
in advance of a day's work, taking their outer garments in pledge of the work
to come. Then, though the family completes the day's work, the employer
refuses to return to them their valuable garments. Our strangers, if they are
bold enough, might dare to take their case to the elders of the community in
which all this has taken place; perhaps these elders will be found willing to
meet, hear the disputants, and make a judgment. But what are the chances
that the elders will believe the word of such strangers against the testimony
of their own kinsfolk? After all, outsiders were often viewed with suspicion
and antipathy. These strangers have no kinsfolk standing by to ensure that
justice is done, and their antagonist might well influence the elders of his
community, perhaps by enlisting popular support, or by brute force, or by
underhanded bribes (cf. Gen 19:9). Who should argue the case for our
dependent strangers?

In fact, *the law itself* argues for them. Within Deuteronomy's law of judicial procedure (Deut 1:16-17; 10:17-19; 24:17; 27:19), the stranger appears
in four texts that require that the stranger receive a hearing and a judgment
without prejudice on the basis of his or her landlessness or lack of kinship
connection: "Hear cases between your brothers-sisters, and judge justly
between a person and his or her brother-sister *and his or her stranger*"

Kinship with Refugees in Phoenix, Arizona

We briefly leave the ancient world of Deuteronomy to consider an example of kinship with refugees today. In 2017, armed bikers were planning to rally outside a mosque in Phoenix, to burn Qur'ans, to burn images of Muhammad, and to shout insults. Hundreds of participants had signed up on Facebook. (This mosque is the place of worship for hundreds of Syrian refugees, people who are trying to find home and stability in a new and strange culture.) The organizers encouraged people to come prepared to use their firearms.

Two faith leaders, friends of ours, Jim Mullins and Adam Estle, spotted the event on Facebook. They consulted with the president of the mosque, with whom they already had a friendship. Then, just twenty-four hours before the rally was due to start, they called upon Christians to gather at the mosque to be a prayerful and peaceful presence. Their aim was to create a physical barrier of protection with their bodies and a spiritual wall of protection with their prayers. As Jim put it: "Before a bullet could pierce the body of a Muslim person, it would first have to pass through the body of a Christian."

Jim and Adam were deeply moved when around two hundred Christians arrived outside the mosque, wearing blue t-shirts to identify themselves. Christ followers numbered about the same as the protesters. They formed a line between the protestors and the mosque. They prayed deeply, and they engaged the angriest and loudest protesters in conversation, listening carefully to their concerns. Jim spoke with the lead biker, and even got him laughing: "Man, I'm the biggest guy here," Jim said. "If a shot is fired, then it is sure to hit me! So can you please put your gun away?" He did put his gun away, and so did many others. Some protesters turned inside out the t-shirts that had previously read: "F*** Muslims." As Jim said, on this day, "Jesus showed up." What a way for these Christians in Phoenix to demonstrate kinship with refugees![a]

---

[a] A photo was shared on Facebook over six thousand times with the caption: "It is reported that more Christians showed up to stand in solidarity with the #PHx-Mosque this evening than protesters." It appears that the photo was shared mostly by Muslims, living all around the world.

(Deut 1:16 author's translation).[20] The fact that this is the very first stipulation in Deuteronomy demonstrates the immense importance of fairness and justice in legal procedures involving the "dependent stranger." The law insists that such an outsider as this is nevertheless on an equal legal footing with the kinsperson.

The judicial rights of the stranger are also protected in a curse ceremony: "Cursed be anyone who perverts the justice due to the stranger, fatherless, or widow. And all the people shall say, 'Amen'" (Deut 27:19 author's translation). Let's not overlook the significance of this ceremony: since it is always possible that injustice in legal procedure may be hidden from the eyes of the community, the curse here reminds the whole people of Israel that Yahweh, the divine and righteous judge, shall see this evil and intervene. Amen indeed.

Thus, in both the social law and the laws of judicial procedure, Deuteronomy insists as a matter of the highest priority that displaced persons should receive a just hearing and fair judgment at the gates. The guarantee of this fundamental right opened the possibility of the dependent stranger's full economic and social participation within the community. Might Deuteronomy's law of judicial procedure suggest for us the importance, to God, of just processes for refugee-claimants throughout the world, processes that they are too often denied?

THE STRANGER IN FEASTING TEXTS: INCORPORATION

Deuteronomy has some of the best feasts in Scripture. Along with the immediate family, the Levite, fatherless, widow, and stranger were enjoined to journey from the farm to the designated place of worship for a time of joyful cultic feasting (Deut 14:22-29; 16:1-17; 26:1-15).[21] These feasts were jubilant—a huge proportion of the annual supply of meat and wine was set aside for them. And anthropological studies of pilgrimage feasts help us to see Deuteronomy's strategy in explicitly including the stranger in these events. Victor Turner, for example, has shown how in pilgrimage feasts the barriers of traditional social structure and hierarchy broke down.[22] For the duration of the

---

[20]"Brother-sisters": both men and women had the right to give testimony at the gate (e.g., Deut 21:18-20).

[21]Peter Altmann has produced an extensive study of Deuteronomy's feasts in light of ancient Near Eastern feasting texts and anthropology (Peter Altmann, *Festive Meals in Ancient Israel: Deuteronomy's Identity Politics in Their Ancient Near Eastern Context*, BZAW 424 [Berlin: De Gruyter, 2011]). Mark Glanville has argued more thoroughly that these texts are fostering the incorporation of vulnerable people as kindred (M. Glanville, *Adopting the Stranger*, chap. 5).

[22]Victor Turner, *Dramas, Fields, and Metaphors: Symbolic Action in Human Society* (Ithaca, NY:

pilgrimage, social status was suspended, producing what Turner calls *communitas*, a sense of mutual belonging that is "undifferentiated, equalitarian, direct, non-rational."[23] Within this anti-structure of *communitas*, kinship is experienced and friendships are formed that (at least to some degree) ignore the boundaries of traditional social hierarchy.[24] This research deepens our vision of Deuteronomy's harvest festivals, where the whole community shares a pilgrimage feast, forging their identity as the people of Yahweh. The inclusion of the Levite, stranger, fatherless, and widow is dominant in these texts. Deuteronomy urges the incorporation of these vulnerable people as kin so that every person may share the feast before Yahweh.

The festival calendar, Deuteronomy 16:1-17. The Feasts of Weeks (Deut 16:9-12) and of Booths (otherwise known as Tabernacles; Deut 16:13-15) are harvest festivals in which the whole community gathers for joyful feasting in celebration of Yahweh's abundant supply.[25] Georg Braulik states, "The deuteronomic cult order, which is otherwise very reticent about stipulations, never tires of enumerating the participants in sacrifices or feasts." A list of festal participants appears in both Weeks and Booths: "Feast, before Yahweh your God! You, your son, your daughter, your male slave, your female slave, the Levite who is in your gates, the stranger, the fatherless, and the widow who is in your midst!" (Deut 16:11; 16:14 author's translation). The participant lists are given prominence in the text by their length and repetition.[26] In them, the dependent stranger is, *like any other member of the community*, caught up in the joy of the feast. Together with the family, the stranger shares in the fellowship, the ritualized time, the smell of boiling meat, the warmth of wine, the rare flavors of festal recipes, the long pilgrimage with winding conversations, the waiting, the fulfillment, the liturgical richness of poetry and song and chant—all before the face of Yahweh, the Lord of the harvest, Giver of gifts, Founder of the feast!

Cornell University Press, 1974). See also Michael Dietler, "Theorizing the Feast: Rituals of Consumption, Commensal Politics, and Power in African Contexts," in *Feasts: Archaeological and Ethnographic Perspectives on Food, Politics, and Power*, ed. Michael Dietler and Brian Hayden (Washington, DC: Smithsonian Institution Press, 2001), 65-114. John Eade and Michael J. Sallnow have edited a volume that contests Turner's thesis, pointing to ways in which pilgrimage feasts may reinforce societal divisions: *Contesting the Sacred: The Anthropology of Christian Pilgrimage* (New York: Routledge, 1991). To be sure, meals have the capacity to both unite and divide. However, we demonstrate here that Deuteronomy's feasts display elements of *communitas*.

[23]Turner, *Dramas, Fields, and Metaphors*, 47.

[24]Turner, *Dramas, Fields, and Metaphors*, 200-201, 205-6.

[25]See also the analysis in M. Glanville, "'Festive Kinship,'" 141-44.

[26]See further Georg Braulik, "The Joy of the Feast," in *Theology of Deuteronomy: Collected Essays of Georg Braulik, O.S.B.*, trans. Ulrika Lindblad (N. Richland Hills, TX: Bibal, 1994) 27-66, at 52.

The list of participants is structured in concentric circles of natural belonging, progressing from the paterfamilias at the center, outward to the sons and daughters, then to household slaves, then to Levites, and outward again to vulnerable people who also participated in the life of the household. These vulnerable people who were associated with a particular rural household often lived under one roof with the family.[27] Janet Carsten reflects that "kinship is made in houses through the intimate sharing of space, food, and nurturance that goes on within domestic space."[28] The sense from these household lists is that the household becomes a place of inclusion and tenderness, where the stranger is enfolded into the family as a beloved member of the people of Yahweh. It demonstrates that kinship is indeed "an area of life in which people invest their emotions, their creative energy, and their new imaginings."[29]

Gates of welcome. If the list of participants associates the stranger within the household, the phrase "within your gates" (Deut 16:11, 14; cf. 5:14; 14:21, 29; 16:14; 24:14; 26:12; 31:12) additionally associates the stranger within the clan grouping of a settlement, or within a city.[30] In Israel (and the ancient Near East generally) the city gate is where the poor gather to receive charity, to find work, or to seek justice (e.g., Amos 5:12).[31] Similarly, in a village context the gate has both a social and a symbolic function. The village gate is the emblem of shelter and succor for the vulnerable (e.g., Deut 16:14): the third-year tithe is to be stored "within your gates" (Deut 14:28); the fleeing slave may reside "within your gates" (Deut 23:15-16); and the laboring stranger resides "within your gates" (Deut 24:14). These references demonstrate that the phrase "within your gates" can refer to the protective shelter that the village offers to the stranger. In Deuteronomy's social laws, then, the gate is not an exclusionary boundary—as gates often are—but a symbol of social responsibility and care. How wonderful it would be if, today, nations could collaborate to establish appropriate and sustainable gates of welcome for refugees around the world.

---

[27]The size of rural dwellings indicates that an extended family along with some vulnerable people probably dwelled under the one roof. See further Avraham Faust, *The Archaeology of Israelite Society in Iron Age II* (Winona Lake, IN: Eisenbrauns, 2012), 12.

[28]Janet Carsten, *After Kinship* (Cambridge: Cambridge University Press, 2004), 35. It is informative, too, to compare Deuteronomy's festival calendar with other ancient Near Eastern feasting texts, of which there are many. Deuteronomy omits common feasting motifs from such texts and includes others, with the overall effect of diminishing the distinctions between social levels from the *paterfamilias* and the stranger, tending toward mutuality. See further M. Glanville, *Adopting the Stranger*, 163.

[29]Carsten, *After Kinship*, 9.

[30]The phrase "within your gates" in Deuteronomy often, but not always, refers to a local settlement. See M. Glanville, *Adopting the Stranger*, 203-5.

[31]See further Faust, *Archaeology of Israelite Society*, 100, 105-6.

Festivals Today

The closest the authors have come to experiencing the joy of Israel's ancient feasts is in our previous careers as jazz musicians. We would play together in Latino/a bands at large Latino/a festivals (we ourselves were outsiders in this context, experiencing the hospitality of our friends). Thousands from the Latin American community would gather together to dance and eat. When our band began to play, the whole arena would move. Every generation, young and old, knew the traditional dances, and everyone, it seemed, could dance with ease and joy. These sorts of experiences can give us a sense of Israel's ancient festivals. The whole community, rich and poor, young and old, feasted together before the Lord with music and dancing. This festal spirit is suggested by some of the very short psalms, which must have been played and sung again and again for singing and dancing (e.g., Ps 117). Gratefully and joyfully receiving the good gifts of Yahweh is at the heart of a covenant response in Deuteronomy. The other side of the coin of thanksgiving, so to speak, is inclusion and justice for the least.

Festival of the Firstfruits and Egypt, Deuteronomy 26:1-11. The Festival of the Firstfruits (Deut 26:1-11) is a grateful pilgrimage feast before Yahweh in which the Levite and the stranger are, again, explicitly included. The divine gift of land and its abundance are the theological grounds for inclusive celebration: "Feast on all the bounty which Yahweh, your God, has given you and your household—you and the Levite and the stranger who is in your midst" (Deut 26:11 author's translation).

The stranger's inclusion at the Feast of Firstfruits is also embedded in Israel's own formative narrative, recited briefly in what is famously called the "small credo":

> A wandering Aramean was my father. And he went down to Egypt and he dwelled there as a stranger . . . The Egyptians treated us harshly, oppressed us, and imposed hard labor on us. And we cried to Yahweh the God of our forefathers. . . . And Yahweh brought us out of Egypt. (Deut 26:5-8 author's translation)

One key memory was Israel's experience of being a stranger in Egypt. In the time of Abraham and then later in the time of Joseph, the patriarchs migrated to Egypt to escape famine and death in the land of Canaan. As a stranger, Israel was dependent upon Egyptian hospitality and kindness. As strangers, Israel's patriarchs were always a whisker away from enslavement

(Gen 15:13). In this declaration, Israel's own troubled past as a nation of strangers in Egypt echoes the harsh realities faced by the stranger who now lives within Israel (Deut 26:11). This invoking of the kinship of fellow sufferers is meant to motivate Israel to offer the kind of hospitality that she herself longed for during her exile in Egypt (Deut 26:5-7, 11): "Love the stranger, for you were strangers in the land of Egypt" (Deut 10:19).[32]

Israel's self-identification as "stranger" creates genuine relationship and equality. In effect, the stranger within Israel *stops* being a stranger, and Israel moves into a position of vulnerability, a mysterious and empathetic space. Israelites are to have no pretention to power or superiority for they are truly the stranger's sister and brother. This is an experience of being dislodged from a place of privilege.

The second narrative motif in the small credo (Deut 26:5-10) is the story of Yahweh's emancipation of Israel. This narrative is repeated numerous times as motivation for showing compassion to the stranger. It frames the gleaning laws, for example, appearing both before and after: "Remember that you were a slave in Egypt and the LORD your God redeemed you from there; therefore I command you to do this" (Deut 24:18, cf. 24:22).

A recurrent picture of God in Deuteronomy is as the great King who emancipates an enslaved nation: Yahweh the great slave-emancipator.[33] God is a God of compassionate action who sides with the oppressed. The memory of slavery and of Yahweh's redemption was a motivating impulse behind Israel's laws. Israel was to leave the evil practices of Egypt behind them: "the LORD your God redeemed you from there." This new redeemed community must now reflect the justice and compassion of Yahweh, the God of Israel. Israel must "remember" her history of enslavement and of redemption. And the word translated "remember" here means more than mere cognitive memory; it means to live the kind of shared life that is in harmony with the striking reality of Israel's history (see Ex 13:3; Deut 16:12).[34] Yet again, this narrative motif of slavery and redemption is a place of deep connection between Israelites and vulnerable strangers. The point of festal celebration is that we have survived (Deut 16:10-12)! We are all alive; and we are alive together—both the native and the stranger.

---

[32]See also Exodus 22:21; 23:9.
[33]See also Deuteronomy 5:14-15; 10:18-19; 15:12-15; 16:11-12; 24:19-22; 26:5, 11; cf. 17:16.
[34]Nathan MacDonald, *Not Bread Alone: The Uses of Food in the Old Testament* (Oxford: Oxford University Press, 2008), 70-99.

Alasdair MacIntyre insists that ethics have meaning in the context of a narrative. "I can only answer the question, 'What am I to do?' if I can answer the prior question, 'Of what story or stories do I find myself a part?'"[35] Israel's formative story is a story of displacement, enslavement, and emancipation. Israel remains always an emancipated people who serve a God who is in the business of releasing slaves. So, consistent with their own story and with their own God, Israel is always to live as an inclusive and protective community of tenderness. The God of Israel and of Moses is the divine Kinsperson who draws into one family both landed people and landless, those who have much and those who have little, those who have been known to us all our lives as well as "the stranger within our gates."

Third-year tithe, Deuteronomy 14:28-29; 26:12-15. The tithe is a sacred portion of the harvest that is set aside for God in grateful worship. This sacred produce is consumed by the priesthood and is also offered to God in sacrifice. In the third-year tithe provision, the sacred portion is given to the stranger. This provision dignifies the dispossessed with an offering customarily reserved for sacred places and sacred people. Once again, this implies that the stranger belongs to the people of Yahweh (Deut 14:28-29; 26:12-15).

A primary function of these feasting texts is to transform relationships between the vulnerable and the household and clan. The stranger is welcomed to share in the abundance of the seasonal harvests, as the community practices God's love in accordance with the rhythms of the creation. Turner's construct of *communitas* helps to clarify the picture: by means of these stipulations in regard to pilgrimage feasting, Deuteronomy is transforming relationships between insiders and outsiders in the direction of kinship. Yahweh is the divine Kinsperson, and as strangers share in the feast "before Yahweh your God," even consuming the sacred tithe, they are incorporated within the very family of Yahweh. Deuteronomy's vision for the stranger is that she or he is to be grafted into the household, the clan, and the nation.[36]

---

[33] Alasdair MacIntyre, *After Virtue: A Study in Moral Theory*, 3rd ed. (Notre Dame, IN: University of Notre Dame Press, 2007), 216.

[36] The conclusions presented here contest some recent scholarship regarding the figure of the stranger in Deuteronomy. For example, Ruth Ebach concludes that there is only limited inclusion for the stranger in earlier versions of Deuteronomy and that this inclusion is broadened in later versions (Ruth Ebach, *Das Fremde und das Eigene: Die Fremdendarstellungen des Deuteronomiums im Kontext israelitischer Identitätskonstruktionen*, BZAW 471 [Berlin: De Gruyter, 2014]). We contend that Ebach underestimates the extent of the stranger's being included in these feasting texts—that even the so-called outsider is here invited to participate in the religious life of the nation and celebrate "before Yahweh your God" (Deut 16:11, 16-17; 26:10-11; etc.). For a detailed analysis see M. Glanville, *Adopting the Stranger*.

In these festivals, celebration and lament were both expressed, as God's people remembered together the affliction of Egypt (Deut 16:1-8). Loren Balisky, the cofounder of Kinbrace, shared with us how in the early days of supporting refugee claimants, the Kinbrace community determined to nourish a culture of family by regularly sharing meals and celebrations.

Does the Bible Belong to Refugees in a Unique Way?

Lava and her children were scheduled for their refugee hearing the next morning. One of the authors, Mark, was to attend their hearing as a silent supporter. Lava was anxious, and Anika Barlow, Kinbrace's Lead Host, was spending time with her and the kids in the Kinbrace living room. Wanting to ease her anxiety in any small way, Anika said: "It is good that Mark is going with you tomorrow. He is a good, kind man, and very smart." Lava replied: "Yes, but he can't say anything at the hearing." "He can't say anything, but he will be praying in his heart," Anika said. Lava smiled. "You can pray anytime? What do you say?" Anika replied, "Yes, and if I was going to pray for you now I might say 'God, give Lava peace in her heart. Help her and her family to have a good rest tonight. Be with her tomorrow and give them a positive decision.' In fact, I do pray that now." Anika explained that Mark would pick them up at 7:45 in the morning. She put on a YouTube video clip of Mark playing the piano, wanting to reinforce familiarity and trust. After the introductory song, Mark begins to talk about the Hebrew people, enslaved in Egypt.[a] "Did he say 'Egypt'?" Lava asked. "Yes, Mark is talking about the Bible, and the Bible tells the story of God freeing his people from slavery in Egypt. Do you know the story of Moses?" "Mosa?" "Yes, Mosa."

Anika fetched her children's Bible and they sat on the couch. They read the story of Moses and the burning bush, the plagues, and the crossing of the Red Sea. God says to his people "Do not be afraid. I will make a way where there is no way. I will be with you." "This is reading the Bible in exile," Anika later reflected. "Here these stories mean something more." God *is* with Lava and her family. The next afternoon, at the hearing's conclusion, the board member accepted Lava's family as refugees in Canada. The joy and relief that the family felt were inexpressible.

---

[a]Mark Glanville, "A Jazz Talk: How Biblical Law Shapes Missional Communities," *YouTube*, September 28, 2016, www.youtube.com/watch?v=A-fkkNRYzN0&t=4s.

Kinbrace celebrates birthdays. Successful refugee claims are a reason for a party. And yet, Loren says, "Celebration is that close to tears all of the time." (Loren gestures with his palms facing each other closely to indicate close proximity.) There are traumatic memories of fleeing violence, parents separated from children with grave fears for their safety, grandparents dying back at home. In the muddled, agonizing mess of displacement, the Kinbrace community eats and feasts, laughs and weeps together as a makeshift family.

THE STRANGER IN DEUTERONOMY'S
FRAMEWORK (DEUT 1–11, 27–34)

The opening and closing sections of Deuteronomy (1–11, 27–34) provide ladder theological and narrative frame surrounding the legislative material of the middle chapters (it's the outside of the doughnut). Israel is poised on the brink of the Jordan, about to cross over into their new home. This geographical turning point is also a place of decision: Will Israel worship the one true God, or will they worship other gods, abandoning the life of gratitude and justice that Yahweh has set out in the law?[37]

Returning to the various levels of kinship that we discussed earlier, recall that "an individual [in Old Testament society] is the child X, of the clan of Y, of the tribe of Z, of the people of Israel."[38] We saw that the law corpus gives particular attention to the social structures of clan and household. In the feasting formula, the stranger is included within a household. In the writer's use of the phrase "within your gates," the stranger is implicitly included within a clan (Deut 5:14; 14:21, 29; 16:14; 24:14; 26:12; 31:12).

Deuteronomy's framing chapters (1–11, 27–34) take this a step further and include the stranger within the kinship grouping of all Israel with their divine Kinsperson, Yahweh. Two texts from the framing chapters reveal this particularly clearly: Deuteronomy 10:17-18 and Deuteronomy 29:10-15.

Ahav, "love," Deuteronomy 10:18-19. The best-known biblical passage regarding the stranger in Scripture is probably Deuteronomy 10:18-19, which reads: "The Lord executes justice for the fatherless and the widow, and *loves* the stranger, giving them food and clothing. *Love* the stranger, therefore, for you were strangers in the land of Egypt" (author's translation).[39] Notice how the word *love* is used in this passage, regarding the strangers. Just a few verses

---

[37]See J. Gordon McConville and J. G. Millar, *Time and Place in Deuteronomy*, JSOTSup 179 (Sheffield: Sheffield Academic Press, 1994), 44.

[38]Hendel, *Remembering Abraham*, 34.

[39]A similar discussion is found in M. Glanville, "'Festive Kinship,'" 138-41.

Figure 2.1. Including the *gēr* within various levels of kinship: household, clan, and nation

earlier is an affirmation of God's love for God's people: "Yet Yahweh set the divine heart in *love* on your fathers and chose their offspring after them, you above all peoples, as you are this day" (Deut 10:15 author's translation). There is a deliberate association here among (1) God's love for ancient Israel, (2) God's love for the stranger, and (3) Israel's love for the stranger.

This term *ahav*, "love," is deeply significant for understanding Deuteronomy's response to the stranger in three senses. First, the term was used in ancient Near Eastern terminology to express a covenant commitment between nations.[40] Thus, God was making a covenant with the vulnerable stranger—a steadfast commitment of faithfulness! Second, the language of ancient Near Eastern covenant treaties is taken from the very language of kinship. It includes terms denoting love, brotherhood, fatherhood, fealty, and the like.[41] To enter a covenant is "to enter another bond of blood and also to

---

[40]See further William L. Moran, "The Ancient Near Eastern Background for the Love of God in Deuteronomy," *CBQ* 25 (1963): 77-87.

[41]See further Frank Moore Cross, *Canaanite Myth and Hebrew Epic: Essays in the History of the Religion of Israel* (Cambridge, MA: Harvard University Press, 1973), 6-7.

take the partner into one's own."[42] The use of *love* in this passage thus suggests that the stranger is to be enfolded within the web of kin and covenant relations binding Israel to her divine Kinsperson, Yahweh. And third, *love*, in this context, even entails emotional connections between Yahweh, the stranger, and the Israelite (see Deut 10:15).[43] The deep emotional attachments that weave together kinsfolk should entwine those who have been displaced together with God's people.

We could represent these relationships of love in the form of a triangle (see fig. 2.2).

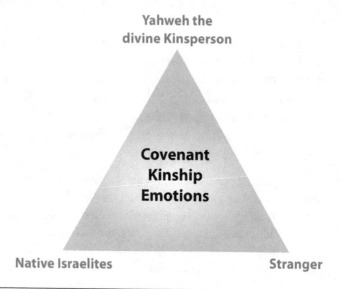

Figure 2.2. A triangle of kinship connections between Yahweh, native Israelites, and the stranger in Deuteronomy 10:15-19

So God makes a *covenant* with the stranger. God makes a steadfast commitment of protection and love with displaced people—what a remarkable revelation of the character of God. What grace! What tenderness! And God calls the people of God to do the same.

The stranger in a covenant renewal ceremony, Deuteronomy 29:10-15. The stranger is even included within the covenant renewal ceremony at Moab recorded in Deuteronomy 29:10-15. (See fig. 2.2.) This text deals with what

---

[42]Gottfried Quell, "διαθήκη," *TDNT*, 2:106-24, at 114.

[43]Jacqueline E. Lapsley, "Feeling Our Way: Love for God in Deuteronomy," *CBQ* 65, no. 3 (2003): 350-69, at 362.

gives a sense of belonging—familial ties in particular (Deut 29:10-11, 13)—and also touches on the implications of an absence of kinship affiliation (Deut 29:11, 14).[44] The stranger is explicitly included in the covenant, and so is also drawn into both the *blessings* of the covenant (Deut 29:13; 30:1, 9, 16) and its *obligations* (Deut 29:9; 30:9). Further, the relationship of the stranger to the nation that now receives him or her is seen to stretch backward into Israel's history so that the erstwhile stranger is grafted into the narrative of the patriarchs themselves, and of the covenant that had been sworn to them (Deut 29:11-12)—the traditional kinship structures of Israel. The stranger is given a place in Israel's family tree, as it were.[45]

In Deuteronomy's framework, as Israel is renewed in covenant with Yahweh, the inclusion of those who had been separated from patrimony and from kindred is a primary goal. The stranger is enfolded within all Israel and is understood to enjoy the kinship of Yahweh, Israel's divine Kinsperson. Rainer Albertz summarizes the careful balance that Deuteronomy strikes between the nation's cohesiveness as the people of Yahweh and a dynamic of inclusivism:

> Their idea that Yhwh, the universal ruler for the world, had elected just Israel
> from all the nations and separated it from them (Deut 7:6-11; 10:14-15) did not
> lead them to the conclusion, that those aliens who resided in Judah, should be
> hated, tortured, and thrown out; on the contrary, the theologians concluded
> from Israel's election, which took place in the release from Egyptian slavery,
> that Yhwh himself loved the aliens and wanted Israel to do the same ([Deut]
> 10:17-19).[46]

God's call upon Israel to extend kinship to the stranger demonstrates for us today how national identity can be malleable, maturing and extending itself for the sake of including those seeking a home. Indeed, this is the desire of Yahweh.

---

[44]The group referred to by the phrase "whoever is standing here with us today before the Lord our God" (Deut 29:15) is grammatically linked with the one referred to as "your stranger." The singular collective form ישנו (Deut 29:14) corresponds to the singular collective form וגרך (Deut 29:10).

[45]Other texts from Deuteronomy's framing chapters that concern the stranger are Deuteronomy 1:16-17; 5:12-15; 27:19; 28:43-44; 31:9-13.

[46]Rainer Albertz, "From Aliens to Proselytes: Non-Priestly and Priestly Legislation Concerning Strangers," in *The Foreigner and the Law: Perspectives from the Hebrew Bible and the Ancient Near East*, ed. Reinhard Achenbach, Rainer Albertz, and Jakob Wöhrle, BZABR 16 (Wiesbaden: Harrassowitz, 2011), 53-70, at 55.

Does Deuteronomy Differentiate Between
Legal and Illegal Immigrants?

A small number of scholars, including James Hoffmeier, argue that the stranger is a person who has been given the *legal authority* to reside within a community, and who on that basis has the right to benefit from the protections prescribed in Deuteronomy. This person has, in Hoffmeier's words, "followed legal procedures to obtain recognized standing as a resident alien."[47] This theory is not taken seriously in the scholarly discussion of the stranger in Deuteronomy. Yet, as we noted in our introduction, it has proven influential, not least in that it has been incorporated into a Bible study run by Capitol Ministries for members of the US Congress and also in a memo on "the Bible and the wall," written by Capitol Ministries at the request of White House cabinet members who participate in the Bible study.[48] Hoffmeier's argument is put to work in this Bible study and memo to justify the expulsion of undocumented immigrants in the United States. This now includes undocumented immigrants fleeing gang violence and domestic violence—primarily women fleeing Central America—since one of the Bible study sponsors, Attorney General Jeff Sessions, ruled in 2018 that such violence should no longer be considered grounds for asylum.[49] It is important, therefore, that we address Hoffmeier's theory and explain clearly why it is wrong.[50]

First, the stranger in Deuteronomy is most certainly *not* a person who had "followed legal procedures to obtain recognized standing as a resident alien." Rather, we have shown that the stranger is simply someone who is vulnerable and seeking a home. It is the Israelite's responsibility to offer the stranger a home, not the stranger's responsibility to adhere to legal procedures for immigration according to Deuteronomy.[51] Certainly, it is possible that at certain

---

[47]James K. Hoffmeier, *The Immigration Crisis: Immigrants, Aliens, and the Bible* (Wheaton, IL: Crossway, 2009), 52.

[48]Ralph Drollinger, "What the Bible Says About Our Illegal Immigration Problem," *Members Bible Study, U.S. Capitol*, Capitol Ministries, September 26, 2016, http://capmin.org/wp-content/uploads/2016/09/Illegal-Immigration-9.26.16.pdf; and idem, "The Bible and the Wall," *Ministry Updates*, Capitol Ministries, January 26, 2019, https://capmin.org/the-bible-and-the-wall/.

[49]Katie Benner and Caitlin Dickerson, "Sessions Says Domestic and Gang Violence Are Not Grounds for Asylum," *New York Times*, June 11, 2018. The "Bible study sponsors" are listed in Drollinger, "What the Bible Says About Our Illegal Immigration Problem," 1, 12.

[50]While Hoffmeier refers to numerous Old Testament books, here we focus our critique by referring to the book of Deuteronomy. The following chapter demonstrates a similar ethic from other Old Testament books.

[51]M. Daniel Carroll R. (Rodas) also critiques Hoffmeier's contention that the Old Testament required a legal immigration process: review of *The Immigration Crisis: Immigrants, Aliens, and the Bible*, by James K. Hoffmeier, *Denver Journal* 13 (2010), https://denverseminary.edu/article/the-immigration-crisis-immigrants-aliens-and-the-bible/.

times and places throughout Israel's history some restrictions on entering its territory were put in place (though this is not found in the biblical text). Yet, it is also clear that there was relatively free movement for much of Israel's history (e.g., Ruth 1:22). The point is that Scripture calls for God's people to extend kinship to vulnerable people, not to insist upon legal processes as Hoffmeier claims.

Second, Hoffmeier's claim that a displaced person who had *not* obtained such legal standing would remain outside the protections codified in the law is diametrically opposed to Deuteronomy's call to protect the *most* vulnerable.[52] Hoffmeier's hypothetical *illegal* immigrant within Israel would be among the most vulnerable in society. It cannot be true that Deuteronomy, which (as we have seen) relentlessly seeks to protect the weak and vulnerable, would deliberately exclude the *weakest* and *most* vulnerable.

Third, cheap farm labor was often sought after in the ancient Near East, especially at harvest time, for a person's labor was worth more than her or his bread.[53] The concern of Deuteronomy was not to ensure that vulnerable workers entered the country, city, or village legally but to ensure that vulnerable laborers were not exploited.

Hoffmeier's approach is anachronistic. He problematically reads present-day conceptions of territorial bordering and legal and illegal immigration into ancient Near Eastern social structures, resulting in an argument that mirrors and justifies restrictionist claims about immigration that are commonly heard in his home country, the United States. But restrictions upon Israel's border crossing are never mentioned in Deuteronomy, nor in any other Old Testament book. To reread the stranger in Scripture as a person who has pursued legal processes for immigration is a sleight of hand that inverts the clear meaning of the biblical text (which is a call to kinship). Deuteronomy advocates not for border restrictions but for taking responsibility: to offer kinship to vulnerable people who are seeking a home.

More troubling still is what is missing from Hoffmeier's book. There is little attempt to give a human face to forced migration, no mention of the life-threatening hazards that force people to move. There is also no discussion

[52]Hoffmeier, *Immigration Crisis*, 76.
[53]See further I. J. Gelb, "Household and Family in Early Mesopotamia," in *State and Temple Economy in the Ancient Near East: Proceedings of the International Conference Organized by the Katholieke Universiteit Leuven from the 10th to the 14th of April 1978*, ed. Edward Lipiński, OLA 5 (Leuven: Dept. Oriëntalistiek, 1979), 1-98, at 23-24. Yet in times of destitution dependents were a burden, and we would expect that under these circumstances there would be little capacity to support nonfamily members (Gelb, "Household and Family," 61).

of the racism that has informed US immigration policy historically—no acknowledgment of how the United States is often implicated in the instability, poverty, and violence in Central America that drives people to seek home elsewhere without documentation; no mention of the deterrents and impediments that are increasingly placed in front of asylum seekers and other migrants seeking to enter the United States legally; and no recognition of the troubling treatment of undocumented migrants, which more recently has included the separation of children from parents. And there is certainly no effort to reconcile such practices with Scripture's call to protect the most vulnerable no matter their status.[54] We grapple with each of these issues in parts three and four.

BECOMING THE PEOPLE OF YAHWEH

We have seen in Deuteronomy the working out in ancient Israelite society of the reality that kinship is not static but is constantly being renegotiated for new circumstances. Deuteronomy displays tremendous creativity in ritual, in law, and in covenantal texts in order to make possible the incorporation of the stranger. It demonstrates that kinship is indeed "an area of life in which people invest their emotions, their creative energy, and their new imaginings," as Carsten claims.[55] This biblical book has shown us that national identity can be malleable and can extend itself for the sake of including those without a home. Indeed, Deuteronomy has shown us that this is the vision and desire of Yahweh.

But what sort of community is Yahweh shaping in this book? Clearly, it is not to be just a gathering of those fortunate enough to have wealth, land, and lineage. Yahweh is forming a community *identified primarily by its positive response to the Torah* (e.g., Deut 31:9-13), extending justice to the least among its people, and finding its identity in the life stories of the patriarchs, the exodus from bondage, and the wilderness wanderings of the people of Yahweh. The criteria for inclusion apply across clan lines and even across national boundaries. At the heart of Deuteronomy is *being and becoming the community of God*. Yahweh's ultimate goal is to shape not a nation-state or an ethnic group but a people responsive to Yahweh's Word.

This raises the question of whether the stranger would have been required to "convert" to the worship of Yahweh as a prerequisite for inclusion in the

---

[54]These points are made powerfully in Carroll R., review, *Immigration Crisis*, by Hoffmeier.
[55]Carsten, *After Kinship*, 9.

community, as some scholars have suggested. Crucially, in the twenty-two references to the stranger in Deuteronomy, this is not so much as mentioned. And, in any case, to pose the question in this way betrays a Western and individualistic bias inappropriate to a clear view of the interconnected, communal culture of ancient Israel. Rather than "conversion," as Westerners tend to think of it today, Deuteronomy's vision for strangers was that they were to be enfolded in the joy, the feasting, the community, the story, the ritual, the abundance, and the gratitude of the family of Yahweh. Deuteronomy fosters the renewal of Israel in light of the gracious rule of Yahweh—and the stranger is simply swept up in the divine invitation. Who *wouldn't* want to join such a feast?

In fact, Deuteronomy is more concerned with the Israelites' faithful inclusion of the stranger than with the stranger's conversion (Deut 16:11, 14). According to Deuteronomy, Israel has no right to come before Yahweh for worship unless the stranger is standing alongside them. This is just as true of household cultic feasts (Deut 16:9-15) as it is for national covenantal assemblies (Deut 29:10-15); the stranger must be there. There is a sense in which the stranger is, in some way, purified by participation in Israel's cultic rituals. Yet there is an even stronger sense in which *the stranger purifies Israel,* and there are many dimensions to this reality: cultic ritual may only be rightly performed with the stranger as a full participant (Deut 16:9-15); the stranger is Yahweh's covenant partner (Deut 10:17-19); the stranger is present because Yahweh prefers to commune with the humble rather than with the proud (Deut 8); the stranger symbolizes Israel's vulnerability in Egypt, which must continue to be a lived reality (Deut 24:17-22); the stranger gives Israel opportunity to share Yahweh's gifts (Deut 14:28-29); and so on. Christ followers today must take this requirement for worship with the utmost seriousness: How may God be approached? God may only be rightly approached alongside the stranger, who is being enfolded within the community. This is right worship, according to Deuteronomy.

Interpreting the Old Testament Ethically, for Today

It is time to detour for a moment to touch on how to interpret these texts for today. In our exploration in this chapter and the next, we are not assuming that God's design for ancient Israel should be applied directly to nation-states today, or even directly to the church. Rather, we are exploring God's vision for *this particular ancient people.* Yet, the vision of the Old Testament always has the "ends of the earth" on its horizon (Is 45:22). Through this ancient people, God was displaying to all of creation the divine vision for the world, that of a beloved community. Through the freshness of the Torah and the abiding presence of Yahweh, Israel was to be a garden in a desert wasteland, a garden whose vines and blossoms would one day bring life, in full bloom, to the whole of creation.

So, how do the ethics of the Old Testament apply to other nations, both then and now? We might liken Old Testament ethics to jazz music. Each of the authors of this book started out as a professional jazz musician: Mark as a pianist, Luke as a drummer. In learning to play jazz, we each spent thousands of hours immersed in the sounds, harmonies, and rhythms of jazz music. We learned the tradition, felt it in our bones, hummed it, and tapped it everywhere we went. Now, each time we come to play, we draw deeply from the tradition, and yet each time we play we also create something new. Each fresh jazz performance rechoreographs the sounds, the time, and the harmony of this African American art form for a new moment. As we play, we are also listening intensely within a new context, interacting dynamically with a saxophonist, a guitarist, or a bass player.

We might liken the jazz tradition that runs deep within every good jazz performance to the ethical tradition that is expressed throughout the narrative arc of Scripture in all of its variety. Biblical ethics, of course, reflect the loving and generous personhood of God.[56] In the Old Testament, this "tradition," God's ethical path, is expressed in a wide variety of ways that are all deeply shaped by specific historical contexts and moments. We have sought in this chapter and will seek in the next to discern the core ethical trajectories regarding displacement in the Old Testament as they are expressed in this variety.

Having discerned the core ethical trajectories within Scripture, we need to move to the present context. Moving beyond Scripture, Old Testament ethics will never "sound" exactly the same when they are applied to another historical context, such as our own context of churches, sovereign states, and a global crisis of forced displacement. Our task, then, is to discern the tradition, so to speak; the core ethical trajectories within the Old Testament that also echo the loving character of God. It will be the task of later chapters to discern how this tradition may be performed within our present context. What fresh creativity is required of us today? What fresh and beautiful sounds and rhythms should the tradition birth in us?

---

[56]God's loving character is also mirrored in the core values that somehow run deep within the warp and woof of creation itself, as we explain in the following chapter.

Let's return to our imagined family on the move, Jonathan, Abital, their children, and Abital's mother, who have found work and lodging within a local settlement during the spring harvest. What will be the outcome for this vulnerable family? Will they receive their daily allotment of grain? Will they be enslaved by their hosts? If their hosts take God's word seriously, the future looks promising: Deuteronomy's social law requires Israelites to take kinship responsibility for these people. The law of judicial procedure secures justice at the gates for them. And through cultic feasting, Deuteronomy promotes the embrace of these strangers within the household and the clan. Deuteronomy's framing chapters enfold them within all Israel. And this ethic of inclusion is embedded theologically both within Israel's narrative-history and also *within Yahweh's own actions and character.*

Picture for a moment Deuteronomy's inclusive feasts in action. Smell the aroma of boiling meat, see the dance, feel the percussion, witness this community in all its diversity, strangers *included.* This is the meme that captures the spirit of Deuteronomy: the whole community, in all its diversity, gathers in the presence of God for joyful feasting. Deuteronomy's vision for community is a vision of festive kinship.[57]

---

[57]M. Glanville, "'Festive Kinship.'"

2

REFUGE UNDER
YAHWEH'S WINGS

"I WANT TO BE A PAEDIATRICIAN," says Joury Al Yehyia, a thirteen-year-old Syrian refugee in Lebanon. "I want to help sick children."[1] One in seven people in Lebanon today is a refugee. This is largely the result of Lebanon opening its doors to more than a million people fleeing the horrors of the Syrian civil war since 2011. Indeed, there are more Syrian school-aged refugees in Lebanon than there are Lebanese school-aged. Hundreds of Lebanese schools have responded to this situation with remarkable generosity, operating a second shift each day in order to provide schooling for 220,000 Syrian children.[2] Joury is one of those children. So are her younger brothers, Imam, who wants to become a dentist, and Ahmed, who dreams of being an astronaut.[3]

Lebanon's welcome of Syrian refugees is an inspiring example of showing love and extending kinship to displaced people, even at great cost. But there is only so much that Lebanon is able to do. And as the Syrian civil war has dragged on and Western states—as well as others in the Global North—have

---

[1]Quoted in "Families Give Cash Assistance High Marks," *Reliefweb*, June 1, 2018.
[2]See David Miliband, *Rescue: Refugees and the Political Crisis of Our Time* (New York: TED Books, 2017), 77-80; and Rima Cherri and Houssam Hariri, "Lebanon Puts in an Extra Shift to Get Syrian Refugees into School," UNHCR, June 26, 2018, www.unhcr.org/news/stories/2018/6/5b321c864 /lebanon-puts-extra-shift-syrian-refugees-school.html.
[3]"Families Give Cash Assistance High Marks," *Reliefweb*.

failed to demonstrate solidarity with Syria's neighbors and share responsibility in caring for the displaced, Lebanon has begun to withdraw its welcome, closing its borders to additional newcomers and encouraging Syrians to return home despite the ongoing violence.[4] Might we in the West be willing to show greater love and extend kinship to greater numbers of displaced Syrians to complement the efforts of Syria's overwhelmed and tired neighbors? Should we? Once again, we turn to Scripture in order to discern God's heart on such matters.

This chapter moves beyond Deuteronomy to investigate eight other books from the Old Testament. Our key question is: How did the Old Testament call Israel to think about and to relate to non-Israelites, especially the most vulnerable? Anticipating later parts of this book, we also begin to ask: What does this ancient ethic communicate about God's desire for our response to displaced people today?

Our desire to read the Old Testament honestly means that we can't build a case with only one or two passages that are attractive to us. Rather, we must acknowledge books that seem to encourage the exclusion and even destruction of foreigners, such as the books of Joshua and Ezra–Nehemiah. We will see how different historical challenges have elicited very different kinds of responses to outsiders in various books of the Old Testament. Yet within both Judaism and Christianity the Old Testament is considered to be a coherent whole, and so we will also seek to tease out how these books fit within the Old Testament canon. We hope to explain clearly how these ancient texts functioned. The books of the Old Testament are far more creative, fresh, inspiring, daring, and multidimensional than many Christians realize.

In Exodus, some of the heroes of Israel's founding stories are non-Israelite. Leviticus scrambles the presumed priority of caring for citizens. The Canaanite destruction texts reimagine Israel in non-ethnic terms, redefining Israel on the basis of obedience to the law. In Ruth, God is a *maternal protector* of outsiders. Ezra–Nehemiah helps us understand how vulnerable communities may at times need to adopt strategies of exclusion for their own preservation. Jonah challenges us to reframe our thinking and consider whether it is actually the "insiders" among God's people that need saving, rather than "outsiders." Finally, Job teaches Israel to listen to outsiders (something that we practice at the end of the chapter by listening to the beautiful

---

[4]Bassem Mroue, "Lebanon Tells EU It Will Encourage Syrians to Return," *Associated Press*, February 26, 2019.

response of fishermen from Aceh to the cries of Rohingya refugees stranded at sea in 2015). In chapter nine, we will circle back to the book of Genesis, observing how it demonstrates the inherent dignity of all people and nations and provides the basis for a conception of kinship with all humanity.

EXODUS: THE NON-ISRAELITE MOTHERS AND FATHERS OF ISRAEL

As with Deuteronomy, the book of Exodus provides for the protection and support of strangers. These provisions are found in the law code that forms the center of the book (Ex 22:21; 23:9, 12). Yet not only the law but also the narrative of Exodus is distinctive: many of the great heroes of Israel's formative stories are foreigners. We won't dwell long on these characters, but they are worth observing as they confirm so much of the ethic of kinship toward the displaced that we retrieved in Deuteronomy. Exodus is all about the emancipation and formation of the ancient people of God, as Yahweh freed Israel from slavery in Egypt and brought the nation to Mount Sinai so that they might receive the Torah. God's laws shaped Israel to be a contrastive community, starkly different from Egypt's oppressive regime. Israel was to embody how God had always intended communities to operate: as kin.

Foreigners play crucial roles both on behalf of Israel and within Israel in this book. A "mixed multitude" left Egypt with the Israelites (Ex 12:38 ESV). These people seem to have been non-Israelites who became incorporated into the community. These outsiders stood at Sinai to receive the law as the community of ex-slaves became the people of God. By this detail, the author seems to be showing that Israel has been incorporating strangers into the heart of the community from the very beginning.

An unlikely hero of this book is Pharaoh's unnamed daughter. She is responsible for Moses' life and thus for the Israelites' ultimate escape (Ex 2:10). Another hero is Zipporah, Moses' wife, one of the seven daughters of Reuel, the priest of Midian (Ex 2:16-22; Reuel is later referred to as Jethro in Ex 18:1). One night as Moses returned to Egypt, the Lord sought to kill him.[5] Zipporah acted assertively, cutting off her son's foreskin with a flint and touching Moses' feet with it. Zipporah seems to work as a skillful priest, evident by her use of the flint and by her knowledge of the circumcision ritual (Ex 4:24-26).[6]

---

[5] We should probably understand Yahweh's actions against Moses in this event as a jolting reminder to Moses that he should revere Yahweh through circumcision. It was the Midianite Zipporah, not Moses, who was attentive in this faithful act.

[6] Carol Meyers, *Exodus,* New Cambridge Bible Commentary (Cambridge: Cambridge University Press, 2005), 63.

Perhaps the most remarkable of all is the story of Zipporah's father, Jethro. It is well known that Jethro instructs the Israelite community on organizing its judges and leaders (Ex 18:1-27), but it is rarely noticed that the *very words* of Jethro are taken up and sacralized within Israel's own laws—in the Torah itself (Deut 1:8-18).[7]

In sum, many of the mothers and fathers of Israel are foreigners. These "foreign" heroes of Israel's communal memory reinforce the ethic that we observed in the previous chapter: the call to enfold displaced people as kindred.

LEVITICUS SCRAMBLES THE PRESUMED ORDER OF CARE

Governments must give "the interests of their citizens precedence over those of strangers," Mark Amstutz contends in a recent book offering a Christian perspective on American immigration policy.[8] This is a common sentiment, to be sure. But the book of Leviticus scrambles this presumed order of care: "If any of your kin fall into difficulty and become dependent on you, you shall support them; they shall live with you as though strangers and resident aliens." (Lev 25:35-36 adapted from NRSV).

We learn quite a lot about displaced people in ancient Israel from this short verse. It is assumed here that Israelites were already supporting displaced people, as a matter of course. The words, "as though they were strangers," display a cultural norm: Israelite households were used to enfolding and caring for impoverished strangers. This cultural practice brings to mind the hospitality of the many Lebanese and Jordanian households where refugees found welcome in the early years of the Syrian civil war. In the Leviticus text, this established law and custom of welcoming vulnerable strangers is the starting point from which God now calls Israelites to similarly welcome fellow Israelites and fellow clansfolk. Foreigners were so protected that the way Israel treats strangers is the benchmark for how they are to treat the poor!

This term "stranger" (Hebrew: *gēr*) has two distinct meanings and usages in Leviticus.[9] The less common usage refers to the figure that we encountered

---

[7] See Mark R. Glanville, *Adopting the Stranger as Kindred in Deuteronomy*, AIL 33 (Atlanta: SBL Press, 2018), 114, 118.

[8] Mark R. Amstutz, *Just Immigration: American Policy in Christian Perspective* (Grand Rapids, MI: Eerdmans, 2017), 102.

[9] Leviticus 17:8, 10, 12, 13, 15; 18:26; 19:10, 33, 34 (2x); 20:2; 22:18; 23:22; 24:16, 22; 25:23, 35, 47 (3x). For further reading, see Rainer Albertz, "From Aliens to Proselytes: Non-Priestly and Priestly Legislation Concerning Strangers," in *The Foreigner and the Law: Perspectives from the Hebrew Bible and the Ancient Near East*, ed. Reinhard Achenbach, Rainer Albertz, and Jakob Wöhrle; BZABR 16 (Wiesbaden: Harrassowitz, 2011), 53-70.

in Deuteronomy: someone who is displaced, impoverished, and dependent. It is with this meaning that Leviticus stipulates: "love the stranger as yourself" (Lev 19:33-34). As we saw in chapter two, the call to "love the stranger" is nothing less than a call to offer kinship solidarity. This is parallel to the command "love your neighbor as yourself" (Lev 19:18 author's translation).

In Leviticus, whoever has need of love, of care, of kinship, should receive it, for every person is created in the image of God. Indeed, this is how Jesus lived and taught, as we will see in chapter five. Jesus echoed Leviticus when he said, "love . . . your neighbor as yourself" (Lk 10:27), all the while demonstrating by his life that one's neighbors are especially those who are on the margins of society (Lk 15:1-2).

The more common use of the term "stranger" in Leviticus was for a person who did not belong to the *religious* community but who nonetheless lived within the social community. This person may be of some means (Lev 25:35-38; cf. Lev 17:8-9; 22:18-19).[10] Such a person was to be on an equal footing with Israelites: "You shall have the one law for the stranger and for the native" (Lev 24:22 author's translation).[11]

Leviticus displays an ancient cultural norm of offering displaced people support and housing that is *stronger* even than the norm to care for clansfolk. Readers today might allow this ancient practice to challenge the common presumption that countries should prioritize the care of citizens over more vulnerable foreigners. We will wrestle further with this idea in chapter seven.

CANAANITE DESTRUCTION TEXTS AND OUTSIDERS

"But, what about the Canaanites!?" you may well ask. The question refers to a group of texts in the books of Deuteronomy and Joshua where Yahweh gives the Canaanite kings and people into Israel's hands so they might possess the land. Particularly difficult is the repeated phrase "devote to destruction" (e.g., Deut 3:6; 7:2; Josh 10:1 ESV). The Hebrew word for "devoting to destruction"

---

[10]See further Nadav Na'aman, "Sojourners and Levites in the Kingdom of Judah in the Seventh Century BCE," *ZABR* 14 (2008): 237-79, at 257.

[11]Yet, these strangers must act in ways that preserve the purity of the community and of the land (Lev 17:10, 13, 15; 20:2; 24:16; see further Mark G. Brett, *Political Trauma and Healing: Biblical Ethics for a Postcolonial World* [Grand Rapids, MI: Eerdmans, 2016], 107). The issue of slavery is more complex. Leviticus provides for the release of Israelite slaves, but not for non-Israelite slaves, in the year of Jubilee (Lev 25:35-55). Nonetheless, the provisions for the stranger are aimed at preventing the enslavement of foreigners due to indebtedness in the first place. The imbalance is also tempered by Deuteronomy's provision that Israelite settlements must offer a home to fleeing slaves—a stipulation that prioritizes the rights of slaves over their owners (Deut 23:15-16). On fleeing slaves, see M. Glanville, *Adopting the Stranger*, 78-81.

is *herem*. One example is the defeat of Sihon, king of Heshbon: "And we captured all his cities at that time and devoted to destruction [*herem*] every city, men, women, and children. We left no survivors" (Deut 2:34 ESV).

Some members of Mark's worshiping community in Vancouver are presently reading through the Bible over two years. Upon reading the book of Joshua, one person exclaimed, "How can anyone call their son 'Joshua'? Have they *read* this book?!" These stories have been used to justify horrific deeds. Some early Puritan preachers in America, for example, referred to indigenous people as Canaanites, using these narratives to justify conquest and murder.[12] How can we square these texts with the compassionate ethic of kinship for outsiders that we have been observing in the Old Testament?

In answering this question, we don't intend to deny or diminish the horror of these passages. While we don't here wrestle with the horrific violence portrayed, such wrestling should certainly be done.[13] We want instead to focus on the *meaning* of these texts, and specifically the claim that these passages might prove false the argument that Old Testament Israel was called to welcome and enfold the vulnerable stranger as kin.

Think of these Canaanite texts as *texts*.[14] Try to forget the horror of the narrative for a moment. What were these *texts* doing as they were read, memorized, and cherished in ancient Israel all those years? Why were they kept, declared sacred? The Canaanite groups had ceased to exist for most of the period of Israel's monarchy, and yet these texts were cherished throughout the periods of the monarchy, the exile, and beyond. Why? Here's why: these texts were shaking up the identity of the people of Israel, re-forming the family of Yahweh as a community that heeds the Torah. Although we tend to think of this story of conquest and destruction in terms of ethnic purity, the story is actually about *Israel's identity*. In these texts, Canaanites become Israelite, and Israelites become Canaanite, and the determining factor is their obedience to the word of Yahweh.

Rahab: The Canaanite who was Israelite. In the story of Rahab and the spies (Josh 2), Rahab, a Canaanite inhabitant of Jericho, is more Israelite than

---

[12]Robert Allen Warrior, "Canaanites, Cowboys, and Indians: Deliverance, Conquest, and Liberation Theology Today," in *Native and Christian: Indigenous Voices on Religious Identity in the United States and Canada*, ed. James Treat (New York: Routledge, 1996), 93-100.

[13]For example, see Warrior, "Canaanites, Cowboys, and Indians," 93-100.

[14]For a more detailed analysis, see Mark R. Glanville, "*Ḥērem* as Israelite Identity Formation: Reading the Canaanite Destruction Texts in Light of the Stranger (*Gēr*) in Deuteronomy and Joshua," *CBQ* (forthcoming).

the Israelites.[15] Rahab is the key initiative taker around whom the story iron-ically revolves. Joshua sends the spies "secretly"—that is, secret from *Israel* (Josh 2:1).[16] This raises a question around Joshua's timidity at the very outset of the conquest (cf. Josh 1:7). Joshua's command, "go, view the land, especially Jericho" (Josh 2:1), is followed by an immediate and ironic switch of verbs: the spies "went" and "entered" the house of a prostitute named Rahab—from which they will not emerge until the end of the story! As for Rahab, she shrewdly hides the spies on her roof, carefully arranging stalks of flax in what is presented as an Israelite priestly cultic performance.[17]

While the Israelite spies lazily prepare for sleep (Josh 2:8), Rahab declares: "I know that the LORD has given you the land" (Josh 2:9). She is using words from Israel's own covenant document, the book of Deuteronomy. She then says: "The LORD your God is indeed God in heaven above and on earth below" (Josh 2:11), echoing numerous precious covenant expressions.[18] Rahab is pre-sented as an exemplary observer of the law, for with these phrases she is de-claring the very words of Moses. She demands that the spies swear an oath that Israel will spare her household. As a result of the spies' lack of trust in Yahweh's promises, they have no choice but to entrust their lives to Rahab (Josh 2:14).[19]

The story is picked up in Joshua 6, which describes the destruction of Jericho and Rahab's deliverance. Ominously, *herem* is threatened upon *Israel* should they take from what has been devoted to Yahweh (Josh 6:18). The threat of *herem* upon Israel (also Deut 7:26; 13:17-18) is ironic given that Rahab, not Israel, should ordinarily be subject to *herem*.

Many writers think that Rahab's words and actions are a confession or conversion story.[20] Indeed, if the story were written without irony, we might

---

[15]A more detailed examination of Joshua 2 is found in M. Glanville, "*Ḥērem* as Israelite Identity Formation."

[16]Joachim J. Krause, "Vor wem soll die Auskundschaftung Jerichos geheim gehalten werden?: Eine Frage zu Josua 2:1," *VT* 62, no. 3 (2012): 454-56.

[17]Leviticus 1:12; cf. 1:7, 8; 6:5; 24:3, 4, 8. This challenges Crowell's suggestion that the author has a "colonial stance" that characterizes Rahab as a "good girl." Bradley L. Crowell, "Good Girl, Bad Girl: Foreign Women of the Deuteronomistic History in Postcolonial Perspective," *Biblical Interpretation* 21, no. 1 (2013): 1-18, at 8, 14.

[18]Exodus 20:4; Deuteronomy 5:8; see also Deuteronomy 3:24; 4:39; 10:14; 26:15; 1 Kings 8:23; cf. Joshua 7:9.

[19]The spies say to Rahab: "Our life for yours! If you do not tell this business of ours, then we will deal kindly and faithfully with you when the LORD gives us the land" (Josh 2:14). The spies' words, "when the LORD gives," could also mean, "if the LORD gives" (cf. a similar construction in Josh 2:19-20).

[20]See for example David G. Firth, "Models of Inclusion and Exclusion in Joshua," in *Interreligious Relations: Biblical Perspectives*, ed. Hallvard Hagelia and Markus Zehnder (London: T&T Clark, 2017), 71-88, at 79, 82.

assume that it *is* simply a beautiful conversion story. However, the ironic mockery of Israel in Joshua 2 signals that deeper issues are at stake: Israelite identity is being re-formed. Rahab's story is told in order to transform traditional conceptions of what it means to be Israel. One's identity as Israelite is not a matter of ethnicity. Rather, *Israel is being reimagined around the Torah*. And, if Israel is being re-envisaged around the Torah, then this also deeply reinforces the ethic of inclusivity that is found in the Torah (cf. Josh 14:6-12).[21]

Achan: The Israelite who was Canaanite. No sooner is Jericho destroyed than we are immediately informed: "But the Israelites broke faith in regard to the devoted things" (Josh 7:1 ESV). Achan is Israelite, with impeccable kinship connections (Josh 7:14, 16-18). He takes some of the booty from Jericho that is devoted to Yahweh. As a result of Achan's transgression, all Israel becomes devoted to destruction (Josh 7:12). Israel has become Canaanite!

"Israel"—those who heed the Torah. The Canaanite destruction passages in Deuteronomy and Joshua are intimately connected with the call for Israel to obey the Torah. In the story of the conquest, it is *Israel's* disobedience—not that of the Canaanites—that is put up in lights! Yahweh is giving the Canaanite kings and people into Israel's hands so that Israel may possess the land. But Israel's possession of the land is dependent upon their obedience to the Torah.[22] And there is a deeper message yet, beneath the surface of the text: *Israel is being redefined* around obedience to the law. Many who seem to be Israel are, in fact, not Israel; and many who seem not to be Israel, in fact, are.

The message of the Canaanite destruction texts. So, what is the purpose of these texts? At a literary level, Canaanites have become Israelite and Israelites have become Canaanite, and the determining factor in these transformations is obedience or disobedience to the word of Yahweh. This transposition of identities declares loudly and clearly that the land belongs to those who are faithful to the beautiful vision held out in the law. *Canaanite* becomes nothing more or less than a metaphor for unfaithful Israel. The metaphor declares that *Israel is not an ethnic group*: the true Israel is that people that *heeds the law of Yahweh*. "Israel" will ultimately include people of many ethnicities, and some of those who are Israelite by "natural descent" aren't

---

[21]This challenges Pitkänen's recent explanation of the inclusion of outsiders in Joshua from a Settler-Colonial perspective. Pekka Pitkänen, "Reading Genesis–Joshua as a Unified Document from an Early Date: A Settler Colonial Perspective," *BTB* 45, no. 1 (2015): 3-31, at 10.

[22]To illustrate, relating to conquest of Sihon king of Heshbon, Israel is twice said to have "rebelled against the command of the LORD" (Deut 1:26, 43), and Israel's rebellion results in Moses' exclusion from the land (Deut 1:37; 3:26). While booty is taken when Heshbon is destroyed, this motif links to *Israel themselves being subsequently taken as booty* (Deut 1:39, cf. 1:26; 2 Kings 21:14).

really Israelite at all. That's the message. There is only one more vital piece here, just in case you missed it: a core command of the Torah is that God's people enfold the stranger. Because the *herem* commands hold God's people to the law, they also hold God's people to this ethic of inclusion—which is illustrated in the inclusion of Rahab, among others.[23]

Here is an analogy, to help us to understand what it means to redefine Israel. Imagine that a book begins to circulate in Australia about what it means to be *Australian*, written by someone who could create interest—Crocodile Dundee, maybe? From now on, we are told, eating Vegemite and having an Australian passport no longer counts for being Australian. What *does* count is welcoming asylum seekers arriving by boat in search of a home. Those who offer this welcome, and only those, are Australian, the book says. To return to ancient times, the *Canaanite* texts were as much as saying, "The only thing that counts for being 'Israel' is obeying Yahweh's word." We have seen that this obedience will include welcoming displaced people.

It ranges from difficult to impossible to explain these extremely complex texts in a short space. The reader is referred to our other publications on this issue.[24] However, it is clarifying to recall that the historical arc of the Old Testament traces the decline of the nation of Israel, because of their unfaithfulness to the Torah.[25] *Israel's* call—and their failure to fulfill that call—is the focus of Old Testament history. The account of the Canaanites is not some strange addendum to this narrative arc, as if for a moment the Old Testament historians become very interested in the demise of the Canaanite people groups. Rather, *Canaanite* is a metaphor for unfaithful Israel, and the narrative of the destruction of the Canaanites functions as a mirror through which to see and understand the destruction of Israel (in 722 BCE) and then Judah (in 586 BCE). The Canaanite destruction texts explain *why* Israel was destroyed. Crucially, the Canaanite destruction texts are *all about Israel*.

RUTH: SEEKING REFUGE UNDER YAHWEH'S WINGS

Famine ravaged the land of Israel. Working in his field, the best that Elimelech could do was rearrange the dust. So, Elimelech—an Ephrathite from Bethlehem—along with his wife, Naomi, and his two sons, Mahlon and Chilion, packed a few vital belongings on their backs and set out on foot to make a new life in Moab. This is akin to what is sometimes referred to as

---

[23]See also Joshua 8:33, 35; 20:9.
[24]See M. Glanville, "*Ḥērem* as Israelite Identity Formation."
[25]Deuteronomy 1–2 Kings 25.

"survival migration." The fractures, the tearing, the loss for this family are inexpressible, for they have broken with clansfolk and with the land where their ancestors were buried.

In Moab, Elimelech dies. Life must go on, and Mahlon and Chilion each marry Moabite wives: Ruth and Orpah. Naomi, the new head of the family, doesn't restrict her sons to Israelite spouses. How could she? Yet, by what ingenuity was she able to find wives for her sons at all, we wonder, as an outsider with no patrimony in Moab and with very little means? Naomi is a skilled survivor, operating in perilous circumstances. We are also led to wonder about the surprising welcome that Moabite families must have shown to Naomi's family in giving their daughters in marriage to Elimelech's family.

Things go from bad to worse. Naomi's two sons die, leaving Naomi, Ruth, and Orpah widowed. Hearing that the famine has ended in the land of Israel, Naomi makes plans to return to her country of origin. In this culture, Ruth and Orpah would naturally have stronger connections with their natural mothers and with their natural siblings than with their mother-in-law (see Ruth 1:8), especially as they are childless. So Naomi sends them back to their mothers' households, expressing her hope that they will find husbands among their own people. The three women share in a ritual of kissing and weeping that signifies the ending of kinship ties (Ruth 1:9-14).

Orpah returns home, but Ruth determines to stay with Naomi. Ruth makes a declaration of kinship with Naomi,[26] and her expression of loyalty has resonated through the centuries:

> Where you go, I will go;
>   where you lodge, I will lodge;
> your people shall be my people,
>   and your God my God.
> Where you die, I will die—
>   there will I be buried. (Ruth 1:16-17)

What devotion to her new kin! Ruth throws her lot in with Naomi, asking to be adopted into Naomi's clan, even choosing Naomi's land, which she has never seen, for her burial! How are we to understand Ruth's life-changing decision? Is Ruth converting to the faith of Israel here?[27] It is more accurate

---

[26]Mark S. Smith, "'Your People Shall Be My People': Family and Covenant in Ruth 1:16-17," CBQ 69 (2007): 242-58, at 258.

[27]The word *conversion* better suits modern Eurocentric-Western cultures, which tend to be more individualistic and compartmentalized than communal cultures. Lau suggests that Ruth's conversion may be accurately described as one that takes place over a period of time. Peter H. W. Lau, *Identity and Ethics in the Book of Ruth: A Social Identity Approach*, BZAW 416 (Berlin: De Gruyter, 2011), 92.

to see Ruth's decision as a shift in kinship, a shift that in this instance also entails a religious shift of some sort.[28] As Naomi returns to her clan of Ephrathah, she feels herself an outsider even among her own people, a "childless widow and a marginalized repatriate."[29]

Leaving Home

Raúl Gatica used to work as the community mobilizer at Kinbrace. He now supports temporary foreign workers in Canada. Raúl shares his grief over fleeing from home:

> People leave their country all the time. But to be forced to move, the moment has you unprepared: physically, mentally, culturally, in every way. There are a lot of ruptures: a break with your job, with your identity, with your culture, with your roots. You are not prepared to break with these things. When you fly to another place, you carry all of these fractures in your soul; even your tears are not enough to express all of your sadness in leaving your homeland, the rivers, the mountains; there are not enough tears to express the sadness, honestly. That is why your body tries to express the sadness of your soul, even if you cry a river; your body gets skinny or fat, or responds in other ways. You don't know immediately all of those broken things, you think more about the difficulties. We don't notice immediately all of those broken things in our soul—they happen later. We realize: Oh, where is my family? Where is the big porch where we used to prepare to have the celebration together? That is when you start to notice that you have been broken.

Back in Judah. The story of Ruth now takes us to the land of Judah in early spring, the time of the wheat and barley harvest. In ancient times, impoverished people could sometimes gain permission to glean in the field behind the harvesters, collecting what they could in order to survive another day. Ruth gleans in a field belonging to a man, Boaz. Boaz inquires with the supervisor about Ruth, and the supervisor praises her hard work. As with many migrants today, Ruth's tireless work is recognized and appreciated by others.[30]

---

[28]See further Smith, "'Your People Shall Be My People,'" 258.

[29]Lau, *Identity and Ethics in the Book of Ruth*, 124-25.

[30]M. Daniel Carroll R. (Rodas), "Once a Stranger, Always a Stranger?: Immigration, Assimilation, and the Book of Ruth," *IBMR* 39, no. 4 (2015): 185-88, at 186.

Boaz blesses Ruth with a most remarkable phrase: "May you have a full reward from the Lord, the God of Israel, under whose wings you have come for refuge!" (Ruth 2:12).

This metaphor of Yahweh's sheltering wings evokes the care and protection of Yahweh, and it appears a number of times in the Old Testament.[31] Only here is it applied specifically to an *outsider* who is seeking a place to dwell and flourish. Whatever Ruth's understanding of Yahweh and Yahweh's people had been before arriving in Judah, Boaz seems to think that Ruth has come to the right place. According to Boaz, Yahweh's protective wings extend to shelter and embrace even the outsider who comes seeking a home. The image is of a mother bird who shelters her chicks under her wings. Yahweh's care is a kind of *maternal nurture*: the tender devotion and fierce protection of a mother. And here this intimate covenant phrase is applied to non-Israelites: Yahweh enfolds and protects vulnerable outsiders with maternal care. Furthermore, Boaz's phrase doesn't apply just to Ruth. Rather, Boaz seems to be pointing to a reliable characteristic of Yahweh, who will step into the protective role of mother, for the outsider. This phrase will reappear shortly in the story.

When Ruth reports Boaz's generosity to Naomi, her mother-in-law says, "The man is a relative of ours, one of our nearest kin" (Ruth 2:20). Naomi gives instructions to Ruth to prepare herself and to secretly approach Boaz by night as he sleeps on the threshing floor. Ruth is to uncover Boaz's feet and lie down beside them. With her sound knowledge of local marriage and redemption customs, Naomi is guiding Ruth toward Boaz. (This moment in the story makes visible two crucial elements that enable displaced people *today* to effectively integrate in their new society: local knowledge and social networks.)[32] When Boaz wakes with surprise, Ruth answers, "I am Ruth, your servant; spread your cloak over your servant, for you are next-of-kin" (Ruth 3:9). The Hebrew word for "cloak" used here is the same as the word for "wings" that was used by Boaz earlier (Ruth 2:12). Ruth is picking up Boaz's own phrase, as much as saying: *You* be the answer to your own prayer, Boaz! *You* be the wings of Yahweh in providing my mother-in-law and me refuge!

---

[31]Other references to "Yahweh's wings" refer to God's care for Israel. For example, the psalmist takes refuge under the shadow of Yahweh's wings (Ps 61:4-5; cf. Ex 19:4; Ps 36:7-9; 57:1; 63:7; 91:4; Mal 4:2). Psalm 36 applies this idea to all of humankind: "The children of mankind take refuge in the shadow of your wings" (Ps 36:7 ESV).

[32]Katherine E. Southwood, "Will Naomi's Nation Be Ruth's Nation?: Ethnic Translation as a Metaphor for Ruth's Assimilation Within Judah," *Humanities* 3 (2014): 102-31, at 107-8, 117-19; Carroll R., "Once a Stranger, Always a Stranger?," 186.

Ruth and Naomi's needs are very specific, and they extend well beyond small gestures of charity. In this culture, a widow needed a kinsman who would take responsibility for her. That is to say, Ruth needs a husband who will be willing and able to redeem Naomi's property, which Elimelech had leased out.

When the sun rises, Boaz springs into action. Boaz redeems Elimelech's field and marries Ruth, preserving Elimelech's name. Boaz's clansfolk pronounce a blessing that likens Ruth to the very matriarchs of the people of Israel: "May the LORD make the woman who is coming into your house like Rachel and Leah, who together built up the house of Israel" (Ruth 4:11-12).

In due course, Ruth has a son, Obed. Ruth's marriage to Boaz and, in turn, her giving birth to Obed are two further steps that complete Ruth's incorporation into the community. For, in ancient Israel it was through childbirth that a woman became fully integrated into her new kin grouping, the family of her husband. Ruth's determination and risk taking provided a home for the next generation of her family. Her son Obed's experience will be very different from hers, for her bravery and ingenuity have created a pathway for her son to enjoy a life in a new land.[33]

There is a deep mutuality, a deep interdependence within this story. Naomi is dependent upon Ruth for her reassimilation into Israelite culture (initially, upon returning from Moab, Naomi was self-isolating; Ruth 1:20), and in turn Ruth is dependent upon Naomi for her own assimilation.[34] Of course, something similar may be said about our mutual interdependence with migrants in Western nations today.

What is more, the book of Ruth takes pains to point out that *the whole story of Israel* is dependent upon a migrant woman. Ruth's son Obed becomes the father of Jesse, the father of David, king of Israel.[35] This mixed genealogy *blurs* the idea of Israelite ethnicity at the symbolic heart of the nation, the genealogy of the king himself.[36] God's ancient people, Israel, is not defined so much as an ethnic group but as a people whom God shelters under God's wings—and non-Israelites find their own shelter there.

---

[33]Carroll R., "Once a Stranger, Always a Stranger?," 187.

[34]Southwood, "Will Naomi's Nation Be Ruth's Nation?," 120.

[35]Perez also appears in the genealogy, and his non-Israelite mother, Tamar, is explicitly mentioned (Ruth 4:12).

[36]Naomi nursed her grandson, Obed (Ruth 4:16). Breastfeeding transferred kinship in ancient Israelite culture. (See Cynthia R. Chapman, *The House of the Mother: The Social Roles of Maternal Kin in Biblical Hebrew Narrative and Poetry* [New Haven, CT: Yale University Press, 2016], 125-49.) It may be that an author inserted this reference to Naomi's breastfeeding because Deuteronomy's law of the king states that the kings of Israel must not be foreigners (Deut 17:15)—a law that seems to entail a rejection of the oppressive domination of the kings of Assyria over Israel.

EZRA–NEHEMIAH: EXCLUSIVISM AS SKILLED SURVIVAL

The books of Ezra and Nehemiah demonstrate an exclusivity that seems to challenge the argument that we have been making thus far. In marked contrast to other parts of the Old Testament in which Israel is called clearly to enfold outsiders, Ezra stipulates unambiguously that foreign wives and their children are to be sent away (Ezra 10:3).

While we have been focusing on the call to *inclusion* and the provision of safety, sustenance, and belonging for displaced people, there may be times in which communities threatened with cultural extinction need to adopt strategies aimed at their own *preservation*. A vulnerable community may find that it needs to limit the entry of ill-intentioned outsiders, for example, in order to preserve the well-being of its members. Think of historical victims of European colonialism, for example, many of whose cultures were destroyed, communities were shattered, and bodies were violated by wars, land thefts, and atrocities that accompanied mass migration out of Europe to the colonies.

The felt need for strategies of preservation in times of dire communal stress is visible in Ezra–Nehemiah.[37] These books tell the story of some reforms within the postexilic community. In the years surrounding 586 BCE, the Babylonian Empire forced thousands into exile. The population was reduced to a tenth of its preconquest levels—literally decimated—precipitating a long struggle for religious and cultural survival.[38] But the Persians, who came to power in 538 BCE, had a policy of reestablishing people groups in their native land, allowing Ezra to return to the land, bringing with him the book of law with the goal of reforming the community under Torah.

As for Nehemiah, his efforts to rebuild the wall and ensure the integrity of the community met with stern resistance from Sanballat, the ruler of the more powerful province of Samaria to the north, and Tobiah, the Ammonite ruler (Neh 4). There was also conflict between returnees and the people who had remained in the land after the Babylonian conquest (Ezra 9:1-4; Neh 10:30-31). Intermarriage had consolidated the shared power between Sanballat, Tobiah, and the Jerusalem clergy.[39] It is possible that the strange stipulation in Deuteronomy—"No Ammonite or Moabite shall be admitted to the

---

[37]See further David L. Smith-Christopher, "Between Ezra and Isaiah: Exclusion, Transformation and Inclusion of the 'Foreigner' in Post-Exilic Biblical Theology," in *Ethnicity and the Bible*, ed. Mark G. Brett (Leiden: Brill, 2002), 117-42, at 119, 125, 127.

[38]Avraham Faust, *Judah in the Neo-Babylonian Period: The Archaeology of Desolation*, ABS 18 (Atlanta: SBL, 2012), 270.

[39]Joseph Blenkinsopp, *Ezra–Nehemiah*, OTL (Philadelphia: Westminster, 1988), 365.

assembly of the Lᴏʀᴅ" (Deut 23:3)—originally addressed Nehemiah's conflict with Sanballat (a Moabite) and Tobiah (an Ammonite).[40]

It seems that Ezra was concerned with intermarriage between returning Jews and the Jews that remained in the land. Those who remained were taken to have polluted true worship (Ezra 9:2).[41] Ezra insists that those men who have intermarried must separate from their "foreign wives" (Ezra 10:11), citing Deuteronomy's warning that intermarriage will lead to a dilution of the faithfulness of the community (Ezra 9:12-14). This practice of restricting marriage to the in-group is known as endogamy. While endogamy may seem strange and even offensive to Western readers, it remains common within communal societies today.[42] It is likely that Ezra did not have the authority to enforce his decrees. The command to send away wives and children is probably a forceful literary device, calling for purity.[43]

Yet, what are we to make of Ezra's actions? Whether exclusion is ethical surely depends on the relative vulnerability of the groups in question. The example of mass migration that accompanied European imperialism mentioned above, which was so destructive to indigenous peoples and cultures, suggests that an ethic of inclusivism ought not to be *absolutized*. That is, it ought not to be demanded without taking heed of where power imbalances lie. Applying this insight today, we might conclude that vulnerable indigenous communities, such as those found in the United States, Canada, Australia, and New Zealand, should be permitted to insist on a degree of exclusivism. Reflecting upon the realities that indigenous communities face, Mark Brett suggests that a nation or people group can justify focusing upon the "recovery of self . . . when a communal identity has been pushed to the edge of its very life."[44] We have seen that God makes a covenant commitment with

---

[40]Many scholars, but not all, date Deuteronomy 23:1-8 to the postexilic period, as a later addition to Deuteronomy. See, for example, Thomas C. Römer, *The So-Called Deuteronomistic History: A Sociological, Historical and Literary Introduction* (New York: T&T Clark, 2007), 171.

[41]See David L. Smith-Christopher, "The Mixed Marriage Crisis in Ezra 9–10 and Nehemiah 13: A Study of the Sociology of the Post-exilic Judean Community," in *Second Temple Studies*, vol. 2, *Temple and Community in the Persian Period*, ed. Tamara C. Eskenazi and Kent H. Richards, JSOTSup 175 (Sheffield: JSOT Press, 1994), 243-65, at 257. See further Ezra 4:1-4; 9:1-2, 11; 10:2, 11; Nehemiah 10:28-31.

[42]On endogamy, see Smith-Christopher, "The Mixed Marriage Crisis in Ezra 9–10 and Nehemiah 13," 246-53. Religious concerns overlapped with the preservation of property among the remnant, for intermarriage granted wives certain property rights in some circumstances. See further Samuel L. Adams, *Social and Economic Life in Second Temple Judea* (Louisville, KY: Westminster John Knox, 2014), 26.

[43]See further Blenkinsopp, *Ezra–Nehemiah*, 179.

[44]Brett, *Political Trauma and Healing*, 161.

vulnerable groups and with vulnerable individuals. Biblical ethics always tilts in favor of vulnerability, whether of vulnerable people who are displaced from their homes or of vulnerable cultures that are seeking to *preserve* their home.

But those of us in our secure and wealthy Western nation-states who are not members of vulnerable indigenous or diasporic communities should be careful not to misapply this insight. US Attorney General Jeff Sessions invoked Nehemiah's wall building to justify the Trump administration's immigration policies, which at the time included separating children from parents and guardians who entered the country without documentation, including those claiming asylum.[45] This will not do. We in the West need to acknowledge our privileged, powerful positions. In our identity as *Christians*, we may feel small, as though the church is being increasingly marginalized in Western culture. Yet, *as members of our national communities*, we are far from vulnerable and therefore far from justified in excluding vulnerable outsiders for our own benefit.

Returning to the ethics of ancient Israel, not everything that key characters in the Old Testament do is to be imitated, and this is probably the case with Ezra and Nehemiah. The voices of the various books in the Old Testament canon speak in concert, mutually informing one another. While Ezra stipulated thoroughgoing endogamy, the book of Leviticus—a book that was no less concerned with individual and communal purity—permits intermarriage with foreigners for all Israelites excepting the priesthood (Lev 21:14), and Ezekiel even provides that the foreigners will be incorporated as natives and allotted land inheritance among the tribes within postexilic Israel (Ezek 47:22).[46] The contrast between these two examples and Ezra's approach highlights the importance of *context* for understanding Ezra, for he wrote in a context of extreme communal stress.

JONAH: GOD'S PEOPLE IN A STORM

The book of Jonah was another text that called ancient Israel to rethink their relationship to non-Israelites. This book isn't about evangelism (as is often assumed) but about Israel's posture toward outsiders and the relationship of outsiders to Yahweh: it challenges a rigid them-and-us mentality with the knowledge that God is at work in the world.

---

[45]Tal Kopan, "Sessions Cites Bible to Defend Immigration Policies Resulting in Family Separations," *CNN*, June 14, 2018.

[46]Brett provides an excellent discussion of Leviticus and Ezekiel 47:22 (*Political Trauma and Healing*, 106-9).

God said to Jonah, "Go at once to Nineveh, that great city, and cry out against it; for their wickedness has come up before me" (Jon 1:2). Nineveh was the capital city of the Assyrian Empire, and Assyrian rule was brutal. The Assyrians exacted tribute from ancient Palestine to such a degree that Israelite households could barely subsist.[47]

When God gives this command, Jonah runs in the opposite direction, "from the presence of the LORD" (Jon 1:3). Jonah thinks that he can run from God by going to sea, yet as a storm begins to rage, he (perhaps sheepishly) admits to the sailors on the boat that he worships "the LORD, the God of heaven, *who made the sea* and the dry land" (Jon 1:9).

Jonah is a comical character who drags his feet the whole way. He is the opposite of the hilarious character Bottom in Shakespeare's play *A Midsummer Night's Dream*. Within Shakespeare's play, a play is performed, and Bottom wants to be all of the characters. So Bottom keeps breaking out into the different parts. Bottom wants all the roles; Jonah doesn't want to play any role!

A storm rages. While the (non-Israelite) mariners cry out to their gods and throw the cargo overboard, Jonah is fast asleep in the hold of the boat (Jon 1:5). The captain wakes Jonah: "Call on your god!" he yells (Jon 1:6). Now the sailors cast lots, only to discover that it is Jonah who has made the gods furious. So the sailors "cry out to the LORD." The sailors, not Jonah, are using Yahweh's name (Jon 1:14)! Kurtis Peters notes that the contrast is laughable: "They pray, they respond, they sacrifice, and they vow to Yahweh. Jonah runs, hides, and gets dropped in the sea."[48] These non-Israelite sailors show more wisdom in relation to Yahweh than does the Israelite, Jonah.

At last in Nineveh, Jonah prophesies that the great city will be overthrown for its wickedness. Hearing this, the king rises from his throne and sheds his royal robes, casting aside these symbols of his sovereign rule—and sits in the dust (Jon 3:6).[49] This is not so much a case of a foreigner converting to Yahwism but of a brutal king acknowledging the greater sovereignty of the God of gods and repenting of the violence that his empire has perpetrated (Jon 3:8).[50]

The upright character of the foreign mariners and of the king contrasts to Jonah's foolishness. This suggests to us that Jonah may have been written at a time when a hot question within Israel was: How are we to relate to outsiders,

---

[47]Many scholars date the book of Jonah later than the fall of the Neo-Assyrian Empire (609 BCE), suggesting that the book is addressing circumstances under the Persian Empire (550–330 BCE) or even the Hellenistic period (323–31 BCE).

[48]Kurtis Peters, *The Book of Jonah*, unpublished book.

[49]See further Hans Walter Wolff, *Obadiah and Jonah* (Minneapolis: Augsburg, 1986), 151.

[50]See further Christopher-Smith, "Between Ezra and Isaiah," 134.

and what is their standing in relation to Yahweh? Perhaps a group of people wished to join Yahweh's community (maybe Samaritans), and there was much resistance. The figure of Jonah represents Israel.[51] The book of Jonah is saying to Israel, "You are in a storm. The 'sailors' are watching—the people around you are watching. They can see that you are not in communion with your God, and you are out of sync with your true identity as the people of God as an *inclusive* people. You are running from God. You are asleep." Similar to the Canaanite destruction texts, the book of Jonah is more about Israel's own attitude toward outsiders than it is about the other nations. Israel's God cannot be contained within any one nation, for this is the God of the heavens: this God is on the move.

The book of Jonah is meant to provoke exacting questions, not only of ancient Israel but also of the church today: Is it possible that the church today is in a storm, without knowing it? Is it possible that the church is asleep in the bottom of the boat while others are busy on the deck? Are we running from God, forsaking our identity as the body of Christ in the world? Might it be *Christians* who need to repent and turn to God? And, if Christ followers fail to show the love of God to displaced people, are we truly proclaiming *Christ*? Perhaps we still need to see that evangelism-without-welcome does not really proclaim the gospel of Jesus Christ at all but is a distortion of the truth, a disfigurement of Christ's beauty. The book of Jonah, by its literary allure and by its warm familiarity as a children's story, tricks us into first thinking that this book is all about our saving sinners; in fact, it is all about saving ourselves.

JOB: LISTENING WELL

A universal impetus is also found in the book of Job, which begins, "There was once a man in the land of Uz whose name was Job" (Job 1:1). Job is a non-Israelite from the East, described as "blameless and upright, one who feared God and turned away from evil" (Job 1:1). But in the opening chapters of the book, Job loses everything.

In the first cycle of speeches, Job's friends do a poor job of comforting him, and they become more and more exasperated as the dialogue unfolds. Job's suffering is an indication that he must be wicked, whether knowingly or unknowingly, they say (Job 11:13-20). The friends assume an overly rigid

---

[51]In Hebrew, the name *Jonah* is the same as the word *dove*, a term that can refer to Israel (Hos 7:11; cf. 11:11).

interpretation of Deuteronomy's principle that obedience will lead to blessing and wickedness to curse (e.g., Lev 26; Deut 28).[52]

Job assumes the same. However, Job, believing that this system of blessings and curses is flawed somehow, goes *to* God.[53] From Job 7 on, Job speaks to God with second-person address, "you," up close and personal. Ironically, the friends tell Job that he should pray to God (Job 5:8; 11:13), yet Job *is* praying— Job is weeping and raging on the Father's knee, as it were.[54] Job is the only character to speak directly *to* God in the book; his friends speak *about* God.[55]

This foreigner is teaching the Israelite readers of the book to speak *to* God, not simply to *explain* God. And he is challenging their tit-for-tat assumptions. Job's wisdom is remarkable: he has even discerned Yahweh's desire for justice for those who are weakest, and he has put this into practice: "If I have withheld anything that the poor desired, / or have caused the eyes of the widow to fail . . ." (Job 31:16).

Where does Job gain this knowledge of Yahweh's will? Job seems to observe the law but without any access to the law (as a non-Israelite). He points his interlocutors to creation itself as his source of knowledge: "Speak to the earth, and it will instruct you, / and the fish of the sea will declare to you" (Job 12:8 author's translation).

The Hebrew word for "instruct" here is used more commonly for instruction in the law of Yahweh (Ex 24:12; Lev 10:11; Deut 33:10).[56] Yet, how can creation instruct a person? There is a carved order in the creation. There is a way that the biosphere functions and that time unfolds that can't be dodged or relativized, at least in the day to day (e.g., Prov 26:27). There are seasons and cycles, and both in their predictability and in their untamed magnificence they grant wisdom, instructing humanity in God's ways (Is 28:23-29). The word translated "wisdom" in the Old Testament means learning the ways of the earth so that we can live skillfully in God's world (e.g., Prov 3:19-20).

In the book of Job, then, are two lessons about Yahweh's relationship to non-Israelites: first, a source of divine knowledge is universally available, and this knowledge has challenged a simplistic (moralistic) reading of the Torah.[57] Second, a foreigner has revealed something about Yahweh to Israel.

---

[52]Andrew Zack Lewis, *Approaching Job* (Eugene, OR: Cascade, 2017), 72, 74.

[53]Lewis, *Approaching Job*, 94.

[54]See David R. Jackson, *Crying Out for Vindication: The Gospel According to Job* (Phillipsburg, NJ: P&R, 2007); and Lewis, *Approaching Job*, 41.

[55]Lewis, *Approaching Job*, 42.

[56]See further Brett, *Political Trauma and Healing*, 130.

[57]This way of knowing through the creation, which is visible to all, relates theologically to the universality of the divine image, whereby all human beings, from every ethnicity, are created in the image of God (Gen 1:27).

Any Israelite who sat through a reading of Job had effectively *listened* to the wisdom of foreigners, whether historical or fictional, for a full forty-two chapters. Imagine an ancient gathering where the book of Job was read aloud. "I wonder what I might learn from my Moabite neighbor!" some might have reflected as they departed from this occasion. One tacit implication of the book of Job is that Yahweh desired the ancient people of God not only to welcome people of other ethnicities but also to listen deeply and to learn from them.

LISTENING TO FISHERMEN FROM ACEH

We learn from the book of Job that listening to those who don't share the faith of Israel may lead to greater insight into our own Scriptures. Let's put this into practice now by listening in and learning from the modern example of some fishermen from Aceh, Indonesia. Let's listen humbly, seeking to gain a richer understanding of Christ's call.

In May 2015, Acehnese fishermen rescued 1,807 Rohingya who had been forcibly displaced from Myanmar and abandoned at sea by people smugglers.[58] Indonesian, Malaysian, and Thai authorities had refused the Rohingya permission to land, providing them with fuel, water, and other provisions and returning them to sea in a manner that mimicked neighboring Australia's policy of turning back boats of asylum seekers. The fishermen found the stranded Rohingya in waters north of Aceh, Indonesia. On May 10, fishermen from the village of Seunuddon helped bring 578 passengers to shore. Indonesian authorities responded by warning Acehnese fishermen not to participate in such rescues. But five days later, fishermen from another village helped bring another boat of asylum seekers to shore. Indonesian authorities punished some of these fishermen by seizing documentation such as licenses and proof of boat ownership. Yet, a further five days later, fishermen from yet another village helped bring another boat of asylum seekers to shore. By this time, the rescues were attracting praise from local and international media. Under this new scrutiny, Indonesian authorities refrained from punishing the fishermen any further.[59]

The Acehnese fishermen explained their compassionate and costly acts in terms that echo many of the themes of our book. Myusup Mansur, who was

---

[58]This story is beautifully told and analyzed in Anne McNevin and Antje Missbach, "Hospitality as a Horizon of Aspiration (or, What the International Refugee Regime Can Learn from Acehnese Fishermen)," *JRefS* 31, no. 3 (2018): 292-313.
[59]McNevin and Missbach, "Hospitality as a Horizon of Aspiration," 295-96.

involved in the second rescue, put it simply: "We helped them because they needed help. What is more human than that?" Another, Suryadi, insisted that they needed to act in spite of the risks and costs: "If we find someone in the ocean, we have to help them no matter who they are. The police did not like us helping, but we could not avoid it. Our sense of humanity was higher. So we just helped with the limited resources that we had at the time." Some identified their own past experiences of persecution at the hands of Indonesian government forces and displacement during the 2004 tsunami as reason for caring for the persecuted and displaced, thus unconsciously echoing Deuteronomy: "You shall also love the stranger, for you were strangers in the land of Egypt" (Deut 10:19). Some Acehnese locals celebrated the welcome and comfort that they were able to provide. "We bought them a big bunch of bananas and water, and they all bathed in our homes," said Saipal Umar. "They were so weak, especially the small children. They were traumatized." Others evoked simply the idea of kinship. "We treated them like family," said Sulaiman.[60]

The selfless rescue and generous welcome that the Acehnese fishermen and villagers offered vulnerable Rohingya enhanced Acehnese communal pride, strengthened communal bonds, and reinforced their self-identity as a community that welcomes.[61] It also sparked a change of heart among neighboring countries. There were still several thousand Rohingya stranded at sea. The Philippines announced that it would not deter them from entry and would provide shelter for three thousand. Malaysia and Indonesia jointly declared that they would provide temporary shelter, so long as the international community organized repatriation or resettlement within one year. These states worked with the United Nations' refugee and migration agencies, United Nations High Commissioner for Refugees (UNHCR) and International Organization for Migration (IOM), to construct emergency camps, determine the status of displaced people, and assist with returns and resettlement. Acehnese leaders offered to continue to host Rohingya refugees if resettlement could not be arranged in the first year. Indonesian officials responded by agreeing to provide temporary protection beyond the first year while resettlement was organized.[62]

---

[60]McNevin and Missbach, "Hospitality as a Horizon of Aspiration," 298-99; and Kate Lamb, "'We Helped out of Solidarity': Indonesian Fishermen Come to Aid of Boat Migrants," *Guardian*, May 18, 2015.
[61]McNevin and Missbach, "Hospitality as a Horizon of Aspiration," 299-300.
[62]McNevin and Missbach, "Hospitality as a Horizon of Aspiration," 296.

The Acehnese fishermen and villagers embraced their own vulnerability and extended kinship to the vulnerable. They could only do so much, but they accepted risks and costs to do all that they could. The village of Seunuddon that provided temporary care to 578 Rohingya, for example, was home to only 1,500 people.[63] What a contrast can be seen with wealthy Western states that seek so obsessively to minimize risks to their security and to calculate so precisely the meager contributions they are willing to make to alleviate the global crisis of forced displacement. Not only do they place strict limits on their quotas for resettlement—quotas that arguably don't even match the numbers of people whose displacement they generate via global injustices—but they do all they can to prevent unwanted others from claiming asylum, allocating absurd sums of money to deterring and detaining vulnerable people, money that might otherwise be spent on temporarily protecting, safely repatriating, or embracing and enfolding displaced people as kin (as we discuss further in parts three and four).

COVENANT AND ELECTION

Before we leave the Old Testament, it is helpful to relate our observations on God's care for outsiders to Israel's election. How do these two theological realities fit together: Israel's election and God's universal care? To be sure, Yahweh had chosen Israel for a unique role: to be a light to the nations (Deut 4:6-8; Is 42:6). As Willie J. Jennings puts it: "At the threshold of Israel's land, in the presence of Israel's God, the story of every people ruptures, cracks open, revealing a second layer, an underlying layer of reality bound to this God."[64] And Yahweh made a covenant with Israel for this purpose (Gen 12:1-3; 17:1-4). And yet, God also made a covenant with all of humanity: the covenant with Noah was a generous grace extended to all of humankind (Gen 9:8-10). As well as making a covenant with all people, God covenanted, with fierce loyalty, with vulnerable foreigners (Deut 10:17-19). God's particular covenant with Israel, then, is a question of role and of degree. This covenant is exceptional, and yet it is not the only covenant. In so far as Israel's relationship with Yahweh is exceptional, this is not for the sake of Israel alone but precisely *for the sake of* the other nations, that all people groups may enjoy this communion and blessing (Gen 12:1-3). And Israel was to extend that same covenant love to displaced people that Yahweh, their covenanting King, extended (Deut 10:18-19).

---

[63]McNevin and Missbach, "Hospitality as a Horizon of Aspiration," 305.
[64]Willie J. Jennings, *The Christian Imagination: Theology and the Origins of Race* (New Haven, CT: Yale University Press, 2010), 258.

In this chapter we have been inquiring into how God shaped ancient Israel, through various books of the Old Testament, to respond to displaced people who were seeking a home. Where does all this lead us? We offered in chapter two the metaphor of playing jazz as a way of conceiving how to interpret the Old Testament ethically for today. Running with this metaphor, in chapters two and three we have discerned a core tradition (cf. the jazz tradition), or ethic, in the Old Testament: a call to enfold displaced people as kin. In the later chapters we will begin to "create" with this ethic for our present historical moment, creatively considering the responsibilities and opportunities that church, national, and global communities have to extend kinship to displaced people. Next, however, we will turn to the New Testament to explore Jesus' creative practices of kinship.

3

JESUS' KINSHIP

THE PEOPLE OF JESUS' PLACE AND TIME in history, N. T. Wright tells us, "had their minds full of poverty and politics, and would have had little time for theological abstractions or timeless verities."[1] Thus, when Jesus announces the coming of God's kingdom, he does so in his attitudes and actions as well as in his teaching. To heal the sick, to cast out demons, to eat and drink and socialize with society's outcasts—his actions communicate just as clearly as do his words, and their message is the same: the Lord of lords is establishing a new kingdom, some of whose people may not have known the privileges of *belonging* in any human realm. The Father, through his only Son, is calling into being a *new family* whose members come from many different human families. The themes of kinship were at the very heart of Jesus' message, and we would do well to keep that clearly in mind as we consider the meaning of his gospel as it was understood by its first hearers, as well as its implications for us in our own place and time.

In this chapter, we narrow in on the Synoptic Gospels, rather than all four Gospels, in order to gain focus. We give particular attention to Luke's Gospel because, from his vantage point in the first-century urban centers of the Roman East, Luke speaks to the very issues of poverty and marginality that concern us today.[2]

---

[1]N. T. Wright, *Jesus and the Victory of God* (Minneapolis: Fortress, 1996), 85.

[2]Philip Francis Esler, *Community and Gospel in Luke-Acts: The Social and Political Motivations of Lucan Theology*, SNTSMS 57 (Cambridge: Cambridge University Press, 1987), 197-200.

KINSHIP AND THE KINGDOM OF GOD

We have seen that kinship is about solidarity. To whom can we turn for support, and who can turn to us? With whom do we share a sense of mutual commitment, belonging, and identity? When the context in which these questions arise is the Mediterranean world of the first century CE, the answers are complicated. Blood ties, while extremely important to a sense of kinship, were not the only consideration. In the world into which Jesus was born, the sense of who was inside and who was outside the circle of trust and fellowship was qualified not only by how close one's ties were to the tribal or family relationships but also by such concepts as honor and shame, purity and impurity, health and infirmity.[3]

Honor-shame. In the communal Mediterranean cultures of the first century, it was imperative to seek honor and to avoid shame.[4] Honor was the highest social good and was ordinarily shared within the circle of one's kin. Honor was an element of family heritage, like a bequest from one's forebears; thus the loss of honor (either through misfortune or through deliberate misdeed) meant the loss of inherited status. And the cultural attitudes toward honor and shame were further complicated by the highly competitive and violent character of the surrounding culture, in which honor came to be perceived as something like a commodity in limited supply and thus something that could become the prize of competition, especially between men. One person could gain honor only at the expense of another. In such a conflict-ridden, agonistic culture, it was crucial to know where loyal support could be found: within one's kinship group. In first-century Palestine, one's kinsfolk may be blood relations or friends bound by the ties of adoptive kinship (such as patron-client relations).

Marginality. In first-century Judaism, marginality and hierarchy—who was acceptable and who was not—were carefully defined. A first-century Israelite would have considered any Gentile or Samaritan to be completely

[3]On kinship in first-century Palestine, see John Davis, *People of the Mediterranean: An Essay in Comparative Social Anthropology* (London: Routledge & Kegan Paul, 1977), 176-238; K. C. Hanson, "BTB Readers Guide: Kinship," *Biblical Theology Bulletin* 24, no. 4 (1994): 183-94; and Bruce J. Malina, *The Social Gospel of Jesus: The Kingdom of God in Mediterranean Perspective* (Minneapolis: Augsburg Fortress, 2001), 1-36.

[4]On honor-shame, see David D. Gilmore, ed. *Honor and Shame and the Unity of the Mediterranean* (Washington, DC: American Anthropological Association, 1987); Bruce J. Malina, *The New Testament World: Insights from Cultural Anthropology*, 3rd ed. (Louisville, KY: Westminster John Knox, 2001), 27-57; and Bruce J. Malina and Jerome H. Neyrey, "Honor and Shame in Luke-Acts: Pivotal Values of the Mediterranean World," in *The Social World of Luke-Acts: Models for Interpretation*, ed. Jerome H. Neyrey (Peabody, MA: Hendrickson, 1991), 25-66.

beyond the pale, not even *registering* as acceptable to God (Mk 7:24-30). But there were finer gradations within Israel, and every single Jew was placed somewhere between the intimacy of the innermost circle and the perimeter defenses of the people of Yahweh. At the center, we have the Pharisees (Mk 7:3-5; Lk 18:11-12), the scribes and priests (Lk 10:31-32), and the chief priest himself (Jn 18:19; Heb 7:18-28). On the periphery are morally compromised Israelites: tax collectors and sinners (Lk 15:1-2; Mt 9:10-13).[5] No better than these were the physically "unclean": lepers (Mk 1:40-45; Lk 17:11-14) and menstruants (Mk 5:25-34).

Imagine, for example, that you suffer from deformity or blindness—common enough maladies in this place and time. Depending upon your circle of support, you might or might not be able to perform the requisite rituals to keep yourself ritually clean. Some would suspect that the cause of your malady is your own sinfulness (Jn 9:2); perhaps you were in the grasp of demons. Add to this the (then) almost universal belief in the "evil eye." Any invalid (presumably envying the good health of others) was thought to have this power to bring calamity on those whose good fortune they envied, a power exercised by merely staring at those more fortunate. If you were thought to have the evil eye, passers-by would defend themselves against your curse by spitting at you.[6] Your vulnerability and loneliness as one of the least in first-century Jewish culture can hardly be overstated.

The community of Jesus. Jesus came preaching that he had come to renew Israel, and he did so using the language of kinship. That language had immediate cultural resonance in his day. Jesus was forming a community who would faithfully embody the redemption he promised. He was not content merely to heal the individual, for individuals by themselves are not able to embody the communal dimension of God's kingdom. When he taught his disciples to pray, he taught them to say "our Father" not "my Father," and this plural form occurs nine times in the Lord's Prayer as recorded in Matthew's Gospel (Mt 6:9-13). The familial kinship group of Jesus' disciples has one heavenly Father. This Father has revealed God's own character and desires for

---

[5]On moral impurity, see Thomas Kazen, *Jesus and Purity Halakhah: Was Jesus Indifferent to Impurity?*, 2nd ed., ConBNT 38 (Winona Lake, IN: Eisenbrauns, 2010), 4, 201; and Jonathan Klawans, *Impurity and Sin in Ancient Judaism* (Oxford: Oxford University Press, 2000), 26-36.

[6]E.g., Job 30:10; Galatians 4:14. See John H. Elliott, *Beware the Evil Eye: The Evil Eye in the Bible and the Ancient World*, vol. 2, *Greece and Rome* (Eugene, OR: Cascade, 2016), 176; idem, *Beware the Evil Eye: The Evil Eye in the Bible and the Ancient World*, vol. 3, *The Bible and Related Sources* (Eugene, OR: Cascade, 2016), 242-49; and David D. Gilmore, "Anthropology of the Mediterranean Area," *ARA* 11 (1982): 175-205, at 197-98.

God's people in the story of Israel. The phrase "hallowed be (or *sanctify*) your name" means nothing less than "gather and revitalize your people!" The community that Jesus formed around himself demonstrated the in-breaking kingdom of God every bit as much as did Jesus' miracles, meals, and teaching.

Jesus' followers became a kinship group within the larger kin grouping of national Israel. The genealogies recorded in the Gospels imply that Jesus' human parents had inherited honor on the basis of their prestigious Israelite royal lineage (Mt 1:1-17; Lk 3:23-38). But Jesus redefined *his* family as "those who do the will of God" (Mk 3:35). In short, Jesus' kinship group becomes that community that truly follows the way of Yahweh for Israel. While Jesus' natural family—Mary (who is emphasized), Joseph (who is not), and the four named brothers and sisters—can be found in the Gospels, his attitude to his own natural family would have been outright shocking in a Mediterranean communal context. "Who are my mother and my brothers?" Jesus asks. "Here are my mother and my brothers! Whoever does the will of God is my brother and sister and mother," he says to those sitting around him (Mk 3:33-35).

Jesus referred to those who recognized in his life and teaching the way of God, and who followed in obedience, as his adoptive kin. The primacy of this new adopted kin made his blood kin secondary. The essential identity of Jesus' followers was no longer to be sought within their natural kinship groupings. Rather, followers of Jesus found their first kinship with Christ and with the divine Father and then with each other. The cost of leaving one's natural family in that cultural context can hardly be overstated. To leave one's family would be seen as socially deviant behavior. Yet, as Simon Peter says, he and his partners "left everything and followed" Jesus (Lk 5:11). Thus, we can see the importance of Jesus' promise that his disciples will ultimately receive "houses, brothers and sisters, mothers and children, and fields" (Mk 10:30)—a hundredfold more than they had abandoned to follow him. However, whole households also aligned themselves to the Way of Jesus. Grafted-in family groups of Jesus followers became fundamental to carrying out the ministry of Jesus and, in time, to spreading the gospel from Jerusalem to Rome (Mk 1:16-20, 29-34; Lk 10:38-42; 24:10; Acts 15:12-13).[7]

Many of his followers gave up much in order to follow him. But perhaps the more remarkable thing about Jesus' adoptive family is how many of those

---

[7] See further John H. Elliott, "Temple Versus Household in Luke-Acts: A Contrast in Social Institutions," in Neyrey, *Social World of Luke-Acts*, 211-40, at 225-26.

whom Jesus and his followers sought out as kindred had little or nothing (in the way of material or social advantages) to offer. These others, the "least" of the people of Israel, became a focus of Jesus' ministry, as we can observe in the Gospel record of Jesus' approach to meals, to the question of ritual purity, to healing, and to parables and other forms of teaching.

MEALS THAT UNITE AND MEALS THAT DIVIDE

Meals, for all of their everyday-ness, are a highly charged social force. Cultural anthropologists have shown how meals reflect, condense, and even shape social relations: "If food is treated as a code, the messages it encodes will be found in the pattern of social relations being expressed. The message is about different degrees of hierarchy, inclusion and exclusion, boundaries and transactions across the boundaries."[8] If meals encode social structures, we should strive to understand those meals chronicled in the gospels in the light of the patterns of social relations in the culture. Jesus' meal practices embodied the social dimension of the kingdom of God in a way that could not go unnoticed or unaddressed—especially by his enemies.

Jesus' meals with "sinners." It is sometimes said that Jesus ate his way through the Gospels. Jesus did more eating in Luke's Gospel than he did teaching—and often he did both at the same time. It is always important to pay attention to the matter of whom Jesus ate with. Jesus had a reputation for eating with those who were socially shunned, as Luke records: "The Pharisees and the scribes were grumbling and saying, 'This fellow welcomes sinners and eats with them'" (Lk 15:2).[9] It was scandalous, for example, for Jesus to dine at the house of Levi the tax collector (Lk 5:27-32; Mt 9:9-13; Mk 2:13-17), for such a person had *negative honor*, with one foot in the devil's camp. Jesus seeks out just these sorts of people, sharing at table with them, nourishing kinship. With the command "Follow me!" Jesus invites Levi to break from his erstwhile kinship network for the sake of joining Jesus' own itinerant kinship group. As we saw with Deuteronomy's feasts, sharing a meal doesn't merely celebrate Levi's adoption into Jesus' fellowship; it brings this kinship into reality!

---

[8]Mary Douglas, "Deciphering a Meal," *Daedalus* 101, no. 1 (1972): 61-81, at 61.

[9]Cecilia Wassen has argued that the term *sinners* denotes "people who transgress the laws and are therefore outside of the covenant, according to the specific perception of the writer" (Cecilia Wassen, "Jesus' Table Fellowship with 'Toll Collectors and Sinners,'" *JSHJ* 14 [2016]: 137-57, at 148; see citations there). In the plurality of Jewish religious groups, the term *sinner* denoted anyone outside of one's own group (see Klawans, *Impurity*, 79-82).

For years I (Mark) have pictured these "sinners' meals" in my imagination. I have imagined Jesus' loving warmth toward this motley crew, and I have always imagined that tax collectors would have made joyful and loud company. And Jesus would have laughed with these men with a laugh full-hearted and loud! Remember, though, that Jesus didn't invent these fellowship meals. Rather, these meals recall the ancient call to inclusive kinship meals. Jesus is simply being what Israel had always been called to be!

To be sure, many of those with whom Jesus ate went on to repent of their sins, like Levi himself and Zacchaeus (Lk 5:28; 19:8, cf. 18:13). Jesus' mission to renew Israel was morally stringent. However, such repentance was not a prerequisite for sharing a meal with Jesus, as is demonstrated by the many tax collectors and "sinners" who ate with Jesus at Levi's house (Mt 9:11).[10] As Richard Bauckham remarks: "This is what distinguished his practice from Jewish leaders who would not have denied that people like tax collectors could repent and obtain forgiveness from God."[11]

Two meals at a Pharisee's house, Luke 14:7-24. Luke 14:7-24 is the story of two meals. The first is a real meal, hosted by a prominent Pharisee—a story unique to Luke's Gospel. The second meal is fictional and is described in the parable of the wedding banquet that Jesus tells *during* the meal that he attends. At the Pharisee's house, the guests follow the customary status-conscious practice for dining, choosing for themselves places of honor (Lk 14:7). First-century Greco-Roman and Jewish cultures were based on a rigid social hierarchy, clearly evident in the way that food and drink were served and eaten.[12] Seating reflected status: the guest of highest social status was seated nearest to the host; other places were assigned in turn according to declining status (cf. Lk 14:7). A guest's rank might also be signaled by the quantity and quality of food offered to him or her (cf. Gen 43:33-34). The formal meal was a public arena where one might display the social honor one possessed already—or compete for greater honor.

Seated at the Pharisee's table, Jesus shames those guests who have used the occasion to jockey for places of honor. Jesus' words are a reversal of that common social practice: "All who exalt themselves will be humbled, and

---

[10]For a discussion of the ongoing debate over whether Jesus required "sinners" to repent, see Mark Allan Powell, "Was Jesus a Friend of Unrepentant Sinners?: A Fresh Appraisal of Sanders's Controversial Proposal," *JSHJ* 7 (2009): 286-310.

[11]Richard Bauckham, *Jesus: A Very Short Introduction* (Oxford: Oxford University Press, 2011), 45.

[12]In the Greco-Roman world, kinship included not only traditional familial associations but also structures of patronage, which were highly hierarchical. The structure of meals signified the vast disparity in status between the patron and client.

those who humble themselves will be exalted" (Lk 14:11; cf. Mk 10:35-40). Jesus then shames the host as well, criticizing him for having invited only those who could be expected to repay the favor. This would have been the norm at the time, to offer a kindness in a cultural system of "balanced reciprocity." Jesus teaches instead: "When you give a banquet, invite the poor, the crippled, the lame, and the blind" (Lk 14:13).

Then Jesus describes the events of a banquet like the one he is attending, but this parable is the story of a symbolic meal of the kingdom of God (see Lk 14:15). In the parable of the great dinner, the host invites his wealthy friends to dine with him, but they make excuses and refuse to come. The host then invites the poor, the crippled, the blind, and the lame to come in place of those who had first been invited. The people in this second guest list have no social status whatever, and the elite risk being cut off from social networks and even from family should they deign to eat with those of a lower status. The host in Jesus' parable risks a rift with family and friends.[13] In this reversal the unresponsive elite are excluded from the feast of the kingdom of God while those whom nobody would think of inviting have the place of honor (Lk 14:24).

The parable strongly undermines the exclusivist and honor-seeking motives present in first-century Judaism as well as in the surrounding pagan culture. The coming of Yahweh to Zion is profoundly joined to Jesus' person and actions. He refers to the great banquet in his parable as "my" banquet (Lk 14:24). None of those who had exalted themselves are to savor Jesus' feast, but those who had been shunned by first-century Israelite insiders will be welcomed. Jesus' deliberate inversion of these categories of insiders and outsiders could not be more dramatic.[14]

To understand the meaning of these two meals at the house of the Pharisee, we need to keep the underlying theme of kinship in mind. Not all meals bring people together. Meals can both unite and divide.[15] This is visible in Luke's contrasting the Pharisee's agonistic jostling for status (in the actual meal served in his home) against Jesus' portrayal (in his parable) of the feast of the

---

[13]See Bruce J. Malina and Richard L. Rohrbaugh, *Social-Science Commentary on the Synoptic Gospels*, 1st ed. (Minneapolis: Fortress, 1999), 366.

[14]The parable amplifies what Jesus says earlier in Luke's Gospel: "Then people will come from east and west, from north and south, and will eat in the kingdom of God" (Lk 13:29).

[15]Michael Dietler, "Theorizing the Feast: Rituals of Consumption, Commensal Politics, and Power in African Contexts," in *Feasts: Archaeological and Ethnographic Perspectives on Food, Politics, and Power*, ed. Michael Dietler and Brian Hayden (Washington, DC: Smithsonian Institution Press, 2001), 65-114, at 77.

kingdom of God. Nonetheless, the theme of kinship is evident in both meals. Those who attend the Pharisee's meal are listed as friends (clients), brothers (perhaps blood kin), and relatives (perhaps referring to fictive kin) (Lk 14:12).[16] While the categories are blurred, these three words refer to kin relations. Patron-client relations were also experienced in terms of kinship: "father" to "son." Kinship was thus the natural frame of reference for relationships in the ancient Mediterranean world. In the second, status-inverting parabolic meal, the social affront is precisely that *the banquet signifies kinship with the "impure" outsiders* invited by the host. Jesus overturns the expectations of his hearers precisely so that they (and we) will ask the important question: What kind of kinship is entailed in the feast in the kingdom of God (Lk 14:15)?

The Pharisee host and his "nobler" guests practiced a form of "balanced reciprocity."[17] Guests invited to such a feast would have been under a strong social obligation to return the favor to their host: it was simply expected. Jesus plays off this expectation in the parable of the great dinner by painting a picture of what cultural anthropologists might refer to as "generalized reciprocity."[18] Here, the interests of the *guests* are paramount; the feast is shared by the host *without any expectation of return.* Generalized reciprocity in anthropology pertains to household relationships and describes such vital matters as the care and feeding of children (for instance). In other words, the great dinner described by Jesus resembles the intimate kinship of a private family meal rather than the competitive, status-seeking public feast. In Jesus' teaching, the kingdom is a place where meals are shared without the thought of payback. Is this an evocative and appropriate image for how nations might respond to refugees? What would happen if the West were to adopt a generalized-reciprocity model as the paradigm for responding to our global crisis of displacement? We will explore such ideas further in chapters six through ten.

Consider for a moment the broader picture of Jesus' meals in the Gospels. By his actions and his words Jesus upends the current assumptions concerning the great disparity in rank and status between servants and hosts and elite guests. Jesus not only serves at table from time to time but also draws attention to himself undertaking a deliberate social humiliation, and this as

---

[16]K. C. Hanson and Douglas E. Oakman, *Palestine in the Time of Jesus: Social Structures and Social Conflicts*, 2nd ed. (Minneapolis: Augsburg Fortress, 2008), 69.

[17]See further Marshall D. Sahlins, "On the Sociology of Primitive Exchange," in *The Relevance of Models for Social Anthropology*, ed. Michael Banton (London: Tavistock, 1965), 139-236, at 147-48.

[18]See further Sahlins, "On the Sociology of Primitive Exchange," 147; and Jerome H. Neyrey, "Ceremonies in Luke-Acts: The Case of Meals and Table Fellowship," in Neyrey, *Social World of Luke-Acts*, 361-87, at 372.

a model for those who are to lead Jesus' kinship movement (e.g., Lk 22:24-30). Jesus is at times both host and guest; he serves and is served; he gives and receives (e.g., Lk 7:38). There is a deep mutuality in Jesus' way with people.

Relationships of Mutuality with Refugees

Jesus' rejection of honor seeking and his embrace of relationships characterized by humility and mutuality need to shape our relationships with refugees today. We see the principle of mutuality at work in the contemporary world, in the experience of Emily Parsons Dickau, who is Director of Programs at Kinbrace Community Society and our dear friend. She tells of her relationship with a couple whom she had been assisting with their refugee claim process. The couple invited her into their small suite at Kinbrace to share lunch. They didn't share a common language so Emily and the family simply sat and ate together in silence. It was awkward but also transformative. Emily recalls that from this moment her relationship with these "strangers" significantly changed: a sense of trust, friendship, and kinship began to blossom. Emily describes the difference between being a mere helper and becoming a *friend*: "When I received the gift of lunch from this couple, our lives connected in a way that they hadn't before. For weeks, I had been the person offering support while this family had been receiving it. But now I was the recipient of care, in the form of a delicious Kurdish meal. The 'helper' dynamic was flipped and suddenly we were both giving and receiving. This is one step on the road towards friendship, which is something that all of us need to flourish."

HOW JESUS CHALLENGED PURITY CUSTOMS

Maintaining ritual purity was important to the culture of Jesus' day, though there was some diversity in understanding and practices.[19] While purity ritual was an important expression of holiness, the relative importance of purity practices versus practices of justice and compassion found live debate.[20] In line with the Old Testament prophetic tradition that emphasized social justice for the least, Jesus had a laid-back attitude toward purity laws, and he prioritized moral evil and injustice.[21] He was also constantly dealing with

[19]On the importance of the purity codes in first-century Palestine, see Kazen, *Jesus and Purity Halakhah*, 3. On diversity in purity practices in first-century Palestine, see Thomas Kazen, *Issues of Impurity in Early Judaism*, ConBNT 45 (Winona Lake, IN: Eisenbrauns, 2010), 104-6.
[20]Kazen, *Jesus and Purity Halakhah*, 207-10, 261.
[21]Kazen, *Jesus and Purity Halakhah*, 261.

people that the purity codes would have told him to avoid.[22] Within today's global community, those 79.5 million people who have been forcibly displaced and dispossessed are sometimes, wrongly, construed in similar ways to the impure outcasts of Jesus' time. It is vital, then, that we learn from Jesus' response to the purity customs of his day.

There were three "systems" of purity, which first-century Judaism inherited from the Old Testament.[23] First, there were the laws concerning clean and unclean food (Lev 11). Then, there were the purity laws concerning bodily contact, namely with dead bodies, with leprosy, and with fluid emissions from the body (Lev 12–15; Num 19); contact with any of these would make a person "unclean." Finally, there were the stipulations concerned with moral and ethical purity (Lev 17–20).

Jesus sharply challenged the Pharisees' focus on ritual purity in light of the greater requirement (moral purity) to demonstrate compassion.[24] The key point of Jesus' challenge was the distinction between practices of outward purification and inner cleanness or righteousness: "There is nothing outside a person that by going in can defile, but the things that come out are what defile" (Mk 7:15). The Pharisees had the wrong priority: "Now you Pharisees clean the outside of the cup and of the dish, but inside you are full of greed and wickedness" (Lk 11:39). The Pharisees' food and drink needed to be given to the poor rather than be subject to purification (Lk 11:41).[25] Jesus berated the Pharisees in a similar way for their tithing practices: "For you tithe mint, dill, and cummin, and have neglected the weightier matters of the law: justice and mercy and faith" (Mt 23:23).

Jesus was not dismissing the purity laws altogether, any more than he was teaching people to disregard the tithing laws.[26] Rather, in line with the Old Testament prophets, Jesus was signaling that practices of justice and compassion tower in importance over ritual purity (Lk 11:42).[27]

---

[22]Jerome H. Neyrey, "Idea of Purity in Mark's Gospel," *Semeia* 35 (1986): 91-128, at 91.

[23]For a summary of the purity system, see Kazen, *Jesus and Purity Halakhah*, 1-7.

[24]Kazen states that the Pharisees were a part of an "influential expansionist tendency, and competing with the early Jesus movement for influence in Galilee" (Kazen, *Issues of Impurity in Early Judaism*, 161). Nonetheless, it was the Sadducees and the Qumran community, over against the Pharisees, who compartmentalized ritual law and moral law (Kazen, *Jesus and Purity Halakhah*, 216). Here Kazen disputes Klawans, who argues that "a Pharisee would not agree with Mark 7:15, for the simple fact that what comes out of the mouth does not ritually defile." Klawans, *Impurity*, 150.

[25]Kazen, *Jesus and Purity Halakhah*, 226.

[26]See Matthew 23:23/Luke 11:42; Matthew 5:23-24. See further Kazen, *Jesus and Purity Halakhah*, 249.

[27]Kazen, *Issues of Impurity in Early Judaism*, 133.

Jesus' response to purity laws was always related to people and to their inclusion in God's community. By healing lepers, who had been cast out of the community due to their impurity, Jesus reinstated them into the worshiping community and also with their kinsfolk.[28] And, by sharing table with marginalized people, who may have been "contagious" because of immorality or bodily uncleanliness, Jesus prioritized kinship over purity customs. Further, Israel's food laws had for generations defined the boundary of the people of God. But in the Gospel of Mark, Jesus declares all foods to be clean (Mk 7:19). By this, Jesus was signifying, in the terms of first-century Judaism, that God may be approached by any person and seeks covenant and kinship with all. Jesus was proclaiming that, in his own person and work, the welcome of God to every person has drawn near (cf. Acts 10:9-33). For Jesus, the purity codes did not exist to disrupt kinship groups, community, and table fellowship.[29]

How often today are asylum seekers seen as pariahs akin to the impure rejected by society in the Gospels! They are labeled aliens and illegals, economic leeches and potential terrorists, threats that must be contained. Yet, displaced people detest their status and grieve their shifting identity. Jesus took kinship responsibility for those designated as impure, those living apart from the protections of kinship and community. As he did, Jesus also received the gift of kinship: think of the love that the woman who anointed Jesus showered on him (Mt 26:7), or think of the big-hearted responses of some tax collectors (Lk 19:8). What lavish displays of love Jesus received! Our exploration of Jesus' Way suggests that churches, communities, and nations ought similarly to stand in the gap, taking kinship responsibility for such as these. As we do, we in turn receive the blessing of kinship. Of course, our point isn't that we should extend kinship with expectations of what newcomers ought to offer us in return (many churches have sponsored refugees with unhelpful or unrealistic expectations), but rather that Jesus' way of kinship is a blessing to all who follow in his way.

HEALING AND THE RESTORATION OF KINSHIP

Inseparable from the eschatological horizon of Jesus' miracles is their relationship to community: they served the restoration of the people of God, among whom, in the eschatological age of salvation, no disease is permitted.[30]

---

[28]Leviticus 13:1–14:32; Luke 5:12-16; 17:11-19.

[29]Kazen, *Jesus and Purity Halakhah*, 347.

[30]Gerhard Lohfink, *Jesus and Community: The Social Dimension of Christian Faith*, trans. John P. Galvin (Philadelphia: Fortress, 1984), 13.

In a communal Mediterranean culture, when someone became ill, it involved the whole kinship group. Consider, for example, the widow at Nain, whose son's death meant the loss not only of a precious child but also of her only ally and breadwinner.[31] Because of certain purity regulations, sickness could also isolate a person from his or her immediate kinship group and from the larger village or even national kinship grouping. The leper (e.g., Mk 1:40-45) and the woman who suffered from bleeding (Mk 5:25-34) were untouchable by the purity codes in effect. People with permanent impairments such as blindness, lameness, or paralysis were barred from temple worship (e.g., Mt 8:4).

Jesus taught and demonstrated that God's kingdom, breaking in through his ministry, brought with it bodily healing and wholeness, restoration of purity and fellowship—and in some of the Gospel stories even restoring the dead to life and to their kin. Two stories from the Gospels in particular bring this home. In answer to a leper's plea for help, "moved with pity, Jesus reached out his hand and touched him" (Mk 1:40-45). Why did Jesus touch the leper? He might have healed him with a word. Yet, Jesus was "moved with pity": he *loved* the leper and so he touched him. Touching a leper would normally make a person unclean, but with Jesus it is *wholeness*, not impurity, that is contagious.[32] Jesus possessed within himself a wealth of purity sufficient to purify even the most polluted persons and places. Within first-century Jewish culture, touching the suffering leper and offering compassion and restoration to him would also be explosively offensive to those guardians of the purity code within Jewish society. In touching this "untouchable," Jesus does more than could rightly be expected even of a family member. The story culminates with the former outcast restored to the worshiping community by way of examination by the priests and cultic ritual (Mk 1:44).

Another powerfully illustrative story of Jesus' offering kinship is the case of the man with paralysis (Mk 2:1-12). Jesus healed and restored the man's body and also forgave the man's sins. Healing of infirmity and forgiveness of sins belonged together in the first-century Jewish mind, for when the Synoptic Gospel writers speak of the forgiveness of sins, they mean far more than simply erasing the legal verdict of guilt. The word for "forgiveness" in the

---

[31]See further John J. Pilch, "Sickness and Healing in Luke-Acts," in Neyrey, *Social World of Luke-Acts*, 181-209, at 195.

[32]See further Craig L. Blomberg, *Contagious Holiness: Jesus' Meals with Sinners*, NSBT 19 (Downers Grove, IL: IVP Academic, 2005), 128. While Blomberg conceives of Jesus' own holiness as contagious, Kazen suggests that this is "not inherent holiness of his own person, but the power of the coming reign of God, which Jesus believed overpowered demons and impurities" (Kazen, *Jesus and Purity Halakhah*, 346).

Gospels usually carries a lot more range. It points to the idea of release: release from exile, from infirmity, from rebellion, from the influence of demons, from exclusion and isolation, from impurity, and from every other bond of sin's curse.[33] When this man with paralysis was brought to Jesus, the release from sin, impurity, isolation, and brokenness that comes with the kingdom of God overtook him.

In his concern for people whose illness had robbed them of life in community, Jesus took responsibility for them and took on the mantle of being their kin. Restored kinship is often revealed in the aftermath of the healing. The healed demoniac freed of "Legion" desires to stay with Jesus and become one of Jesus' itinerant kinship group. In this case, Jesus sends him back to his own clan, the natural kinship group from whom, because of his condition, he had been estranged (Mk 5:18-19).

Another revealing aspect of the Gospel stories of Jesus' healings is the boldness shown—by the sick, estranged, shunned, and abhorred—as they dared to approach Jesus. Their boldness makes sense only if Jesus had established a reputation in touching the untouchable and for loving those believed to be under the influence of evil spirits. Jesus demonstrated again and again his willingness to act as kin to those at the margins of society. The kingdom looks like home, hearth, kinship, touch, fellowship, embrace, solidarity, intimacy, brotherhood, entanglement. And, most importantly, all of this with those who appear to be impure: in fact, to those who stink, literally or metaphorically, to the people of that culture.

DOES AN ETHIC OF WELCOME AND OF HEALING EXTEND ONLY TO THOSE WHO FOLLOW CHRIST?

What can we learn of this kinship ethic described in the Synoptic Gospels as central to the ministry of Jesus? Are the welcome and the healing power of God offered only to those who follow Christ? The Gospels make it quite clear that not all those whom Jesus healed accepted him as a prophet of God. Some saw Jesus as a healer merely with access to divine power. We see this for instance in Luke's story of the ten lepers: only one, the lone foreigner among them, returned to give praise to God (Lk 17:11-19). Nine of these healed lepers

---

[33]See the entry "ἀφίημι" in *A Greek-English Lexicon of the New Testament and Other Early Christian Literature*, revised and edited by Frederick W. Danker, 3rd ed. (Chicago: University of Chicago Press, 2000), 156. See further Pamela Shellberg, *Cleansed Lepers, Cleansed Hearts: Purity and Healing in Luke-Acts* (Minneapolis: Fortress, 2015), 111-13; and Robert C. Tannehill, *The Narrative Unity of Luke-Acts: A Literary Interpretation*, vol. 1, *The Gospel According to Luke* (Philadelphia: Fortress, 1986), 103-9.

apparently never returned to Jesus, and yet the healing power of the in-breaking kingdom was extended to them just the same. More surprising still is Jesus' encounter with the rich young man, unwilling to enter the kingdom of God on account of his wealth. This rich man was an outsider in relation to Jesus' group of friends and followers, and yet "Jesus looked at him and loved him" (Mk 10:21). We will observe shortly that *love* is explicitly a term of kinship.[34] Thus, even as this man refuses the invitation to follow in Jesus' way, Jesus acts as kin toward him, in a powerful display of the spirit that animates the kingdom of God.

This is important for how the church must act today. The welcome of God in Christ extended into all the highways and byways of the community of first-century Syria-Palestine. It reached out especially to the impure, and even to those who had no interest in following Jesus. Today, as Christ's church seeks to live as a sign of Jesus' love and authority, we must, like him, offer kinship and healing to all people in need, whether they follow Christ or not. While we'll discuss this further in later chapters, we want to offer here a personal illustration. My (Mark's) family is presently blessed to share time with two families from Iraq who are seeking refuge in Canada; one is Christian and the other is Muslim. Of course, sharing Christian faith with one of these families creates the space for us to share in prayer easily and to share in some other common understandings. Yet, we also find commonality with the Muslim family. Their readiness to laugh, *her* stunning culinary gifts, and the sparkle in *his* eye as he humorously picks up any and every deadly spider and scorpion available—these are a joy and a gift to us.

THE GOOD SAMARITAN, LUKE 10:25-37

Jesus asks a crowd that had come to listen to him which of three characters in a parable—a priest, a Levite, or a Samaritan—had "proved to be a neighbor to [a] man who fell among the robbers?" (Lk 10:36). An expert in the law answers that it was the Samaritan who proved to be a neighbor. The word translated "neighbor" in this passage is a word that carried the meaning of kinship at the level of the clan or village group.[35] To put it in first-century terms, Jesus is asking the lawyer, which person assumes the role of kindred for this man?

---

[34] As Pilch and Malina put it: "Love is the value of group attachment and group bonding." John J. Pilch and Bruce J. Malina, *Handbook of Biblical Social Values,* 3rd ed. (Eugene, OR: Cascade, 2016), 106.

[35] "Neighbor," πλησίον, is a word from the field of kinship, a metaphor referring to the clan/village grouping, which also contains an aspect of ambivalence (Lk 10:29; Acts 7:27). See further Johannes P. Louw and Eugene A. Nida, "πλησίον," *Greek-English Lexicon of the New Testament: Based on Semantic Domains* (New York: United Bible Societies, 1996), 11.89.

A *Samaritan* acted as a neighbor?! This would be jaw dropping simply because of the way that Palestinian Jews looked upon the Samaritans. This scribe Jesus spoke with couldn't bear to even say the word *Samaritan*, referring to him instead as "the one who showed him mercy" (Lk 10:37). Samaritans' ethnicity alone destined them for hellfire. Jesus' hearers would have thought of this Samaritan as most probably a trader, one who frequented taverns and lived a life of disrepute.[36] Such a despised figure is an ironic foil to the other figures in the story: the priest and the Levite who had crossed the road to avoid the suffering man. It is probable that these two men would not only have seen themselves as holy but would have been considered holy by Jesus' hearers. Yet both priest and Levite failed to follow the teaching of the Torah (Old Testament law) to show mercy to a person in need. The priest and the Levite who passed by the injured man on the other side of the road may simply have intended to preserve their own purity, for touching a near-dead man could render a person ritually unclean.[37] In criticizing the priest and the Levite, Jesus was saying that God prioritizes compassion over purity rules every time.[38] In this way, the reference of the parable is multilayered: on the one hand, Israel's distorted piety is shown up by a Samaritan; on the other hand, Jesus implies that Israelites should welcome outsiders such as this Samaritan by virtue of the ethic that this Samaritan is exemplifying! Jesus is destabilizing his hearers, in their self-assumed piety. By repositioning a Samaritan merchant as the merciful host, Jesus is relocating the mercy of God in God himself (rather than in Israel), inviting his hearers to get on board with what God is busy doing. In other words, Jesus' hearers will never be the saviors of people lying by the roadside; rather, Jesus' hearers will be saved by the act of serving such people—by walking in the Way of Christ.

This story amplifies Jesus' answer to this lawyer's question concerning how to inherit eternal life: "You shall love the Lord your God . . . and your neighbor as yourself" (Lk 10:27; cf. Mk 12:30; Mt 22:37-39). The love language found

---

[36]Malina and Rohrbaugh, *Social-Science Commentary on the Synoptic Gospels*, 347.

[37]See Richard Bauckham, "The Scrupulous Priest and the Good Samaritan: Jesus' Parabolic Interpretation of the Law of Moses," *NTS* 44, no. 4 (1998): 475-89. See Snodgrass's reservations about this interpretation in Klyne R. Snodgrass, *Stories with Intent: A Comprehensive Guide to the Parables of Jesus* (Grand Rapids, MI: Eerdmans, 2008), 355. Kazen also argues that concern for purity was the reason for the priest and Levite avoiding the man (Kazen, *Issues of Impurity in Early Judaism*, 140-48). Kazen shows that there were likely a variety of opinions and behaviors in regards to responsibility toward a corpse: this was, "a discursive context in which the story of the 'good Samaritan' would fit very well" (Kazen, *Jesus and Purity Halakhah*, 195).

[38]To put it another way, Jesus subordinates the purity law of the Pentateuch (e.g., Lev 11–15) to the social law that concerns the vulnerable (e.g., Deut 24).

in the Gospels here also derives from kinship language. The parable illustrates the Pentateuch's teaching on those to whom kinship love is due under the covenant that we examined in the preceding chapters. Love is due to God (Deut 6:5), to one's neighbor (that is, one's kinsperson; see Lev 19:18), and also to the stranger (the outsider who is to be enfolded as kin, including the impure person; see Lev 19:34; Deut 10:18). These three loves are interdependent, the expression of an organic covenant life that is emphatically oriented toward others and in particular toward the weakest among us. So, at its heart, the parable of the good Samaritan obliterates the boundary markers between those who should and those who should not receive our love, compassion, and service. Jesus' response to the self-righteous lawyer undermines the question itself: "Who is my neighbor?" Neighbors are defined not by self-serving social maps but in our response to their need. Kinship, in other words, is created by willing acts of loving kindness and service. Klyne Snodgrass, a biblical scholar who has written one of the most useful books on the parables, puts it this way: "Boundaries are an important means by which we establish our identities, but an identity growing out of Jesus' sense of being a neighbor obliterates boundaries that close off compassion or that permit racism and attitudes of superiority."[39]

When we think of Jesus' teaching here in relation to the topic of refugee welcome, we should not miss the detail that the Samaritan provided for the injured man out of his own means. What might it look like for churches and nations to provide for asylum seekers out of their own means? Perhaps Pope Francis's call for every Catholic parish in Europe to house at least one family of refugees represents a good start—and we note that he modeled this call by housing a refugee family in the Vatican.[40] Perhaps Chancellor Angela Merkel's decision in 2015 to open Germany's border to more than one million asylum seekers fleeing the Syrian civil war and other crises might be fruitfully replicated elsewhere: "Germany is a strong country—we will manage," Merkel famously declared.[41] We will wrestle with Merkel's controversial decision in chapters eight and ten. And in chapter seven, we will wrestle further with the parable of the good Samaritan, pondering particularly the claim made by some that the parable demands only that we care for those that we encounter, not that we should care for vulnerable people displaced on the other side of the world.

---

[39]Snodgrass, *Stories with Intent*, 358.

[40]Anthony Faiola and Michael Birnbaum, "Pope Calls on Europe's Catholics to Take In Refugees," *Washington Post*, September 6, 2015.

[41]BBC News, "Migrant Crisis: Merkel Warns EU of 'Failure,'" *BBC*, August 31, 2015.

Sheep and goats, Matthew 25:31-46. In the parable of the sheep and the goats, at the finale of the Matthean teaching passages, there is a stark final separation of sheep and goats that is determined by how each group assisted the needy (as it is in the parable of the rich man and Lazarus, Lk 16:19-31). The parable also conveys Jesus' moving identification of himself with those in great need: "For I was hungry and you gave me food, I was thirsty and you gave me something to drink, I was a stranger and you welcomed me, I was naked and you gave me clothing, I was sick and you took care of me, I was in prison and you visited me. . . . Truly I tell you, just as you did it to one of the least of these who are members of my family, you did it to me" (Mt 25:35-36, 40). "Welcome the stranger" is the most common tagline used by Christian refugee advocates to express the biblical call to welcome (cf. Mt 25:35).

A common view is that Jesus' phrase, "the least of these my brothers-sisters," limits the scope of the text to the needy among Jesus' own disciples. Others suggest that the phrase refers to Christian missionaries. However, there are good reasons to query these interpretations. Klyne Snodgrass demonstrates that a number of times in Matthew when Jesus says "brother-sister," it carries the broader sense of "neighbor." For example, Matthew 5:22, "everyone who is angry at his brother or sister."[42] Few would disagree that Jesus implies neighbor in such passages. Matthew's Gospel portrays Jesus' group as a place of love and compassion whose care extends beyond the boundaries of the community itself. As for the suggestion that the intention of the passage is limited to that of hosting Christian missionaries, this would seem to be a strangely narrow focus for Jesus to have on the day before he was betrayed.

Here Jesus again identifies with the needy, describing the actions toward "the least of these my brothers-sisters." *These* are his kin. In the communal culture of Jesus' day, he identifies so closely with the poor and the stranger that what is done for *them* is what is done for *him*—this is how kinship worked in that culture. As noted New Testament scholar Richard Hays states: "Caring for the poor (or, alternatively, Jesus' poor followers) is somehow equivalent to encountering the presence of God."[43] Jesus is teaching that all of those who have Jesus' Father as their Father must care for Jesus' needy kinsfolk. Of course, all these actions—clothing, feeding, visiting in prison— are acts that befit kinsfolk.

---

[42]Snodgrass, *Stories with Intent*, 556.
[43]Richard B. Hays, *Reading Backwards: Figural Christology and the Fourfold Gospel Witness* (Waco, TX: Baylor University Press, 2014), 47.

Welcoming Christ at Kinbrace

Anika Barlow recalls: Last month, on a Friday evening "after-hours," a mother and daughter came through our doors. We learned that there was no linguistic common denominator between us, and so we called up an interpretation service in Toronto. Soon, we had a Lingala speaker on the line and we began our three-way conversation. After explaining to these women where exactly they had just arrived and how the Kinbrace community operates, we asked if they had any questions. The mother was eager to speak, her words impassioned. Then came the pregnant pause of the interpreter. "Thank you. Thank you. Thank you. We praise God for you. In the Bible God tells us to welcome the stranger. Thank you so much for welcoming us." Not what I was expecting to hear. And as I led them to their new apartment (a far cry from the prison cell where they had been kept in detention) I wished I had kept the interpreter on the line for a few more minutes, because I want to say: "Yes, God does tell us that, but God also tells us that when we open the door to a stranger, it is God we are welcoming. So thank *you* for knocking, and for stepping through our doors tonight."

There are many other parables and teachings in the Synoptic Gospels that call God's people to act as kin for people in need. We don't have the space here to discuss, for example, the parable of the rich man and Lazarus (Lk 16:19-31). All of this teaching, however, demonstrates that the Way of Christ, both then and today, is cruciform. Jesus said, "I am among you as one who serves" (Lk 22:27). As Hays states: "Because Jesus uses power to serve rather than to be served, authentic power is shown forth paradoxically in the cross. Those who exercise power to dominate others, to kill and oppress, are shown not only as villains but also, surprisingly, as pawns of forces beyond their control" (e.g., Herod, Mk 6:14-29; Pilate, Mk 15:1-15; cf. Mk 10:45).[44] It is chilling to recall that Jesus was crucified by the Roman government, but in partnership with the orthodox. Will we use our power to destroy or to serve? The cross of Christ is an invitation to us to serve people who are seeking a home, even at a cost to ourselves, even at a great cost. How can the church (and our society for that matter) soften our self-protective reflexes so that we are free to serve displaced people? As we come to the cross for forgiveness,

---

[44]Richard B. Hays, *The Moral Vision of the New Testament: Community, Cross, New Creation: A Contemporary Introduction to New Testament Ethics* (San Francisco: HarperCollins, 1996), 90.

can we allow the crucifixion to pierce the barriers that we have put up around our routines? Can we, who Christ serves, be set free to serve others?

JESUS' KINSHIP WITH THE LEAST IN OUR TIME

We will further discuss issues of interpretation and application surrounding Jesus' ethic of kinship in the Gospels in subsequent chapters, but let us consider here some of the implications of the Gospels.

"You will always have the poor among you," Matthew 26:6-13, Mark 14:3-9. Some have interpreted this observation of Jesus as diminishing the impact of the social ethic of the Gospels. Some have used these words to justify subordinating social ethics to acts of worship.[45] US Congressman Roger Marshall (Kansas) recently used this text in his effort to argue that many poor and homeless people don't want to receive healthcare.[46] The context of this saying is Jesus defending the woman who anointed him at Bethany. The disciples had criticized the woman, suggesting that the ointment she used could have been sold and the money given to the poor. The disciples' criticism of the woman actually displays a strong positive ethic for sharing material goods with the poor, observed by Jesus' followers. This is the disciples' assumption here. Jesus is quoting from Deuteronomy 15:11 (ESV), where the same observation is offered as the motivation for open-handed generosity: "For there will never cease to be poor in the land. Therefore, I command you, 'You shall open wide your hand to your brother, to the needy and to the poor, in your land.'" Thus, rather than a resignation to the reality of poverty, Jesus' words anticipate that his disciples will *always be acting as kin* to the poor. This is to be a defining feature of Jesus' followers. In terms of the woman's actions, Jesus is saying that she rightly honors Jesus at the very moment when the rulers plot to strip him of *all* honor.

Who is responsible to embody Jesus' ethic? The immediate context of Jesus' teaching and example was to gather and equip his followers. The Gospels demonstrate that Jesus was gathering a renewed people—first from within Israel but later in the New Testament with others grafted in—that was to be a light to the nations (Is 49:6; Mt 5:14-16). Jesus intended his community to be the faithful witness that Israel was always called to be. As a foretaste of the kingdom of God, Jesus' community also reflected God's *telos,* God's ultimate purpose—for all of humanity—of reconciliation and flourishing.

---

[45]For a discussion of this scholarship see Wolfgang Schrage, *The Ethics of the New Testament*, trans. David E. Green (Edinburgh: T&T Clark, 1988), 71-73.

[46]Abigail Abrams, "GOP Congressman Says the Poor 'Just Don't Want Health Care,'" *Time*, March 9, 2017.

For these reasons, Christ's church today must be deeply shaped by the *Way of Christ*. The Way of Christ is, in a sense, an embodiment of what Israel was always supposed to be, an embodiment of God's telos for humanity in relationship. In Jesus' ministry, which was a proclamation and enactment of the in-breaking reign of God, outsiders experienced healing, honor, and inclusion. Like Jesus' disciples who followed directly in his footsteps some two thousand years ago, Christ followers today are invited to be Jesus' students, to study Jesus and his Way. For he is the truth, the healer, the "mender of all things."[47] And as we are conformed to his likeness, we too begin to embody in our life together the healing reign of God.

Further, God's desire for "mending" extends beyond the people of God, even to encompass society and politics. For, as Jesus', ministry was a proclamation and enactment of the in-breaking reign of God, his ministry reflected God's desire and end-goal for humanity in relationship with one another. So, God desires that Christ's tenderness characterizes every sphere of society—including domestic politics, global politics, economics, etc.—even in those places where Christ is not acknowledged as Lord. How can the church first seek to embody Christ's Way itself, and then from that compelling and attractive posture seek changes in the surrounding society, toward tenderness?

One way that Mark's church has tried to follow in Jesus' Way is by birthing and supporting Kinbrace, which provides housing, community, and advocacy for refugee claimants. The newcomers with whom we share life experience enormous stress. One of the biggest stressors for refugee claimants relates to loss of identity. They have left a home where they had an identity and in doing so have also lost vocational credentials, the familial role that kept them busy on a daily basis, gender-based roles, and more. Having stable housing and community greatly reduces the stress that newcomers experience. Among other things, Kinbrace offers a modicum of stability in this way for people as they walk through the process of making a refugee claim and preparing for their hearing.

> It is characteristic of Jesus that he constantly established community—precisely for those who were denied community at that time, or who were judged inferior in respect to religion.[48]

We've looked at the Synoptic Gospels here through the lens of kinship. The world of first-century Judaism abounded with rigid social and religious boundaries, and everyone knew where they stood: in or out, near or far.

---

[47]The phrase "mender of all things" is taken from a song by that name by Tom Wuest (not released).
[48]Lohfink, *Jesus and Community*, 88.

Those who were blind, lame, diseased, or paralyzed were often thought to be impure, with one foot in the devil's camp. It was considered right that they should be despised and excluded. The purity map held the Jerusalem elite at its center: they were the icons of purity and wholeness. But Jesus turned that map inside out. Those whom first-century Judaism shunned, Jesus embraced as his own, his kin. And Jesus taught that those who would follow in his Way should be as humble servants, taking kinship responsibility for the needy and undefended.

How may we describe the boundary lines of the Jesus group? They could refer to strangers and even to enemies as brothers-sisters (e.g., Mt 5:47). They were called to extend kinship love not only to one another (the in group) but also to those who were culturally deemed unlovable (Mt 25:40) and to those who could not be expected to reciprocate a favor (Mt 18:21). Thus the Jesus group was most clearly defined by its center rather than by its outer boundaries. On the one hand, Jesus' followers were identified as those who threw their allegiance behind Jesus in obedience and love—and the demands upon them could seem fearsome (see for example the radical discipleship commands of Mt 5:22, 28; 18:5-6, 21-22; Mk 10:21). On the other hand, the outer edges of the group were blurred in at least two ways. First, kinship love could be shown to those outside the group, and even to its enemies. Second, and most important, the marginalized—those who were without the means of subsistence or honor—seem to have had a place at the table of Jesus and of his followers. Of course, such lack of discrimination in the matter of who should be accepted by Jesus as his followers would have been considered utterly disgraceful by the elite elements of this society, obsessed as they were with outward displays of honor. That such a mixed-caste group as these Jesus followers should refer to one another as "brother-sister" must have seemed very beautiful to those who had come from the outside to follow him. But to his enemies, in the terms understood by their culture, it was utterly foolish and profoundly shameful.

By locating himself in culturally unlikely places, Jesus entirely shifts and even reverses the insider-outsider dynamic. Jesus shares honor with those who are deemed undesirable by others, and he shames those who grasp after honor. In this way, Jesus shifts the center, to the margins of culture. This is where God is to be found, and where true and permanent honor is granted.

For Jesus, entry into the kingdom of God is a matter of simply accepting and reflecting Jesus' welcome, knowing that, in Jesus, the Father is bringing his healing rule to earth. Yet, this impetus toward inclusion and healing (visible in meals, parables, exorcisms, teaching, and healing) extends even to those who have not themselves accepted Jesus. Jesus demonstrates that our responsibility toward others extends beyond "our own," to include those who are not like us or of us. We do have a responsibility to displaced people who are not of us—not of our nationality, even not of our faith. For neither ethnicity nor faith was a barrier to Jesus' own welcome.

PART TWO

THE CHURCH

4

CREATIVE KINSHIP
IN THE CHURCH

Raúl Gatica formerly worked as the Community Mobilizer at Kinbrace, and he now leads Dignidad Migrante, an organization that seeks justice for temporary foreign workers in Canada. Raúl was for many years persecuted for advocating for the poor in Mexico. He has been imprisoned thirteen times, and at one point tortured to the edge of death. He tells the story of a priest who risked his life for him many times.

One day in 1994, the army arrested Raúl. The priest rang the church bell at eleven in the morning and announced on the loud speaker that Raúl had been arrested by the army. Over two thousand people gathered at the church and marched to the army barracks together in order to protect Raúl. On another occasion when Raúl was incarcerated, this same priest robed himself "in full costume," to use Raúl's words—collar, cloak, and so on—and arrived at the police station. "I want to see Raúl," the priest demanded. The sergeant asked, "Why?" "Because I want to get his confession," the priest responded. The priest was ushered to Raúl's cell and asked the police to leave them alone. He had made a hollow in the pages of his Bible to conceal a padlock, which he gave to Raúl so that Raúl could lock his own cell, preventing the police from secretly taking Raúl away to murder him.

Raúl himself is not a Christ follower, yet he is deeply thankful for this priest's bravery and kindness. Leaving Mexico, Raúl became a refugee. The priest's inspiring example of protecting Raúl in Mexico raises the question of the church's role in receiving and protecting refugees like Raúl when they become displaced and are seeking a home.

The purpose of this chapter is to examine, biblically, what the church's response to global displacement might be. You will quickly see that this is not merely a question of something that the church *does* but a question of the *very identity* of the people of God. We are seeking to forge a *missional theology* for responding to displacement. This chapter is the fulcrum of our book, for the theme of mission provides a transition point from considering a theology of kinship to the implications for nations and the global community. Here we will offer practices for nourishing worshiping communities toward creative kinship. And we will offer a biblical foundation for church-based advocacy for refugees. We finish the chapter with more stories of people and churches that have lived and acted in solidarity with refugees in the hope that these examples will inspire fresh imaginings for your own worshiping community. But to begin, let's address two fundamental questions: What is the gospel? And what is mission?

THE GOSPEL AND MISSION

The comprehensive scope of the gospel. The gospel or "good news" that Jesus preached was the message that God was, at last in his own person, acting in power and love to restore all of human life and all of creation to again live in loving relationship with one another under God's benevolent rule as it was intended in the beginning. The gospel is comprehensive in its scope: Christ's healing embrace enfolds all of creation. The introduction to Mark's Gospel states: "The beginning of the gospel of Jesus Christ, the Son of God" (Mk 1:1 ESV). As Mark's Gospel unfolds, it is as if we see God striding around creation bringing healing to brokenness. Think about the joy that must have filled the streets of Galilee where Jesus walked. Think of the healing that Jesus left in his trail: A blind boy sees again, gazing at the trees, at the sky, at the faces of his family! A former leper embraces his family for the first time since the day of his diagnosis! Even the nonhuman creation responds to Jesus' gracious rule: the storm that Jesus calms is an image of the "creation in thrall to evil."[1] All of this demonstrates the good news that Jesus preached—that in him the Father is busy recovering God's purposes for the creation.

---

[1]Gunton uses this phrase in regard to Jesus' miracles. Colin E. Gunton, *Christ and Creation: The Didsbury Lectures, 1990* (Eugene, OR: Wipf & Stock, 1992), 18.

If one is tempted to *narrow* this glorious gospel, a gospel that is cosmic in its scope, to only the forgiveness of sins, we must remember what we learned in the previous chapter: that the word *forgiveness* in Luke's Gospel means "release"—release from demons, from oppression, from guilt, from infirmity, and so on. To be sure, the gospel includes God's judicial forgiveness of the transgressions of the covenant people, and yet it also includes release from sin's curse of the whole person—the whole people of God. We must also understand the gospel as the climax of salvation history as revealed in the Old Testament. According to the apostle Paul, the gospel is the fulfillment of God's purposes for the world that God has been working through the story of ancient Israel. This story reaches its climax in the life, death, and resurrection of Israel's Messiah (see Rom 1:1-4; 1 Cor 15:1-5; 2 Tim 2:8). Our understanding of the gospel, therefore, cannot be separated from the story of the Bible as we have witnessed in chapters two and three of this book. Think of all the beauty, the freshness, the community, the kinship, that we have seen in the Old Testament—all of this is fulfilled in the gospel. As we have seen in our investigation of kinship in the biblical story, a part of this good news is that God is, in Christ, restoring human sociality to relationships of love and protection as befits kindred.

Mission is central to the arc and purpose of the biblical story. Mission is the encounter with the world of a community gathered by Christ to be caught up in God's reconciling purpose for all of his creation, a community living by the Spirit as a sign, instrument, and foretaste of Christ's restorative reign.[2] Following the resurrection, the Spirit of Christ was sent upon the Christ followers to empower them to play a particular role in this present period in world history (Acts 1:6-11). Christ's church, both then and today, is located in the era between the ascension of Jesus and his return to renew all things. This is a time of witness, when God's people exist as a sign to the Lordship of Christ. Mission is not an add-on, something that the church *does* among many various activities. No, mission is a part of the very identity of the church: we are a *sent* people. When Christ said, "As the Father sent me, I am sending you" (Jn 20:21), he showed us that to be the people of God is to be *sent*, to live as a sign to the healing rule of Christ. Yet, we should quickly add that God's

---

[2]"Sign," "instrument," and "foretaste" are Newbigin's characteristic images of the church, first articulated in Lesslie Newbigin, *The Household of God: Lectures on the Nature of the Church* (London: SCM Press, 1953), 166. See also Mark R. Glanville, "A Missional Reading of Deuteronomy: Communities of Gratitude, Celebration, and Justice," in *Reading the Bible Missionally*, ed. Michael Goheen (Grand Rapids, MI: Eerdmans, 2016), 124-50, at 125.

mission to restore the creation was also core to the calling of Israel, in the Old Testament. Israel was to be a kingdom of priests, a holy nation (Ex 19:6). Through God's ancient people, God was displaying to all of creation the divine vision for the world, that of a beloved community (Ex 20:3-17; Deut 10:17-19). Somehow Israel, through the freshness of the Torah and the abiding presence of Yahweh, was to be a garden in a desert wasteland, a garden whose vines and blossoms would one day multiply to fill the earth, and so return all of creation to its original beauty, fragrance, and fruitfulness (Gen 12:1-3; Heb 2:14).

Mission is first of all *God's* mission, for this is our Father's world. Broken and corrupted it may be, yet it belongs to God. In Christ, God is busy recovering the divine purposes for the creation: "From him, through him, and to him are *all* things" (Rom 11:36). Because God's healing work is comprehensive in its breadth, God's people witness by our lives, our words, and our deeds (Acts 2:43-47; 4:32-37; 11:19-30; 13:1-3). What does it mean to witness in life, word, and deed? In our shared *life* as Christ's people, a local church embodies the kinship and the hope of the kingdom of God. In our *words* we call attention to the gracious, healing rule of Christ. In our *deeds* we bring the healing of Christ to our neighborhoods and our world, while also receiving healing from others. The story of Israel and the ministry of Jesus show us that a faithful witness involves every part of our lives as we seek to embody the restoring rule of God, in Christ. The church is called to *be* the witness, *say* the witness, and *do* the witness.[3]

Ethics and God's mission. In order to discern the nature and shape of mission, we need first to discern what God is busy doing throughout Scripture and then discern how this revelation of God in Scripture intersects with our own lives and cultures. In chapter two, we used the analogy of jazz music for interpreting Scripture ethically for today. Each time the authors come to play jazz, we draw deeply from the tradition of jazz and the blues. And yet each time we play we also create something new. In interpreting Scripture ethically, our task is to discern the "tradition," the core ethical (restoring, healing, joining) trajectories within God's word. We then discern how this tradition can inspire fresh "performances" within our present context of global displacement. What fresh creativity is required of us today?

As for the tradition, we have seen that God forms allegiances in response to human vulnerability and displacement. For example, in Deuteronomy

---

[3]Darrell L. Guder, *Be My Witnesses: The Church's Mission, Message, and Messengers* (Grand Rapids, MI: Eerdmans, 1985), 91.

God makes a covenant with the stranger. This is a steadfast commitment of kinship, solidarity, protection, and love (e.g., Deut 10:17-19). On the basis of God's covenant with the stranger, God called ancient Israel to make a covenant with the stranger (Deut 10:19). How can the mission of the church be inspired and energized by this vision? What fresh and beautiful harmonies and rhythms can the Spirit birth in us? As a community emancipated and enfolded by God, the church always remains a receiving community that engages, especially, the most broken parts of our neighborhood and our world. How can we live into our identity with creativity?

HUMAN MOVEMENT AND GOD'S MISSION

One argument often made in favor of welcoming refugees is that through human migration God is bringing unreached people right onto our doorstep, in the West. While we are used to beseeching God to send missionaries out from the West, God is now sending migrants here—a ready harvest for the gospel. How foolish it is, then, for Christians to sour this opportunity for the gospel by putting up barriers against newcomers!

There is an important truth to this argument, and yet there is also a deeper historical reality. In our lifetime, the axis of global Christianity has shifted completely. Today, around half to two-thirds of Christians live in the Global South and East.[4] In fact, Western nations only contribute 15 percent of the global church today.[5] Missiologist Lamin Sanneh estimated that the Western church dwindles by 4,300 people per day.[6] Churches from the Global South and East contribute the majority of crosscultural missionaries. These churches also tend to be more theologically orthodox than Western churches, which have been corroded by consumerism and secularism.[7]

For this reason, we need to shift how we see diasporic communities: these are often God's own people on the move! And these diasporic communities are being used by God to revitalize the church in North America, Australia, and Europe. Throughout history, God has been renewing and revitalizing the church from the margins. The Holy Spirit is especially active there. In Europe,

---

[4]Philip Jenkins, *The Next Christendom: The Coming of Global Christianity*, 3rd ed. (Oxford: Oxford University Press, 2011), 2-3.
[5]Michael W. Goheen, *Introducing Christian Mission Today: Scripture, History and Issues* (Downers Grove, IL: InterVarsity Press, 2014), 17.
[6]Lamin Sanneh, *Whose Religion Is Christianity?: The Gospel Beyond the West* (Grand Rapids, MI: Eerdmans, 2003), 15.
[7]See Soong-Chan Rah, *The Next Evangelicalism: Freeing the Church from Western Cultural Captivity* (Downers Grove, IL: InterVarsity Press, 2009), 164-70.

for example, Christian refugee communities from the Middle East are being used by God to bring life to formerly stagnant churches. Churches that serve these newcomers are experiencing renewal while churches that ignore the opportunity often remain moribund.[8] As Sam George and Miriam Adeney state, "Christian mission is a boundary-breaking phenomenon, diffusing across cultures and geographies relentlessly."[9] For this reason, forced displacement has always played a key role in shaping and renewing the church. A foremost historian of mission, Andrew Walls, concludes: "Migration is a more significant factor in Christian history than the Reformation itself."[10]

The church's commonality with migrants. When we as the church are living into our identity as a *sent people*, we will have a natural affinity with people who are on the move. God's people have always been on the move throughout salvation history.[11] This experience has been one of weakness, not strength. In Scripture, God's people on the move have been incarcerated, famished, and sexually exploited. They have fled to survive (Gen 12:10), lied to survive (Gen 12:12-13), shown extraordinary ingenuity (Gen 40), worked tirelessly (Ruth 2), learned languages (Dan 1:4), embraced new identities (Dan 1:5), and cherished old identities (Dan 1:8). We share an identity with people on the move: we too are "aliens and exiles" (1 Pet 2:11). Whether at home or abroad, Christ calls his people to embrace vulnerability and weakness for the sake of the gospel. As the Apostle Paul states:

> To the Jews I became as a Jew, in order to win Jews. To those under the law I became as one under the law (though I myself am not under the law) so that I might win those under the law. . . . To the weak I became weak, so that I might win the weak. I have become all things to all people, that I might by all means save some. (1 Cor 9:20, 22)

Paul's weakness is not a condescension to others, a temporary act of charity in solidarity, for Paul really becomes weak. He empties himself.[12] He ventures forth not in strength but in weakness, in order that he might display the power of the gospel.[13] Christ followers on mission, whether at home or in a

---

[8]Sam George, "Introduction," in *Refugee Diaspora: Missions amid the Greatest Humanitarian Crisis of Our Times,* ed. Sam George and Miriam Adeney (Pasadena, CA: William Carey, 2018), xvii.

[9]George, "Introduction," xxi.

[10]Andrew Walls, "The Great Commission 1910–2010," a lecture delivered at the University of Edinburgh in 2003, cited in George, "Introduction," xxii.

[11]For example Genesis 12, 39, 40, 45; Exodus 16–18; Deuteronomy 26:5; Ruth 1–2.

[12]Brian Brock and Bernd Wannenwetsch, *The Malady of the Christian Body: A Theological Exposition of Paul's First Letter to the Corinthians,* vol. 1 (Eugene, OR: Cascade, 2016), 221.

[13]Robert W. Heimburger, *God and the Illegal Alien: United States Immigration Law and a Theology of Politics* (Cambridge: Cambridge University Press, 2018), 57.

crosscultural context, embrace vulnerability and discomfort as they seek to love their community, adopting its culture and language while also bearing the offense of the gospel within that community. In such humble obedience, the church experiences affinity with people on the move who may also experience persecution, hunger, loneliness, and tension with the dominant culture. In its relationship with migrant communities, the church is reminded of its missionary character.[14]

Of course, as the church lives into its mission, many of us are called to stay in a particular neighborhood and to witness to Christ's love in that particular place. However, the church's identity as a people who are sent in weakness teaches us that our role in *any* place is that of a servant and a healer. We must reject attitudes of privilege, prejudice, and selfishness, and we must reject postures of power, exclusivity, and pride. In its weakness, the church's primary location will not be places of power but places of the margins, from where the church calls society to compassion and solidarity. Most important of all, we must have the tender heart of Christ.

For these reasons, migrants also remind us of the dangers of having a settled identity as a church. Like migrants, the church is an unsettled people, in our very identity. When Christians are tempted to see people on the move as the other, whom we should keep out, this is likely because we have become settled, become forgetful of own identity as aliens called to serve others in weakness.

Evangelism. The question of evangelism, of speaking of Jesus to refugees, requires thoughtfulness. By now, readers of this book will realize that a biblical response to global displacement is not to persuade the rest of the world to worship as we do but to give ourselves for the welfare of the world. To be sure, Christ as Lord of all tenderly beckons every person to enter into his healing love (Jn 6:51), and we are Christ's ambassadors (2 Cor 5:20). Yet, what does it mean to have Christ's humility when we share our lives with a newcomer who is experiencing extreme vulnerability? How can we avoid signaling an expectation that newcomers will conform to our religion? How can we engage with an appropriate humility, given that our own Western nations so often have been responsible for historical or contemporary injustices that contribute to the displacement of these refugees, injustices that have been and continue to be so often sanctified by our religious leaders? (We explore these injustices and their implications further in later chapters.) Most important, how can we learn, deep in our hearts, that we ourselves need to be

---

[14]Heimburger, *God and the Illegal Alien*, 59.

transformed in relationship with newcomers, that in this person I am meeting Christ (Mt 25:31-46)? This encounter may be more about my own conversion than theirs. Sharing life with refugees is about being fully human in a space of vulnerability.

So *can* we share our faith in Jesus with refugees? Certainly. A helpful lens might be the concept of coherence. Many therapists use the term *coherence* to express an alignment between what therapists experience internally and their external communication, via speech and bodily expression. Good therapists strive to have coherence between their heart (internal) and their affect (external). Perhaps the same can be said for our speech as Christ followers. When we walk intimately with God, inviting Jesus into our daily struggles and joys, then Jesus also enters into our speech, in a way that is unforced and natural—a gentle and authentic coherence. Anika Barlow, Kinbrace's Lead Host, reflects: "I hope the hospitality we offer as a refugee claimant housing provider is not just the stuff of clean sheets and community dinners, but a safe space to encounter God: to strengthen a trusting dependence on the one who is ultimately 'Other.'"

FESTIVE KINSHIP: PRACTICES FOR NOURISHING WELCOMING COMMUNITIES

It is clear that we need to reimagine the shape of missional communities today, particularly in relation to people on the move. We have unfolded a biblical ethic of kinship, but what might this look like in practice for a local church? We want to offer the biblical image of festive kinship in order to reimagine the life of a missional community.

The festival calendar of Deuteronomy (Deut 16:1-17) offers a radical vision of thankfulness, generosity, and inclusion for vulnerable people. Yahweh's generosity in giving the land and the harvest in its season inspires the community to share in feasts of thanksgiving. Deuteronomy's festival calendar gives instructions for three feasts that are timed in response to the cycles of harvest. The Festival of Weeks follows the spring grain harvest in a time of celebration for God's provision:

> You shall count seven weeks. From the time the sickle is first put to the standing grain, begin to count seven weeks. Then you will keep the Feast of Weeks to Yahweh your God with a proportionate freewill offering from your hand, which you give according to the measure with which Yahweh your God blesses you. **And you shall feast before Yahweh your God, you, your son, your daughter, your slave, your female slave, the Levite within your settlements, the stranger,**

the fatherless, and the widows who are among you, at the place Yahweh your God chooses as a dwelling for his name. Remember that you were slaves in Egypt. Observe and keep these statutes. (Deut 16:9-12 author's translation)

A four-part movement characterizes Deuteronomy 16:1-17: (1) God's people lament their suffering in Egypt; (2) Yahweh gives the land and its produce; (3) the people respond in thanksgiving with celebration; and (4) this in turn produces generosity and inclusion for vulnerable people—the stranger, the fatherless, and the widow. These rituals and feasts had one main purpose: *to forge an inclusive and celebrative community in light of the generosity of God.* Let's trace this four-part movement that characterizes Deuteronomy's feasting texts: lament—gift—thanksgiving—inclusive justice.

1. Lament and repentance. Israel's festival calendar begins at the dawn of springtime, with rituals of lament and remembrance: the Passover and the Festival of Unleavened Bread (Deut 16:1-8). The Passover meal remembers suffering and death: the death of the firstborn of Egypt and the death of hundreds of Hebrew boys. The "bread of affliction" (Deut 16:3) recalls flight at night, a desperate (and divine) attempt to escape the horror of slavery and genocide.[15] The festival calendar begins with lament because, for God's people, lament is the beginning of something new. It is only as we face up to the world's groaning that we can begin to seek its healing. In lament, we are opening our doors to the pain of the world and to our own pain. Grief is the axis on which the world changes, and for this reason grief has to be both private and communal. We Christ followers must soften our hearts to recognize our own brokenness and also to recognize the loss and the darkness that surround those who are forced to leave their homes and countries. When we lament, Jesus is with us, for in his life on earth Jesus always preferred broken places and broken people.

As Christ followers, our lament is focused most deeply when we share in the Last Supper of Christ (which was also a Passover meal). Kinship and the cross come together profoundly in the Eucharist meal of the early church as this was the one meal that the poorest among God's people could be sure of.[16] However, before we share in the Eucharist meal, we repent. In our repentance, we are especially required to discern how we have treated the weakest among our fellow human persons (1 Cor 11:28). In our repentance, we take upon

---

[15]Mark R. Glanville, *Adopting the Stranger as Kindred in Deuteronomy*, AIL 33 (Atlanta: SBL Press, 2018), 168.

[16]Philip Francis Esler, *Community and Gospel in Luke-Acts: The Social and Political Motivations of Lucan Theology*, SNTSMS 57 (Cambridge: Cambridge University Press, 1987), 198.

ourselves the death of Christ, dying to our sin. Then, in the Eucharist meal we affirm our identity as those who are alive in Christ. My new identity reconfirmed to me in the bread and wine requires my everything: my heart, my soul, my prayer, my will, my reputation, my sociality, my meals, my thoughts, my desire, my joy, my lament, my skills, my love, my allegiance, my politics, my speech, my money, and my ongoing repentance. My forgiveness cost everything, and now my new life in Christ requires everything from me. Repentance is a vulnerability; it is a vulnerability different from that of forced displacement, and yet it is also the same—a displacement of a different kind. Our new life in Christ may put us in tension with our culture and our government. As we come to the cross of Christ we must remember that Jesus was crucified by the Roman government in partnership with the "orthodox." We who are in Christ, however, are invited to take up our cross and follow Christ.[17]

If lament is the beginning of something new, how do we teach our communities to lament? Liturgies of lament and confession are one indispensable means. These include liturgies that grieve specific areas of brokenness in our society, such as global displacement. Songs of lament and hope are hard to find, but they are crucial for a mature church. Songwriter Tom Wuest writes the most nourishing songs of congregational lament that we have encountered. His songs "O This Night Is Dark"[18] and "Something Like Scales"[19] nourish the church to grieve what Christ grieves in our society and in ourselves. Mark's church occasionally shares in rituals of lament. For example, in 2012 we held a special service of lament in response to the Canadian government passing legislation that mandated harsh treatment of refugee claimants.[20]

2. God who gives. In her book Radical Gratitude, Mary Jo Leddy, a Catholic nun and an advocate for refugees, tells the story of a period in her life when she found it difficult to be grateful. God jolted her out of her dissatisfaction through a refugee family staying with her in her home. A young girl in the family was peering out of Mary's kitchen window. When the girl saw the garage through the window, she asked, "Who lives there?" Mary's world suddenly turned upside down as she recognized that someone could live there:

---

[17]See further James H. Cone, The Cross and the Lynching Tree (Maryknoll, NY: Orbis, 2011), 36, 108, 124, 149-51. See also Emily Askew, "Notes Toward a Theology of Cross/ing," Int 72, no. 2 (2018): 188-97, at 194.

[18]Tom Wuest, "O This Night Is Dark," on Rain Down Heaven, Brass Trumpet Publishing, 2008, https://tomwuest.bandcamp.com/album/rain-down-heaven.

[19]Tom Wuest, "Something Like Scales," on Unless the Seed Falls, Brass Trumpet Publishing, 2006, https://tomwuest.bandcamp.com/album/unless-the-seed-falls.

[20]Bill C-31, Protecting Canada's Immigration System Act, S.C. 2012, c. 17, assented to June 28, 2012.

a number of people in fact. As Mary answered "the car," her world was opened up afresh to the abundance, even overabundance, that she had been given.[21]

The Bible is a story that begins with a gift: at the heart of reality is a God of limitless generosity. We see this in the Festival of Weeks text: "Then you shall keep the Feast of Weeks to Yahweh your God *with a proportionate freewill offering from your hand, which you give according to the measure with which Yahweh your God blesses you*" (Deut 16:10). Truly, as Gordon Spykman puts it, "God's creation is evidence of the caring hand of the Creator reaching out to secure the well-being of His creatures, of a Father extending a universe full of blessings to His children."[22]

How may we nourish worshiping communities whose shared life begins with a gift? The generous gifts of God must be a melody that is sung aloud in biblical preaching: God is good to us, and God seeks the welfare of all; God is committed to this good creation; in Christ, God is recovering the Father's good purposes for the creation.

3. Thanksgiving in celebration. Grateful feasting is the natural response to the divine blessing of land and its abundance. Twice in the festival calendar we read:

> And you shall feast before Yahweh your God, you, your son, your daughter, your slave and your female slave, the Levite within your settlements, the stranger, the fatherless, and the widows who are among you, at the place Yahweh your God chooses as a dwelling for his name. (Deut 16:11, 14 author's translation)

Yahweh commands, "Feast! Kill the lamb! Share the wine!"[23] As the extended household feasted together with joy, relationships were forged and kinship confirmed. God invited ancient Israel to a life of joy, gratefully to receive the divine gifts with inclusive feasting. The whole community, rich and poor, young and old, feasted together before the Lord with music and dancing, becoming kin. Gratefully and joyfully receiving the good gifts of Yahweh lies at the heart of a covenant response in Deuteronomy. Yet there was provision also for serious and deeply thoughtful thanksgiving: worshipers were to come before Yahweh "with a proportionate freewill offering

---

[21]Mary Jo Leddy, *Radical Gratitude* (Maryknoll, NY: Orbis, 2002). This paragraph has been previously published, with minor changes, in: Mark R. Glanville, "One City, One Message," *Light Magazine* 17 (2017). Used by permission.

[22]Gordon J. Spykman, *Reformational Theology: A New Paradigm for Doing Dogmatics* (Grand Rapids, MI: Eerdmans, 1992), 178.

[23]For the interpretation of *śmḥ* (Hebrew) as "feast," see Peter Altmann, *Festive Meals in Ancient Israel: Deuteronomy's Identity Politics in Their Ancient Near Eastern Context*, BZAW 424 (Berlin: De Gruyter, 2011), 205, 180-85.

from [their] hand" (Deut 16:10). Gratitude, both solemn and celebratory, lies at the heart of a covenant response throughout Scripture.[24]

Living gratefully today in the West is a particularly difficult task for we Westerners are immersed in a culture of consumerism. "To increase their capacity for consumption, consumers must never be left to rest. They need to be constantly exposed to new temptations to keep them in the state of perpetual suspicion and steady disaffection," Zygmunt Bauman observes.[25] Walter Brueggemann observes that the church is not exempt: "The contemporary American church is so largely enculturated to the American ethos of consumerism that it has little power to believe or act."[26] But it is possible for a community that is indwelt by the Spirit to resist consumerism and live gratefully. Some Christian communities find creative ways to challenge consumerism, sharing possessions, for example, in order to reduce consumption. As strange as it may sound, we suggest that *feasting* is the best antidote to consumerism. Traditionally, a whole community shares in a feast. In feasting, a community may share together in the deep joy of being gifted by God and being knit together as kin. Such warm experiences of family easily trump the shallow thrills of consumerism. We need to teach our communities how to feast with gratitude and our congregations to pray prayers of thanksgiving.

The festal call to thanksgiving with inclusive celebration highlights the importance of the distinctive *life* of a missional congregation: "Mission is not primarily about *going*," Howard Peskett and Vinoth Ramachandra note. "Nor is mission primarily about *doing* anything. Mission is about *being*. It is about being a distinctive kind of people, a countercultural . . . community among the nations."[27]

4. A shared life, in diversity. As a goal in and of itself, celebrative thanksgiving could turn toward self-indulgence. So it is important to embrace generous kinship inclusion of people who feel on the outside as the fourth of the four movements that characterize the festival calendar. We might say that justice and inclusion are corollaries of thanksgiving, the natural results of gratitude. Twice annually an Israelite household journeys to Jerusalem for

[24]For example, this theme of thanksgiving spills over into Pauline theology. Meye writes that gratitude is the "heartbeat of Pauline spirituality." R. P. Meye, "Spirituality," in *Dictionary of Paul and His Letters*, ed. Gerald F. Hawthorne, Ralph P. Martin, and Daniel G. Reid (Downers Grove, IL: InterVarsity Press, 1993), 906-16, at 915.
[25]Zygmunt Bauman, "The Self in a Consumer Society," *Hedgehog Review* 1 (1999): 35-40, at 38.
[26]Walter Brueggemann, *The Prophetic Imagination,* 2nd ed. (Minneapolis: Augsburg Fortress, 2001), 11.
[27]Howard Peskett and Vinoth Ramachandra, *The Message of Mission* (Downers Grove, IL: InterVarsity Press, 2003), 123.

feasting, and *everybody* participates, including the stranger, fatherless, and widow. We learn here that where Yahweh reigns God's restoring influence not only extends to individuals who suffer but also reaches deeply into social groups and heals through rearrangement. New Testament scholar Richard Bauckham argues that God's love reaches the strong by way of the weak:

> God's love has to reach the strong via the weak, because the strong can receive the love of God only by abandoning their pretensions to status above others.
> . . . As well as the outward movement of the church's mission in geographical extension and numerical increase, there must also be this (in the Bible's imagery) downward movement of solidarity with the people at the bottom of the social scale of importance and wealth.[28]

How may we nurture our communities to place the weakest among us at our very center? How can we walk as our Savior did and have a place of honor for the weakest at our dinner table? Deuteronomy's feasting passages provide us with a crucial clue: we must be reminding one another constantly that at the heart of reality is a God of limitless generosity. The first step toward solidarity with people on the move is thanksgiving.

Many evangelical churches are homogenous, exhibiting very little diversity. Is it any wonder, then, that fear of welcoming refugees and immigrants to our nations exists when we have not been able to make space for others in our churches, of which Paul said, "there is neither Jew or Greek," there is no longer slave or free" (Gal 3:28)? Christ followers will more easily appreciate the gift of diversity for our nations when we have first experienced the gift of diversity within our worshiping communities. How can your own church strive to reflect the diversity of your neighborhood, whether African American, Hispanic, Caucasian, indigenous, Asian, rich, poor, employed, unemployed, and others? One key to increasing diversity in your church is to model this diversity, sharing your life with people who appear to be different from you. Other keys are to pray and teach with this in mind. Consider singing in a variety of languages, for at least one song each Sunday. Also consider using a variety of languages in liturgy. Reflecting the diversity of your neighborhood in church staffing is also key. Sharing life as a diverse church may not be conflict free (neither are homogenous churches conflict free), but with good processes of dialogue, diversity opens up the opportunity for maturity and love.

---

[28]Richard Bauckham, *Bible and Mission: Christian Witness in a Postmodern World* (Milton Keynes, UK: Paternoster, 2003), 53-54.

In the life of our (Mark and his wife Erin's) household in Vancouver, we try to lean into this rhythm of thanksgiving and kinship. If you were to attend the birthday party of Mark and Erin's six-year-old son, for example, you would enjoy seeing a gathering of six-year-old children energetically playing soccer on the green grass. And you would have the opportunity to be blessed by conversation with a number of vulnerable people who have become family with us over the years. We try to avoid falling into the humdrum pattern of homogenous gatherings of middle-class families. We want our lives to reflect, imperfectly, the diversity of Jesus' kinsfolk. When we live in diversity like this, sadness, brokenness, and addiction are also very present, even for our children. But this is real, it is human, and it is the Way of Christ. Our family also experiences the joy of diversity on many Tuesday evenings at the Kinbrace community meal. On these evenings, grief over the suffering of loved ones back home mixes with the joy and hubbub of forty or so people sharing a meal. We often reflect together how wonderful a context this is for our two children to mature and to learn the Way of Christ.

For worshiping communities today, mission begins with a shared life of lament, gift, thanksgiving, and creative kinship. As we live in this way, as a contrast-community, our neighbors notice that something wonderful is going on, and they too get caught up in the joy and healing of the kingdom of God!

The Witness and Advocacy of the Church

While personal, local engagement with displaced people is crucial for our own "conversion," such engagement can also serve as a powerful witness to broader local, national, and even global communities. The church, furthermore, has a profound opportunity and responsibility to advocate in these communities on behalf of the displaced. We will say much more in parts three and four about both *why* the biblical ethic of kinship with the displaced is applicable not only to the church but also to national and global communities, and *how* that ethic might be practically applied to those communities and embedded in their institutions, policies, and practices. That is not our focus here. But in this present chapter our concern is to consider the role of the church in witnessing and advocating for such an ethic.

Of course, the church isn't responsible to usher in the kingdom of God—only Christ can do that. Yet, as we wait for Christ's return, the church can call communities to lament, to humility, and to tenderness toward the displaced through creative practices of witness and advocacy. By the power of the Spirit, the church can offer prophetic witness by modeling the self-sacrificial Way of Christ. The church earned a reputation for this way of life from early on, as witnessed by the fourth-century Roman emperor Julian the Apostate, who complained: "It is disgraceful that, when no Jew ever has to beg, and the impious Galileans support not only their own but ours as well, all men see that our people lack aid from us."[29]

In the Roman Empire, care for the poor was neither required nor valued, yet love for the weakest flowed through the community of Christ followers, not occasionally but in a widespread and ongoing way. How wonderful it would be if Western governments today felt disgrace in the face of the loving witness of Christians who cared for newcomers self-sacrificially.

The suggestion that the church should not only serve as a witness but also advocate for displaced people may raise concerns among people who, perhaps with Romans 13 in mind, worry that Christians ought not to challenge governmental authorities that God has established. We deal more fully with Romans 13 in chapter seven, but it should suffice to note here that Scripture presents us with numerous examples of God's people advocating for the just treatment of vulnerable people. Think of Moses pleading with Pharaoh to grant freedom to the Israelites and Queen Esther petitioning King Xerxes to spare the Israelites from destruction. Think of the Old Testament prophets and also John the Baptist condemning the injustices of rulers, including their oppression of the vulnerable. And think even of Paul, the author of Romans 13, who persistently preached the gospel, despite the threat of imprisonment.[30] Certainly, Christians should advocate with humility and grace, but they should make the most of the opportunities they have to encourage communities and governments to embrace the responsibility and opportunity to pursue kinship with the displaced.

How might our communities be transformed by our witness and advocacy? To explore this question, we take time now to share some stories of creative responses of Christ followers who have sought to act in solidarity with refugees. Beyond this, in chapters six through ten we will explore the questions and challenges surrounding national and global responses to our present crisis of displacement. These chapters will give some specificity and direction to the church's advocacy.

---

[29]Julian, "To Arsacius, High-Priest of Galatia," *Works of the Emperor Julian*, 3.22.
[30]See similarly Stephan Bauman, Matthew Soerens, and Issam Smeir, *Seeking Refuge: On the Shores of the Global Refugee Crisis* (Chicago: Moody Publishers, 2016), 171-72.

SOME EXAMPLES OF CREATIVE KINSHIP

There are many people engaged in the work of welcoming refugees and advocating for them in various ways. It is a joy to share just a few stories. They demonstrate a range of possibilities for expressing solidarity with displaced people: working alongside governments to improve public policy; working through legal channels or engaging in civil disobedience to challenge and change policy; and generously loving refugees who have been resettled in one's country and encouraging others to do the same.

As you read these stories, you will see that living into the biblical vision of creative kinship doesn't mean that you simply *do* something for someone. Instead, you take the risk to walk as closely as you can with someone. You share the privilege that you have—that's when mutual transformation happens.

Kinbrace: National impact in Canada. For Kinbrace staff, living with refugee claimants has been a window through which to see the gaps in the refugee claim process in Canada. It is a privileged place, a kind of listening. Staff have come to realize that while a refugee's future will be decided at their refugee claim hearings, most claimants don't know in advance the most basic things about their hearings: where to go, what to expect, who is going to be there, or how the process will unfold. "Hearing-readiness" is in everybody's interest, and yet an upcoming hearing is so foreign to many applicants that it can be positively terrifying. So, in collaboration with lawyers and the Immigration and Refugee Board of Canada, Kinbrace initiated what is known as the Ready Tour.[31] Fran Gallo, program coordinator for Accessing Refugee Protection, is the organizer. An Immigration and Refugee Board staff member takes refugee claimants into one of the hearing rooms in Vancouver to learn about their upcoming hearing. They learn about the role of each person in the room during their hearing and how a hearing proceeds. Following Kinbrace's example, the Ready Tour is now replicated throughout Canada, supported by different organizations in each major city.

Kinbrace staff soon realized that after claimants left the Ready Tour, they didn't have anything with which to continue the learning process. So Jamie Spray began a process of writing the "Preparation Guide," an easy-to-read pamphlet for refugee claimants attending Ready Tours—many hands have collaborated on the pamphlet since.[32] This pamphlet has been illustrated by

---

[31]See "Ready Tours," *Ready for My Refugee Hearing*, Kinbrace Community Society, accessed April 14, 2020, https://refugeeclaim.ca/en/ready-tours/.

[32]See "Preparation Guide," *Ready for My Refugee Hearing*, Kinbrace Community Society, accessed April 14, 2020, https://refugeeclaim.ca/en/preparation-guide/.

a local artist, Andrea Armstrong, and translated into ten languages. The Preparation Guide has also been picked up by others and adapted for six different regions throughout Canada.

Prior to this collaboration there was an us-versus-them mentality in the refugee protection system in Vancouver, with nonprofits and lawyers pitted against government institutions. Loren Balisky reflects, "One of the graces is that we somehow found our way through that, building relationships of trust and a common objective." We asked Loren what Kinbrace's posture has been as each of these initiatives has gotten off the ground. He answered: "Being faithful. We ask, What is the next thing we need to do so that refugee claimants have a clear pathway to refugee protection in Canada?"

Ebony, Australian lawyer. Ebony Birchall is a gifted and compassionate Christian lawyer in Sydney, Australia. She uses her professional skills in solidarity with refugees. Ebony had always felt a strong calling on her legal work to uphold justice and glorify God, and during the course of 2014–2017 God provided a wonderful opportunity for her to do this: she played a key role in a successful lawsuit against the Australian government for its policy of detaining refugees and asylum seekers in offshore detention facilities.

People arriving by boat to seek asylum in Australia are mandatorily detained in facilities on Manus Island and Nauru. We will say more about the injustice of this policy and the harm that it does to already vulnerable people in chapters seven and eight. The lawsuit alleged that refugees and asylum seekers were falsely imprisoned on Manus Island, in northern Papua New Guinea, since Papua New Guinea's Supreme Court had ruled that their detention was illegal under the constitution of PNG. The legal team within which Ebony worked sought damages for detainees on the basis that, under the care and protection of the Commonwealth of Australia, they had been detained in poor conditions and experienced fear, indignity, or humiliation. The case also alleged negligence in the management of the detention center, including failures in ensuring the safety of detainees and failures in providing adequate medical treatment, housing, food, and water. The almost 1,700 detainees involved in the case were awarded AU$70 million in compensation. And this was not the only achievement of this case. The settlement also gave important recognition to the suffering of vulnerable people made subject by the Australian government to indefinite, offshore detention.

Ebony led the process of the litigation team completing over one hundred interviews with refugees for the case, and this process changed her life. "Now that I have seen, I'm responsible," she says. Since this case, she has worked with refugees in numerous legal claims, political advocacy, and through community organizations. Ebony both serves these refugees and considers working with refugees to be a gift. For example, when she expressed compassion to one Christian refugee, the man said to her: "Don't worry. I know that the Australian government isn't the most powerful thing in the world. I trust in God, and I know that this will end." Ebony was struck in that moment by the contrast between the many Australian Christians who support this policy and this man who is still pointing to God amidst the suffering of detention. Ebony reflects, "There is a gift in knowing that life isn't about buying a house and going on holidays. It is this work that gives me joy and fulfillment. This is the sort of thing that builds my character and my faith in God."

Ebony's perseverance within her local Christian community is inspiring for us. God's heart for the most vulnerable has been crucial in Ebony's journey with Christ. Having personally experienced injustice as a child, hearing about a God of justice initially drew Ebony to God. Her personal journey has made it all the harder when most responses from Christians in Ebony's circles have been discouraging of her work. "Why do you help these refugees on Manus? Aren't they just queue jumpers?" has been a common response. She has also been deeply confused that Christian leaders around her have failed to show and speak love to refugees either in personal contexts or publicly. This has led Ebony to desire to reach a deeper understanding of God's love of justice and love for the stranger theologically, for this is rarely discussed in her church context.

Ebony speaks of her own process: "I am learning to manage my own emotional responses to my work and to take on a teaching role toward those with unloving responses, though these are very difficult things to learn and implement. God has taught me much about grace through this process. And I have taken the approach that even small impacts I can make on my local church's culture are worthwhile. You have to find people who have the same convictions as you; otherwise you will burn out."

Readers of this book may resonate with Ebony's journey within her church community. In order to inspire hopeful ideas in others, we asked Ebony to list some of the ways in which she has tried to engage her church on these issues. Here are the suggestions she offers:

- Seek out Christian organizations working in social justice. There are organizations set up to help equip individuals and churches on justice issues (e.g., for those in Australia, Common Grace is a movement of people passionate about Jesus and justice that seeks to resource local churches on justice issues).

- Regularly speak to your church leaders about their ideas on God's love for justice and how your church is pursuing this. Offer to help your church in this pursuit however you are able.

- Ask your church leaders if they have a considered theology of justice. If they haven't, you could offer to write a position statement for them to consider and approve, as a first step toward including justice as a value within your church's culture.

- If you're involved in teaching at your church, write Bible studies or sermons that include themes related to God's love of justice.

- Invite your church or Bible study group to openly discuss and pray for justice issues.

- Hearing stories of refugees is a great way to introduce people to the issue. There are many great movies/documentaries on refugee issues. Local screening events are quite common, so you could take church members to a screening or host a screening at your own church.

- One-on-one conversations with church members to openly discuss their opinions on justice issues can be powerful. However, these conversations can be very challenging or confrontational.

- Ultimately, if your church is unresponsive to your attempts to recognize and pursue God's love of justice, you may need to consider finding a different church community.

Jarrod, Australian pastor and activist. Jarrod McKenna detected a gap in the system of protection for newcomers in Perth, Australia. Affordable rental accommodation is difficult to find in Perth for many people. Jarrod noticed that this is the case especially for refugees, who have no rental history. So he began the First Home Project. He was able to borrow money to purchase a house in which refugees could live for a period of one year. These newcomers could thus develop a rental history, enabling them to find rental accommodation on their own. Jarrod himself has an apartment in the house, sharing his life with newcomers. He emphasizes that sharing life within his First Home Project family regularly brings him to repentance. "The stranger is our savior," he says, echoing the parable of the good Samaritan, in which the alien Samaritan brings healing. Through the First Home Project, Jarrod's goal is "not only to name the injustice of the mandatory detention of asylum seekers who arrive in Australia by boat but also to show that a different way is possible."

Jarrod has not been hesitant to "name the injustice" though. He has been a key participant in the Love Makes a Way movement, a movement of "Christians seeking an end to Australia's inhumane asylum seeker policies through prayer and nonviolent love in action." Self-consciously following the examples of prayerful civil disobedience set by Martin Luther King Jr. and others, Love Makes a Way protestors have staged "pray-ins" in the offices of Australian politicians, including the prime minister, immigration minister, and leader of the opposition on numerous occasions since 2014. They have sought, in their own words, "to publicly witness to and dramatise the injustice of Australia's asylum seeker policies, to awaken the conscience of the church and wider community, and to point to a better way."[33] Jarrod and his friends express their practice of prayerful protest in a beautifully disarming way:

> Cranky Christians aren't going to burn your office down. We're going to come and sit in it and pray. And awkwardly sing. And we'll be super polite and thank the staff as the police take us away. Then we'll show up to court in mismatched suits and make friends with the bailiffs. If you fine us, we'll pay on time. And we'll pray like crazy, and so will a thousand women named Doreen. . . .
>
> We are powered by the Holy Spirit, and egg sandwiches cut into quarters. We have an infinite supply of both, and we are not giving up.[34]

Mary, loving refugees in the United States. Mary Kaech has been acting in solidarity with refugees in Phoenix, Arizona, for many years. Mary began engaging with newcomers by forming two small groups in her church to sponsor refugee families. These groups set up an apartment, met each family at the airport, and walked with the families for their first several months in their new city. Mary is still friends with those families, eight years later.

Mary has worked hard at educating her church community by teaching small groups about God's heart for the stranger. One effective strategy has been a reading group. The most transformative moment, however, was when refugee friends came and spoke to her church community. Mary reflects: "There is nothing quite as powerful as coming face-to-face with 'the other,' who turns out to be just another human who reflects the image of God." Now

---

[33]"About," *Love Makes a Way*, accessed April 14, 2020, http://lovemakesaway.org.au/who-we-are/. See also the discussion of Love Makes a Way in Erin K. Wilson, "Theorizing Religion as Politics in Postsecular International Relations," *Politics, Religion and Ideology* 15, no. 3 (2014), 347-65, at 362-63.

[34]Chris Bedding with Peter Barney and Jarrod McKenna, "Cranky Christians Against Asylum Seeker Cruelty," *Drum* (blog), *ABC News*, May 20, 2014.

Mary leads Phoenix Refugee Connections, a network of Christians across Phoenix walking in relationship with refugees.

In this chapter we have applied the biblical ethic of kinship, which we retrieved in the opening chapters of the book, to the mission of the church. This chapter plays a pivotal role in our argument, bridging between the biblical exploration of creative kinship and the application of this ethic to the nation and the global community in the chapters that follow. We have seen that mission isn't just another activity that the church *does*; rather, mission is a part of the very *identity* of God's people. For Christ said: "As the Father sent me, I am sending you" (Jn 20:21). We are a sent people, by our very identity, witnessing to Christ's redeeming love in life, word, and deed. God forms allegiances with the vulnerable and the displaced (Deut 10:17-19). So, in an *imago Dei* mirroring, the church is called to practices of creative kinship with the same. Through the metaphor of festive kinship, we have explored practices for nourishing worshiping communities toward welcome: practices of lament, gift, thanksgiving, and inclusive justice. And we have outlined a scriptural basis for, and offered some examples of, church-based witness and advocacy.

Yet, if we take it as established that the church has a responsibility to extend kinship to refugees, questions remain regarding the responsibilities of our political communities. Does a *nation* have responsibility to welcome refugees according to biblical ethics? Does not a government have responsibility merely for its own citizens? And doesn't that require that they secure their borders and strictly regulate and limit the entry of outsiders? These questions will be addressed as we now turn, in part three, to articulate a political theology of national community grounded in the biblical model of kinship with the stranger.

PART THREE

THE NATION

5

NEIGHBOR-LOVING
NATIONS

In October 2015, one month after Chancellor Angela Merkel opened Germany's borders to hundreds of thousands of strangers fleeing violence and suffering in the Middle East and North Africa, former Australian Prime Minister Tony Abbott delivered a lecture in London. "Implicitly or explicitly, the imperative to 'love your neighbor as you love yourself' is at the heart of every Western polity. It expresses itself in laws protecting workers, in strong social security safety nets, and in the readiness to take in refugees. It's what makes us decent and humane countries as well as prosperous ones," he observed. "But—right now—this wholesome instinct is leading much of Europe into catastrophic error. . . . No country or continent can open its borders to all comers without fundamentally weakening itself. This is the risk that the countries of Europe now run through misguided altruism." Abbott recommended that Europe study the approach that his government had taken to a recent influx of asylum seekers: secure one's borders, stop the flow of boats, and "firmly and unambiguously" deny entry. "It will require some force," he admitted. "It will require massive logistics and expense; it will gnaw at our consciences—yet it is the only way to prevent a tide of humanity surging through Europe and quite possibly changing it forever." Such a policy, he said, is demanded by "the moral duty to protect one's own people and to stamp out people smuggling."[1]

---

[1]Tony Abbott, "Transcript: Tony Abbott's Controversial Speech at the Margaret Thatcher Lecture," *Sydney Morning Herald*, October 28, 2015.

Such arguments are often heard. It is a good thing, the thinking goes, for national communities to embrace the biblical imperative to love one's neighbor and to apply it to domestic (internal) policy for the benefit of citizens who are in need and for the advancement of the common good. National governments may even at times have cause to extend neighborly love to vulnerable people beyond their borders, providing aid or refuge to certain strangers and intervening diplomatically or even militarily on their behalf when this can be done with convenience. But governments are ultimately charged with the care of their own people. Thus, they have an unquestionable right and a solemn responsibility to prioritize securing the safety and advancing the well-being of these people and preserving their national character and values. This requires that they exercise strict control over their borders, carefully selecting and limiting the number of strangers that they welcome into the community.

How does this accord with God's desire and design for community? Simply put, it doesn't. Scripture envisages the cultivation of communities marked by the joyful and relentless care of the weakest and the neediest—not only the poorest and most vulnerable within the community but also those displaced and dispossessed beyond it whom they are to welcome and enfold as kin. It is widely held that, in a complex and dangerous world, this model of community cannot be feasibly or justifiably applied at the level of the nation. But it can. And it should. In this chapter and the next, we seek to explain why. In chapter eight, we strive to imagine how.

In this chapter and the next, we outline a political theology of national community, applying the biblical ethic of kinship with the vulnerable and displaced to a world of sovereign nation-states. We grapple with widely held assumptions and arguments that recommend exclusivist approaches to nationhood. These include instinctive assertions of the prerogatives of sovereign authority as well as more thoughtful claims about the importance of prioritizing the care of one's own people and preserving their collective way of life. We suggest, however, that none of these arguments provide good grounds for setting aside or circumscribing the biblical imperative for nations to embrace and enfold vulnerable strangers as kin. In fact, careful consideration of some of these arguments amplifies our appreciation of the mandate to welcome displaced persons as they help us perceive how we are often implicated in the suffering of those beyond our borders. Too often, states have behaved and continue to behave not merely as the priest and Levite who passed by the other side but like the robbers that left the man half dead by the road. This should move us to reimagine our nations as communities that humbly repent of our injustices and embrace the opportunity to make amends as we joyfully seek to love our distant neighbors as ourselves and welcome the displaced as kin.

GOD'S DESIRE FOR POLITICAL COMMUNITY

A Christian understanding of the state today ought to be shaped by the revelation of God's desire and design for political community through the whole testimony of Scripture. To be sure, the model of Israel found in the Old Testament is not fully and directly applicable to any political community today. Those nations through history that have succumbed to the temptation to identify themselves with Israel—with God's elected people—and that have sought to imitate particular chapters of Israel's story through the adoption of theocratic laws and the pursuit of holy wars, have gone disastrously astray. They have failed to recognize that Israel's salvific vocation has already been fulfilled in the incarnation, life, death, and resurrection of Jesus. They have failed to comprehend that Israel's witness to the world is today the mission of the transnational church, rather than of any individual nation.[2] No political community should cast itself as the people of God, as the means to salvation or as the witness of truth to the world. But every political community is implicated in the call to justice for the oppressed, to care for the vulnerable, and to kinship with the displaced, which God gave to Israel and that Jesus modeled to those he encountered. The state does not offer redemption, but it should pursue justice.

The scope of justice. This claim that the state is fundamentally charged with the pursuit of justice echoes Oliver O'Donovan's influential argument about the purpose of political authority.[3] God's rule authorizes political authorities to secure justice, O'Donovan tells us, in order to maintain a social space and preserve a social order in which the gospel can be spread and people be drawn into God's kingdom.[4] He cites Romans 13:4, in which Paul says the governing

---

[2]Joan Lockwood O'Donovan, "Nation, State, and Civil Society in the Western Biblical Tradition," in Oliver O'Donovan and Joan Lockwood O'Donovan, *Bonds of Imperfection: Christian Politics, Past and Present* (Grand Rapids, MI: Eerdmans, 2004), 276-95, at 284-87.

[3]Oliver O'Donovan, *The Desire of the Nations: Rediscovering the Roots of Political Theology* (Cambridge: Cambridge University Press, 1996); idem, "Government as Judgment," in O'Donovan and O'Donovan, *Bonds of Imperfection*, 207-24; and idem, *The Ways of Judgment: The Bampton Lectures, 2003* (Grand Rapids, MI: Eerdmans, 2005).

[4]O. O'Donovan, *Desire of the Nations*, 146-57.

authority is "an avenger to visit wrath on the wrongdoer."[5] When challenged
by Nicholas Wolterstorff that he focuses too much on the need to restrain injustice and neglects to speak of the role of government in also promoting "the
flourishing, the well-being, the *shalom* of the people," O'Donovan replies that
governing authorities should certainly promote human flourishing and suggests that such flourishing should be understood as an aspect of justice.[6] He
even hints that governments might at times rightly seek justice for, and flourishing of, people beyond the national community.[7] But he ultimately insists
that a government is *responsible* for securing justice and flourishing only for
the particular people that it represents.[8]

The responsibilities of political authority are necessarily limited,
O'Donovan claims. "Divine providence has instituted distinct peoples with
distinct identities (conventionally, though by no means exclusively, defined
by territorial borders), to set limits to the pursuit of justice, focusing it upon
conceivable and practicable undertakings." In our own moral reflections, he
says, we are aware of a range of "undischarged responsibilities" for the care
of people beyond the boundaries of our community, but these are burdens of
obligation "for which we could never responsibly take responsibility."[9] The
only alternative to "government with a limited sphere of responsibility," he
declares, "is a world government, literally conceived."[10]

The scriptural model of community that we retrieved in part one, however,
commends to us an understanding of justice that is more relentlessly
outward looking and inclusive. We will consider in chapter ten some specific
ways that responsibilities can and should be allocated among states for the
care of vulnerable people beyond their borders, without the need for the
creation of a world government, but for now let us simply recall what
Scripture tells us about God's desire and design for community. As we found
in chapters two through four, a community that pursues God's vision for
community will certainly be one that cares for its most vulnerable members,
for the poor and the needy, for the widow and the orphan.[11] But this call

---

[5]O. O'Donovan, *Desire of the Nations*, 147.

[6]Nicholas Wolterstorff, "A Discussion of Oliver O'Donovan's *The Desire of the Nations*," *SJT* 54, no.
1 (2001): 87-109, at 106; and Oliver O'Donovan, "Deliberation, History and Reading: A Response
to Schweiker and Wolterstorff," *SJT* 54, no. 1 (2001): 127-44, at 132, 134-37.

[7]O. O'Donovan, "Deliberation, History and Reading," 132-33.

[8]O. O'Donovan, "Deliberation, History and Reading," 130-32.

[9]O. O'Donovan, "Deliberation, History and Reading," 130.

[10]O. O'Donovan, "Deliberation, History and Reading," 132.

[11]We translate *yātôm* as "fatherless" in our textual analysis and as "orphan" in our political-theological
discussion.

extends also to vulnerable people that lack community, the stranger and the marginalized in its midst. More than this, it will welcome these into community, enfolding them as kin. Indeed, it will invite them into the heart of the life of the community, feasting with them and celebrating the cultivation of new kinship.

This was God's desire for nations in the Old Testament, and it is God's desire for communities of Christ followers in the New Testament. It surely remains God's desire for nations today. Israel was given the law as a concrete (and highly contextualized) model of God's vision for community. God's laws are not an arbitrary set of rules for one nation. Rather, as Ryan O'Dowd puts it, "They are a paradigm of God's re-creative initiative to bring righteousness, justice, and wisdom into this world."[12] For the law reflects the will and wisdom of the "God of gods, Lord of lords"—that is to say, the God of every place and every nation (Deut 4:5-8; 10:17). Israel itself was to be a contrastive community, living in the sight of the nations, transformed by the word of Yahweh. The law, including its provisions for the treatment of the displaced stranger, Christopher Wright explains, "was given to Israel to enable Israel to live as a model, as a light to the nations." And "the anticipated result of this plan was that, in the prophetic vision, the law would 'go forth' to the nations, or they would 'come up' to learn it. The nations were 'waiting' for that law and justice of the Lord, which was presently bound up with Israel (Is 42:4)."[13] The accounts of the law in Scripture, thus "render for us a paradigm, in one single culture and slice of history, of the kinds of social values God looks for in human life generally."[14] We may understand the universal impulse of the Scriptures more deeply, again, when we comprehend that the Old Testament was ultimately shaping not a nation-state or an ethnic group but a people who were responsive to the divine word.[15]

As evidence that God desires that all nations—not just Israel—will be marked by justice, consider how God repeatedly held nations to account in

---

[12]Ryan O'Dowd, *The Wisdom of Torah: Epistemology in Deuteronomy and the Wisdom Literature*, FRLANT 225 (Göttingen: Vandenhoeck & Ruprecht, 2009), 40-41.

[13]Christopher J. H. Wright, *Old Testament Ethics for the People of God* (Downers Grove, IL: InterVarsity Press, 2004), 64. O'Donovan likewise remarks that "Yhwh's law can be extended in principle to other nations than Israel" and "the political structures of other nations had the same vocation to just judgment as Israel's did" (O. O'Donovan, *Desire of the Nations*, 65, 68).

[14]C. Wright, *Old Testament Ethics for the People of God*, 65.

[15]Mark R. Glanville, *Adopting the Stranger as Kindred in Deuteronomy*, AIL 33 (Atlanta: SBL Press, 2018), 260. See also Gordon McConville's discussion of the priority of the law over Israel's election. J. Gordon McConville, *Deuteronomy*, Apollos Old Testament Commentary (Downers Grove, IL: InterVarsity Press, 2002), 163.

the Old Testament. God went ahead of Israel and drove out the nations in the lands beyond the Jordan not because of Israel's righteousness but because of the wickedness of these nations (Deut 9:4-5). God likewise condemns the injustice of several of Israel's neighbors in Amos 1:3–2:5. The psalmist even has God giving judgment "among the 'gods'" for the care of the vulnerable:

> "How long will you defend the unjust
> and show partiality to the wicked?
> Defend the cause of the weak and fatherless;
> maintain the rights of the poor and oppressed.
> Rescue the weak and needy;
> deliver them from the hand of the wicked." . . .
> Rise up, O God, judge the earth,
> for all the nations are your inheritance. (Ps 82:2-4, 8)

In neither of these passages does God explicitly judge nations for failing to welcome displaced strangers. We do, however, at least find God judging nations for failing to protect the most vulnerable in their communities. And as Robert Heimburger usefully notes, while the requirement to care for the displaced is not explicitly applied to other nations in the Old Testament, "surely, this account of divine justice and love [required of Israel] would not be displaced by some more generic version of justice required of other nations."[16]

Our point is not that Israel's festivals and legal and institutional structures should be precisely replicated by all nations today. Rather, the arrangements that we find in the Old Testament represent the specific and concrete application of God's vision for community in a particular cultural and historical context. Nations should consider this model carefully and strive again to work out this vision of community in their own cultural and historic contexts today.[17] As we explained in chapter two, the task is like that of a jazz musician— to hear and internalize the "tradition" and to "perform" it anew, with fresh creativity, again and again in ever-evolving contexts.

And, to speak directly to O'Donovan's concern with political *authority*, it seems clear that the consideration and concretization of this vision must be the purpose not only of communities but of their governments. Jeremiah proclaims the word of the Lord to the king of Judah and his officials: "Act with justice and righteousness, and deliver from the hand of the oppressor anyone

---

[16]Robert W. Heimburger, *God and the Illegal Alien: United States Immigration Law and a Theology of Politics* (Cambridge: Cambridge University Press, 2018), 121.

[17]See similarly M. Daniel Carroll R. (Rodas), *Christians at the Border: Immigration, the Church, and the Bible*, 2nd ed. (Grand Rapids, MI: Brazos Press, 2013), 81-83, 96-97.

who has been robbed. And do no wrong or violence to the alien, the orphan, and the widow, or shed innocent blood in this place" (Jer 22:3). Governing authorities are charged with pursuing God's vision for community. They need, therefore, to work to help cultivate communal sentiments and create appropriate institutional and legal structures so as to facilitate the development of communities that are both eager and able to welcome displaced strangers as kin. In chapter eight, we will explore some of the emotional and material obstacles and opportunities that attend this task.

The bounds of community. But what of communal boundaries? What of borders? Don't communities need to be bounded in order for the concept to have meaning? And don't they need to maintain these boundaries and control these borders in some way if they hope to secure a measure of order and justice for the people found within? We have certainly taught ourselves to think this way. But surely the regulation of boundaries is justified only insofar as it serves God's vision for community.

What does Scripture tell us? The parallel accounts of Genesis 10:1-32 and 11:1-9 tell of God dividing the world into a multitude of separate political communities—described as "peoples" or "nations." This division is portrayed in the second account as a product of both grace and judgment.[18] When humanity sought to accumulate wealth and glory by building a city with a tower that reached the heavens, God came down to them and prevented them from carrying out their plans by confusing their language and scattering them over the face of the earth. This act of dividing and scattering, of course, should not be read as establishing communities whose existence and boundaries were at that moment established for all time. But it does provide an early indication of God's interest in the distinct lives of distinct communities.

We are soon told that God provides nations with territory as a gift. Deuteronomy speaks repeatedly not only of the land that God gives to Israel (Deut 1:25; 2:29; 3:20; and many times thereafter) but also of lands given to others. Do not provoke the descendants of Esau, the Edomites, to war, God commands Israel, "for I will not give you even so much as a foot's length of their land, since I have given Mount Seir to Esau as a possession" (Deut 2:5). God says the same for the land given to the descendants of Lot, the Moabites and the Ammonites (Deut 2:9, 19). The territories of nations are given boundaries by God (Deut 32:8), with valleys (Deut 2:14), gorges (Deut 2:24), rivers

---

[18]Karl Barth, *The Doctrine of Creation*, vol. 3, pt. 4 of *Church Dogmatics*, ed. G. W. Bromiley and T. F. Torrance (Edinburgh: T&T Clark, 1961), 313-18.

Shifting Bounds of Community

We sometimes talk about refugee issues today in a way that implies that the boundaries that divide the world into separate political communities have remained more or less fixed across time. But of course we know that is not true.

The idea of shifting boundaries of community was expressed artistically at Grandview Church recently, in the context of a children's drama. Our dear friend Sahel is a brilliant artist from a Middle Eastern country. Sahel received refugee status in Canada as we put the finishing touches on this book. She volunteers at Eastside Story Guild, which is Grandview Church's children's community theatre group (fondly known as ESG). ESG dramatizes biblical stories though Sahel describes herself as a secularist. For the latest performance, ESG's directors wrote a script on kinship and the kingdom of God, contributing to the growing conversation within Grandview Church around the theme of kinship.

Sahel was tasked with creating an art installation that explored kinship and national borders. In a small dark room, she projected a map of the world onto a white sheet. To the left of the map was the year, which moved from 1000 BCE to 2018 CE and back again, over and over. As the years went by, the national borders on the map shifted like wiggly worms, never still. We stood in the small room watching the nations constantly changing shape while we listened to an audio track of footsteps: the footsteps of people who were on

(Deut 2:37), and towns (Deut 2:37) marking their limits.[19] Again, we should not read this as divine endorsement of permanent and unchanging communal boundaries. After all, Israel's territorial boundaries shifted many times during the period of the Old Testament.[20]

Were communal boundaries monitored and regulated in the Old Testament? Well, we do find examples of nations exercising control over those who entered or attempted to enter their lands, both in Scripture and in archaeology of the ancient world.[21] But such records are of nations *other* than

---

[19]See similarly Heimburger, *God and the Illegal Alien*, 116. Recall from chap. 3, however, that the clear demarcation of linear borders, in contrast to more fluid or overlapping boundaries, was universalized only in the modern era, and we shouldn't make the mistake of thinking that political communities have always conceived of strictly defined geographical limits to their territories, much less that they have always obsessed about the flow of people across these limits as they do today.

[20]E.g., 2 Samuel 5:1-5; 1 Kings 4:21; 12:16; 2 Kings 18:13.

[21]James K. Hoffmeier, *The Immigration Crisis: Immigrants, Aliens, and the Bible* (Wheaton, IL:

the move, across all those centuries. Borders on the move, people on the move, always. In the middle of the room a small table was adorned as if for a wedding. Sahel explained that the table was ready for a wedding feast, prepared for all those who will accept other human beings as their fellows. Replicas of passports and cash hung from the roof. These are possessions that force false divisions between people, Sahel explained.

Sahel's projection reminds us that the boundaries dividing the world into separate political communities today have not remained static historically. Nation-states, empires, city-states, and other forms of political community have risen and fallen and have been shaped and reshaped across time. Indeed, the very suggestion that the *borders* of political communities have been changing for thousands of years can be unhelpful if it obscures the fact that the demarcation of linear borders across the globe is a modern phenomenon—a product, scholars tell us, of developments in the practices and technologies of mapmaking, the "rationalization" of territories and frontiers, and the emergence of the territorially bounded sovereign state that displaced earlier, diverse, frequently overlapping, and often nonterritorial conceptions of political authority and community.[a]

---

[a]See for example Jordan Branch, *The Cartographic State: Maps, Territory, and the Origins of Sovereignty* (Cambridge: Cambridge University Press, 2014); and Kerry Goettlich, "The Rise of Linear Borders in World Politics," *EJIR* 25, no. 1 (2019): 203-28.

Israel (e.g., Gen 12:10-20; Num 20:14–21:35). We should be careful not to conclude from this, as some do, that such control was intrinsically or always justified.[22] As for Israel's own territories, the example of Ruth and Naomi's migration indicates that, at least at that time, there were few if any restrictions placed on entry. In considering borders, most important is Scripture's demand that God's people should welcome and enfold people who are seeking a home as kin. As we have seen, this biblical call was embedded in Israel's understanding of God. God had given the land and its abundance as a divine gift, and there was more than enough to share (Deut 16:10-14). And crucially, Israel's retention of the gift was contingent upon their sharing the divine supply with displaced people (Deut 27:19). In a nutshell, according to Scripture, communal boundaries and borders must always serve both those

---

Crossway, 2009), 38-44.
[22]See, for example, Hoffmeier, *Immigration Crisis*, 32-35, 153-54.

within the boundaries as well as those who are outside seeking a place to belong. God desires that the governance of communal boundaries, like the rest of communal life, should be marked by a concern for the flourishing of all people, especially the weakest.

Certainly, boundaries are valuable. They usefully mark the territorial limits of a community, within which people can develop a shared sense of place, belonging, and care. There will often be good grounds for communities to monitor their boundaries. As we suggested in the context of our Ezra–Nehemiah discussion in chapter three, a vulnerable community may need to limit the entry of predatory or ill-intentioned outsiders in order to preserve the well-being of those within, and an impoverished community may need to prevent the entry of those who seek to extract their limited wealth and resources. But efforts to establish borders and limit entry must always be subject to the demands of justice—justice not only for current members of the community but also for vulnerable outsiders who stand in need of community.

Karl Barth on "near and distant strangers." Karl Barth put it well in a discussion of "near and distant neighbors," penned soon after the Second World War.[23] He acknowledged the reality and the importance of the "economic, social, cultural, political, and religious factors" that underlie the existence of a distinct people. And he recognized that everyone should love their own people. However, he insisted that the idea of one's own people should be understood to be "not a fixed but a fluid concept." The existence of a national community should never be considered an end in itself. The nation should not be made "a prison and stronghold," securing its people to the exclusion of all others. Rather, "where the command of God is sounded and heard, the concepts home, motherland and people, while they must retain their original sense, will prove capable of extension."[24] This has clear implications for how we think about the bounds of national community:

> In short, we must understand the concept of people dynamically and not statically even from the standpoint of geographical determination. One's own people in its location cannot and must not be a wall but a door. Whether it be widely opened or not, and even perhaps shut again, it must never be barred, let alone blocked up.[25]

---

[23]Barth, *Doctrine of Creation*, 285-323. Barth's discussion of "near and distant neighbors" is insightfully treated in Heimburger, *God and the Illegal Alien*, 45-53.

[24]Barth, *Doctrine of Creation*, 294, 291, 293.

[25]Barth, *Doctrine of Creation*, 294.

Barth was clearly eager to warn against repeating the errors of earlier theologians, whose sanctification of German nationalism paved the way for the horrific deeds of the Third Reich. He emphasized that no nation should conceive of itself as a sacred, pure, and permanent people.[26] But he was by no means blind to the impact of mass migration on societies. World War II, after all, saw the forced displacement of an estimated sixty million people, and Germany received more than fourteen million refugees in the years following the war.[27] We cannot, therefore, simply write off Barth's fluid and inclusive conception of national community as an impassioned but impractical reaction to the sins of the Nazis. Barth surely knew at least as well as we do today the costs and risks that nations bear when they seek to enfold as kin large numbers of displaced peoples. And yet, he insisted, "The confrontation of the near and the distant, of people and people, is necessarily fluid where the command of God is issued and heard. We have seen that, although this does not mean the removal of boundaries, it certainly means the overthrow of barriers and a certain coming and going."[28]

We will continue to attend to this difficult issue of national boundaries in the chapters that follow. We don't pretend for a moment that it is an easy issue to think through, but we do suggest that the right of a people to control the entry of outsiders is not as self-evident as is commonly assumed. Scripture does not provide any clear and direct warrant for the strict enforcement of territorial borders. What it does provide is a mandate to seek justice for vulnerable people, which includes an obligation to welcome the stranger. Border enforcement is surely only valid insofar as it is necessary for pursuing God's vision for community.

But, of course, thoughtful Christians commonly offer a range of reasons why nations today do not need to be, indeed cannot afford to be, as relentlessly generous and welcoming to vulnerable strangers as we are suggesting. Let's consider several of these reasons in the remainder of this chapter and also in the next.

NATIONAL IDENTITY

One justification commonly given for controlling and limiting the admission of outsiders is that excessive immigration, or the immigration of the wrong

---

[26]Barth, *Doctrine of Creation*, 305-9.
[27]Chauncy D. Harris and Gabriele Wülker, "The Refugee Problem of Germany," *Economic Geography* 29, no. 1 (1953): 10-25.
[28]Barth, *Doctrine of Creation*, 300.

people, risks weakening the shared affinities and loyalties that bind a national community together and risks corrupting the community's shared identity and values. This claim should not be lightly dismissed.

The identities and boundaries of nations, of course, are not timeless and unchanging. National communities are imagined and constructed at particular points in time, and they are reimagined and reconstructed again and again over time.[29] Even with respect to the boundaries of Old Testament Israel, exactly who qualified as "Israel" was sometimes unclear. There was ongoing uncertainty, for example, around the status of the tribes east of the Jordan, Manasseh, Gad, and Reuben, at the time when Joshua was written (see Josh 22).

Nevertheless, while communal identities may be continually reimagined and reconstructed, the bonds that members of these communities share with each other are morally valuable and the customs that they cultivate, insofar as they embody particular expressions of universal human goods, ought to be cherished. Perhaps this provides good grounds for strictly controlling membership of the community? Philosopher Michael Walzer famously frames the argument in terms of a right of self-determination: "Admission and exclusion are at the core of communal independence. They suggest the deepest meaning of self-determination. Without them, there could not be *communities of character*, historically stable, ongoing associations of men and women with some special commitment to one another and some special sense of their common life."[30]

Such arguments are widely heard today, including among thoughtful Christians. Some followers of Christ, it should be said, succumb to the temptation to embrace a pernicious understanding of communal identity, attributing the characteristics of God's chosen people in Scripture to their own nation—a chosen nation with a sacred land, a divine commission, and a glorious destiny.[31] Such a conception of nationhood is at times applied to justify

---

[29]Benedict Anderson, *Imagined Communities: Reflections on the Origin and Spread of Nationalism* (London: Verso, 1983).

[30]Michael Walzer, *Spheres of Justice: A Defense of Pluralism and Equality* (New York: Basic Books, 1983), 62. For a recent and influential defense of this type of argument, see David Miller, *Strangers in Our Midst: The Political Philosophy of Immigration* (Cambridge, MA: Harvard University Press, 2016). Both Walzer and Miller, it should be said, nevertheless insist that self-determining communities do have certain obligations to welcome some refugees.

[31]For an example that leans too far in this direction, see Stephen H. Webb, *American Providence: A Nation with a Mission* (New York: Continuum, 2004). For a critique, see John D. Wilsey, *American Exceptionalism and Civil Religion: Reassessing the History of an Idea* (Downers Grove, IL: IVP Academic, 2015).

the closing of borders, as well as the pursuit of reckless and unjust wars beyond these borders. Other followers of Christ refuse to mix their faith and national identity in such a troubling way but nevertheless believe it is vital that the preservation of communal bonds, national culture, and shared values be central to deliberations about how many and which kinds of outsiders the community should be prepared to welcome. Peter Meilaender, for example, frames it in terms of concern for "the way of life that we share."[32]

Again, shared affinities and loyalties and the cultivation of a sense of belonging are valuable things. And national cultures and customs, insofar as they facilitate the pursuit and fulfillment of universal goods, are to be cherished.[33] But there are good reasons to be wary of allowing our concerns for such valuable things to trump the needs of vulnerable strangers. Let's first consider a few reasons to be skeptical of the prioritization of communal bonds and national identities before suggesting a way forward.

To begin, we should recognize that arguments for the preservation of national culture so often rely on a sanitized portrayal of that culture. The identity and character of each nation is a product of history. And while national histories may be marked by evidence of God's providential care and guidance, they are also often stained by the violent expulsion and exclusion of others. Think of the United States, Canada, and Australia. Not only did European settlers in these territories first establish their communal ties and national cultures on lands stolen from indigenous peoples (about which we will say more in chap. 7), but these ties and cultures have subsequently been shaped and sustained over generations, at least in part, by racially discriminatory immigration controls—controls that are made more troubling by being introduced, in some instances, only once demand for cheap foreign labor declined.[34] Consider the Chinese Exclusion Act of 1882 and the racial quotas established in the Immigration Act of 1924 in the United States, the Chinese Immigration Acts of 1885 and 1923 in Canada, and the White Australia Policy that remained in place from 1901 until the 1970s. The identities

---

[32]Peter C. Meilaender, "Immigration: Citizens & Strangers," *First Things*, May 2007. See similarly Gilbert Meilaender and Peter C. Meilaender, "Fences and Neighbors: A Theological Analysis of Immigration and Borders," *First Things*, August 2018.

[33]O'Donovan adds, "If Israel's experience of government is to be taken as a model for other societies, then we must allow that divine providence is ready to protect other national traditions besides the sacred one." O. O'Donovan, *Desire of the Nations*, 73.

[34]On the fluctuations between hospitality and hostility in the history of American immigration policy, see Ali Behdad, *A Forgetful Nation: On Immigration and Cultural Identity in the United States* (Durham, NC: Duke University Press, 2005). See also Heimburger, *God and the Illegal Alien*, 65-94.

of these nations today are at least partly a product of such racist practices of exclusion. Recognition of this should lead us to pause before concluding that the preservation of these same identities might, yet again, justify the exclusion of outsiders.

We should also be wary of buying into pernicious myths that cast the existing identities of nations as homogenous and uncontested. Arguments for the preservation of a nation's culture and traditions are often actually arguments for the preservation of the culture and traditions of one historically dominant group. The group claims ownership of the national identity and fashions this identity in its own image. In the process it excludes other groups within the community, just as it does those beyond the community. This has been a particularly troubling feature of the resurgent populist nationalisms that have proliferated across the globe in recent years, and it gives us reason to be at least skeptical when cries of asylum seekers are met with calls to preserve national identity.[35]

Furthermore, the suggestion that we need to restrict entry in order to maintain communal bonds and national cultures, at least when it is political leaders making this suggestion, is undermined by the fact that these same leaders eagerly and routinely make exceptions for wealthy and highly skilled outsiders. For example, while they ignore the desperate pleas of all but a few refugees, countries such as the United States, the United Kingdom, and Australia have established programs that grant residency to outsiders in exchange for financial investment, purchase of property, transfer of capital, or establishment of a job-creating business. These programs commonly also reduce the requirements for citizenship and expedite citizenship procedures. Within the European Union, several states have even established schemes by which an investment—€650,000, in Malta's case—leads directly to citizenship. This shift toward the "commodification of citizenship," as it has been termed, clearly undermines the claims of some leaders of such states that restrictive policies toward refugees and asylum seekers are necessary for the preservation of national identity.[36] Indeed, the fact that states will embrace the

---

[35]On the long history of efforts to write racial inequality and subjugation out of America's national story, see Jill Lepore, "A New Americanism: Why a Nation Needs a National Story," *Foreign Affairs*, March/April 2019.

[36]See Ayelet Shachar and Rainer Bauböck, *Should Citizenship Be for Sale?*, Robert Schuman Centre for Advanced Studies Research Paper no. 2014/01, January 2014; Ayelet Shachar, "The Marketization of Citizenship in an Age of Restrictionism," *EIA* 32, no. 1 (2018): 3-13; and Luca Mavelli, "Citizenship for Sale and the Neoliberal Political Economy of Belonging," *ISQ* 62, no. 3 (2018): 482-93.

wealthy and eagerly seek their residency while turning away "the least of these" tells us a lot about their true identity.

How then, should we think about national identity? Put bluntly, national identity is to be affirmed so long as it is oriented toward a biblical understanding of community. This requires that it be disposed not only to the care of the poor and needy within the community but also to the cultivation of kinship with vulnerable outsiders.[37] To be sure, national cultures will always be diverse, and cultures are worth upholding. As Jonathan Chaplin helpfully puts it, cultures are "historically particularized collective human responses to the possibilities enclosed within creation. And since God sustains the goodness and flourishing of creation even in the face of human sin, we will always expect to find *something* of value in *any* culture."[38] Just as we should enjoy the differences that we observe between families or between neighborhood communities, so too should we celebrate differences both within nations and between nations, insofar as they express "the goodness and flourishing of creation." But whatever else each particular national identity, culture, or tradition will be about, God's desire is that they be about the pursuit of justice and flourishing for every person, including the stranger. This is God's desire for human community.[39]

We ought to be wary, then, of the temptation to pursue prideful and uncritical preservation of national identity no matter what. We should instead contemplate our national identities with a posture of humility and a willingness to recognize where we have gone astray. Certainly, we should identify and celebrate what is good about our cultures and strive to maintain these characteristics, in all of their rich diversity. But we should also seek to develop, as Chaplin says, "responsible, critical patriotisms based on national narratives suitably humbled by repentance and grace and always open to critique."[40]

---

[37]For a thoughtful discussion of the relationship between national identity and justice, see Andrew Ross Errington, "Between Justice and Tradition: Oliver O'Donovan's Political Theory and the Challenge of Multiculturalism," *SCE* 27, no. 4 (2014): 417-30.

[38]Jonathan Chaplin, "Beyond Multiculturalism—But to Where?: Public Justice and Cultural Diversity," *Philosophia Reformata* 73, no. 2 (2008): 190-209, at 195.

[39]On the perils of an identity that is not conformed to justice, see O. O'Donovan, "Deliberation, History and Reading," 130-34. In this context, it is worth noting the incoherence of arguments that recommend excluding vulnerable outsiders in order to preserve a nation's *Christian* identity. Such exclusion would be self-defeating since it would violate the biblical imperative to welcome the vulnerable as kin. The nation would thus be forsaking the very Christian identity that it seeks to preserve.

[40]Chaplin, "Beyond Multiculturalism," 196. And as we think of our national identities in this way, so too should we think of our nations themselves. As Newbigin writes, "With affirmation there has to be anathema. We have to reject ideologies which give to particular elements in God's ordering

Andrew Errington puts it plainly: "Although tradition cannot be lightly brushed aside, it can and should be displaced for the sake of justice. . . . Every society must be open to change in the light of what is right."[41] Insofar as our national identities do not promote human flourishing and do not drive us to enfold the vulnerable as kin, we must work to reshape our identities by developing new narratives of who we are and what our collective purpose is.

Of course, the imperative to cultivate an identity marked by inclusivity no doubt generates genuine fears about impact of large-scale immigration on social order and social cohesion and the practicalities of managing these impacts. It also brings with it the potential for real grief that can attend cultural change and the loss of what is familiar and comfortable, even as joy is found in new traditions and new kinship relations. We will address such fears and griefs in chapter eight. For now, we merely emphasize that the cultivation of such a culture of inclusivity seems to be God's vision for humanity in community.[42]

Recall from chapters two and three that God envisioned that the very identity of Israel was to live a life that was inclusive of the vulnerable outsider. Danny Carroll summarizes: "The arrival and presence of sojourners were *not a threat to Israel's national identity*; rather, their presence was *fundamental to its very meaning*."[43] Israel invited the stranger to participate in the very heart of its life—its religion—though participation was not compulsory. It welcomed the stranger's participation in the weekly Sabbath, in the annual feasts, and even in the covenant renewal ceremony (Deut 29:9-15). This was an inclusivity marked by joyful celebration—celebration of the opportunity to enfold the displaced as kin. How wonderful it would be if nations today were similarly marked by a desire to welcome needy strangers into the heart of communal life and to invite them into festive kinship! How beautiful it would it be if this identity as a welcoming people, rather than an identity grounded in ethnic homogeneity, economic power, or military might, provided the foundation for communal bonds and loyalties!

---

of things the central and absolute place which belongs to Christ alone. It is good to love and serve the nation in which God has set us; we need more, not less true patriotism. But to give absolute commitment to the nation is to go into bondage." Lesslie Newbigin, *Truth to Tell: The Gospel as Public Truth* (Grand Rapids, MI: Eerdmans, 1991), 80.

[41]Errington, "Between Justice and Tradition," 429.

[42]Dana Wilbanks expresses it well: Certainly, "we are culture-creating and culture-bearing peoples. We develop a sense of who we are by being related to particular communities, whose identity we come to share." And yet, "for Christians, the claims and interests of nations should always be evaluated by reference to the God whose love and justice is the center of astonishingly inclusive relatedness." Dana W. Wilbanks, *Re-Creating America: The Ethics of U.S. Immigration & Refugee Policy in a Christian Perspective* (Nashville: Abingdon, 1996), 120.

[43]Carroll R., *Christians at the Border*, 97.

Before moving on, it is worth noting how the understanding of national identity that we have presented maps onto the oft-rehearsed debate between cosmopolitanism, which emphasizes the moral significance of the global community of which all humans are members, and communitarianism, which instead prioritizes the significance of people's membership in localized (commonly national) communities.[44] Briefly put, the biblical model of human relations does not recommend an abstract and rootless cosmopolitanism that denies the value of local communal identities, affinities, and loyalties.[45] But neither does it endorse an inward-looking and exclusivist communitarianism that denies the imperative to care for vulnerable outsiders.[46] Rather, the biblical model might be fruitfully cast as a form of "rooted cosmopolitanism"—a cosmopolitan concern for vulnerable people everywhere that is deeply rooted in localized communities.[47] It affirms the value of communal traditions, sentiments, and practices that bind people together and are so important not only for individual well-being but also for motivating the care of the vulnerable. It also accounts for the fact that universal human dignity is typically best advanced through localized structures and institutions. But it insists that communities be outward looking, caring for outsiders as well as their own, marked by a desire to embrace and enfold as kin the stranger in need.

Crucially this requirement to enfold the stranger must be attended with a willingness to be transformed in some way by the stranger. This is something that theorists of rooted cosmopolitanism have not grappled with sufficiently. If national communities are to be welcoming, if their boundaries are to be

---

[44]For an example of a nuanced Christian defense of a cosmopolitanism approach to immigration, see Luke Bretherton, *Christianity and Contemporary Politics* (Oxford: Wiley-Blackwell, 2010), 126-74. For a thoughtful Christian defense of a communitarian approach, see Mark R. Amstutz, *Just Immigration: American Policy in Christian Perspective* (Grand Rapids, MI: Eerdmans, 2017).

[45]The phrase, "rootless cosmopolitanism," comes from Alasdair MacIntyre, *Whose Justice? Which Rationality?* (Notre Dame, IN: University of Notre Dame Press, 1988), 388. Mark Brett additionally warns: "Lessons drawn from colonial history should cause us to draw back from the cosmopolitan utopia that acknowledges no homelands to which particular groups are attached." Mark G. Brett, *Political Trauma and Healing: Biblical Ethics for a Postcolonial World* (Grand Rapids, MI: Eerdmans, 2016), 178.

[46]Barth put it bluntly: "Christian ethics cannot espouse an abstract internationalism and cosmopolitanism. On the other hand, it cannot espouse an abstract nationalism and particularism." Barth, *Doctrine of Creation*, 312-13.

[47]For discussion of the idea of rooted cosmopolitanism, see variously Kwame Anthony Appiah, *Cosmopolitanism: Ethics in a World of Strangers* (New York: Norton, 2006); Toni Erskine, *Embedded Cosmopolitanism: Duties to Strangers and Enemies in a World of "Dislocated Communities"* (Oxford: Oxford University Press, 2008); and Will Kymlicka and Kathryn Walker, eds., *Rooted Cosmopolitanism: Canada and the World* (Vancouver: University of British Columbia Press, 2013).

fluid, then they need to accept the likelihood and ideally celebrate the opportunity of mutual transformation. We consider what this might entail in
chapter eight. But first, let's continue in chapter seven to wrestle with some
more reasons commonly given for diluting the biblical ethic of kinship with
the displaced when applying this ethic to sovereign states today.

6

STRANGER-LOVING
SOVEREIGNS

In June 2018, US Attorney General Jeff Sessions invoked Romans 13 to defend the Trump administration's "zero tolerance" immigration policy, a policy that at the time included separating children from parents or guardians entering the country without documentation, placing these children in shelters or foster care, and prosecuting almost all the adults for illegal entry, including those claiming asylum. "I would cite you to the Apostle Paul and his clear and wise command in Romans 13 to obey the laws of the government because God has ordained the government for his purposes," Sessions declared. "Orderly and lawful processes are good in themselves. Consistent, fair application of law is in itself a good and moral thing and that protects the weak, it protects the lawful. Our policies that can result in short-term separation of families are not unusual or unjustified." Sessions explained to his "church friends" that he was "a law officer for a nation-state. A secular nation-state. . . . It's not a church. . . . My request to our religious leaders and friends who have criticized the carrying out of our laws: I ask them to speak up forcefully, strongly, to urge anyone who would come here to only come lawfully."[1]

Sessions's interpretation of Romans 13 was consistent with that put forward in a Capitol Ministries Bible study. Sessions had been a member and sponsor

---

[1]Tal Kopan, "Sessions Cites Bible to Defend Immigration Policies Resulting in Family Separations," *CNN*, June 15, 2018.

of this Bible study for several years. Vice President Mike Pence, Secretary of State Mike Pompeo, and several other members of President Donald Trump's cabinet have also been longtime members and sponsors.[2] In a study of "What the Bible Says About Our Illegal Immigration Problem," Capitol Ministries declares, "People who are illegals are a threat to the welfare of those who are citizens. . . . For a government to be pleasing to God and receive His blessing, it has no option but to protect its citizenry from illegal immigration per Romans 13:4 and 1 Peter 2:13-14. It must always protect its borders and punish those who enter illegally." The study goes further: "Also based upon Romans 13:4 is the inherent responsibility of a government to advance the country, meaning its leaders will want to enact immigration policies that only allow people into the country who can advance it, not detract from it."[3]

Theologians again and again offer similar interpretations of this passage. James Hoffmeier, whose spurious argument that Old Testament Israel was called to care only for *legal* immigrants we examined in chapter two, draws from Romans 13 that it is "the state's responsibility to enforce its laws and provide for its citizens," and "each country has the right to control who enters it borders and who is denied."[4] Even theologians appealing for more compassionate and generous government policies toward asylum seekers sometimes take for granted that Paul's letter to the Romans instructs governments to strictly control immigration, with one concluding, "our elected officials have a responsibility, according to Romans 13, to keep us safe and to set reasonable limits."[5]

Romans 13 says no such thing. The verses to which these theologians and politicians usually refer say:

> Let every person be subject to the governing authorities; for there is no authority except from God, and those authorities that exist have been instituted by God. . . . For [the authority] is God's servant for your good. But if you do what is wrong, you should be afraid, for the authority does not bear the sword in vain! It is the servant of God to execute wrath on the wrongdoer. (Rom 13:1, 4)

---

[2]Ralph Drollinger, "What the Bible Says About Our Illegal Immigration Problem," *Members Bible Study, U.S. Capitol,* Capitol Ministries, September 26, 2016, http://capmin.org/wp-content/uploads/2016/09/Illegal-Immigration-9.26.16.pdf; and Owen Amos, "Inside the White House Bible Study Group," *BBC News,* April 8, 2018.

[3]Drollinger, "What the Bible Says," 9, 10.

[4]James K. Hoffmeier, *The Immigration Crisis: Immigrants, Aliens, and the Bible* (Wheaton, IL: Crossway, 2009), 142, 144.

[5]Daniel Darling, "Christians Should See in the Migrant Caravan the Bible's Call to Honor the Dignity of All Humanity," *Washington Post,* November 2, 2018.

The passage says nothing about a responsibility—or even a right—of governments to limit immigration. Likewise, it says nothing suggesting a responsibility or right of governments to prioritize the well-being of its people over the well-being of foreigners or to pursue only policies that advance the national interest. Perhaps there are biblical grounds for drawing such conclusions—we have and will continue to explore the possibilities and limits of such grounds throughout this book—but they are not to be found in Romans 13.

But what about Sessions's suggestion that Romans 13 requires that people submit themselves to governing authorities? This is different from the claim that Romans 13 instructs governments to protect their borders, but it is one worth addressing since it is brought up so often in debates about the entry of asylum seekers and other migrants lacking documentation. Is the command to submit to governing authorities to be interpreted as absolute, without exception? New Testament scholar James Dunn suggests, "Here we must recall that [Paul's] advocacy of political quietism is in the context of the political powerlessness of most members of the ancient state."[6] In our contemporary context of modern democracies, we must submit to the authorities in the normal run of things, and yet it is also possible and even responsible to challenge the unjust laws of governments. This idea is suggested by what precedes the passage in question. Romans 12 requires the church in Rome to reorient itself to the will of God that is revealed in Jesus Christ: "Do not be conformed to this world, but be transformed by the renewal of your mind, that by testing you may discern what is the will of God, what is good and acceptable and perfect" (Rom 12:2 ESV). According to Romans 12, to discern the will of God means weeping with those who weep (Rom 12:15), associating with the lowly (Rom 12:16), and feeding one's enemy (Rom 12:20). These two points must not be missed: Christians are called to discern the will of God, including how God's will relates to governmental legislation, and *compassion* should be discernment's defining principle.

Jesus himself on occasion disobeyed the laws of the land, and this especially for the sake of those in need (Mt 12:1-14). Jesus didn't pose the same kind of threat to Roman rule as did the Zealots; he was not leading a rebellion. But, as Richard Cassidy states, he was no less dangerous: "Jesus pointed the way to a social order in which neither the Romans nor any other oppressing group would be able to hold sway."[7] A similar tension is found in the book of

---

[6]James D. G. Dunn, *Romans 9–16*, WBC 38B (Dallas: Word Books, 1988), 774.
[7]Richard J. Cassidy, *Jesus, Politics, and Society: A Study of Luke's Gospel* (Maryknoll, NY: Orbis, 1978), 79.

Acts. Peter and John refuse the Jewish authorities' demand to cease from speaking in the name in Jesus, declaring, "Whether it is right in God's sight to listen to you rather than to God, you must judge; for we cannot keep from speaking about what we have seen and heard" (Acts 4:19-20). In a similar scene in the next chapter, Peter insists, "We must obey God rather than any human authority" (Acts 5:29).[8] As Kavin Rowe puts it, in Acts there is a "complex negotiation between the reality of the state's idolatry and blindness—its satanic power—and the necessity that the mission of light not be misunderstood as sedition."[9]

When considering the biblical role of government, particularly in relation to immigration issues, Western readers often start and finish with Romans 13. Yet, what if we started with Revelation 13 and its portrayal of the empire as a hideous sea monster? This image presents Rome as "a system of tyranny and exploitation."[10] Indeed, in countries where Christ is persecuted, the biblical books most cherished are often the apocalypses—the books of Daniel and Revelation. Mark Brett captures this well: "How anomalous the surface meaning of Romans 13 is when considered against the wider background of the Bible's relentlessly reiterated critique of unjust monarchies and empires, including the Roman empire of Paul's own day."[11] We need to be careful lest, in insisting that undocumented asylum seekers and other migrants obey federal law, we and our nations disobey God's higher law: the call to extend kinship protection to vulnerable people seeking a home.

Not all laws are just. Consider Pharaoh's instruction to Hebrew midwives to murder newborn boys (Ex 1:15-21). David Daube states that the midwives' response is the first example of civil disobedience in recorded history.[12] Consider similarly Nebuchadnezzar's decree that people bow before his image—which some rightly refused (Dan 3).[13] Christians over the centuries have repeatedly insisted that Romans 13 should not be understood as ruling out the

---

[8]See further Richard B. Hays, *The Moral Vision of the New Testament: Community, Cross, New Creation; A Contemporary Introduction to New Testament Ethics* (New York: HarperCollins, 1996), 127-28.

[9]C. Kavin Rowe, *World Upside Down: Reading Acts in the Graeco-Roman Age* (Oxford: Oxford University Press, 2009), 88.

[10]Richard Bauckham, *The Theology of the Book of Revelation* (Cambridge: Cambridge University Press, 1993), 36.

[11]Mark G. Brett, *Political Trauma and Healing: Biblical Ethics for a Postcolonial World* (Grand Rapids, MI: Eerdmans, 2016), 164.

[12]David Daube, *Civil Disobedience in Antiquity* (Edinburgh: Edinburgh University Press, 1972), 5, 7.

[13]See also Matthew Soerens and Jenny Yang, *Welcoming the Stranger: Justice, Compassion & Truth in the Immigration Debate*, rev. ed. (Downers Grove, IL: InterVarsity Press, 2018), 95.

possibility of challenging unjust laws and even disobeying them in certain circumstances. Think of the civil disobedience activities of the civil rights movement in America. Think of missionaries preaching in countries where it is illegal to do so. Indeed, think of the esteem in which—rightly or wrongly— many Americans hold their *revolutionary* founding fathers!

The right to seek asylum is inscribed in international law in the 1951 Refugee Convention and universalized in the 1967 Protocol. At the very least, this should give us pause before accepting the justice of domestic laws allowing the punishment of asylum seekers who cross borders without documentation and the forced separation of children from their parents or guardians—and even more so since these US laws have been accompanied in recent years by a series of increasingly troubling policies aimed at limiting the *legal* avenues for applying for asylum at the US-Mexico border (see chap. 10). Christians have a responsibility to discern the will of God (Rom 12:2) with regard to refugee and immigration legislation and to advocate for compassionate reform where necessary.[14] In some circumstances, Christians may need to defend the rights of those in desperate circumstances who cross borders without a visa. They may need even to break the law themselves to defend the rights of vulnerable people.

Romans 13 provides no justification, in and of itself, for governments to limit the entry of vulnerable outsiders. But might there be other legitimate sources of justification? In this chapter we first examine oft-heard appeals to the principle of state sovereignty to justify the exclusion of outsiders. Like appeals to Romans 13, appeals to sovereignty make the mistake of looking at the way things are—existing laws, in the case of Romans 13, and prevailing understandings of political concepts, in the case of sovereignty—and concluding this is the way things ought to be. After challenging certain habits of thinking about sovereignty, we turn to some more sophisticated arguments that are offered for circumscribing how the biblical call to sacrificial and joyful kinship with the displaced should be applied to states. We will discover that the process of wrestling with these arguments actually amplifies our commitment to the biblical call since we are forced to acknowledge how we in the West are implicated deeply in the past and present vulnerabilities of many displaced peoples. The practice of enfolding the displaced as kin can thus be understood no less as an act of repentance and reparation than it is a joyful opportunity for new relationship and mutual enrichment.

---

[14]See further M. Daniel Carroll R. (Rodas), *Christians at the Border: Immigration, the Church, and the Bible*, 2nd ed. (Grand Rapids, MI: Brazos Press, 2013), 124.

SOVEREIGN STATEHOOD

Political authorities often claim that states, by virtue of their sovereignty, have an absolute right to decide for themselves both who enters their territory and the conditions by which they may enter.[15] In the same month that Sessions delivered his speech, for example, US Ambassador to the United Nations Nikki Haley responded to the United Nations' criticism of the Trump administration's practice of separating children from families with a typical appeal to sovereign prerogative: "We will remain a generous country, but we are also a sovereign country, with laws that decide how to best control our borders and protect our people. Neither the United Nations nor anyone else will dictate how the United States upholds its borders."[16] Christian scholars and commentators are also heard putting forward this argument from time to time. In a recent book offering a Christian perspective on American immigration policy, for example, Mark Amstutz puts it plainly: "The sovereign authority of government is the primary basis for making and applying immigration policies, not the virtues of love and compassion that sustain the church."[17]

Such a claim might be an accurate rendering of how things are, but it is hardly an argument for how things ought to be. In Amstutz's defense, he does offer an argument in defense of regulating immigration that is grounded in considerations of justice, an argument that we will consider later in the chapter. However, throughout his book he leans heavily on the claim that, since the sovereign state is the fundamental unit of the international system, it should not be restricted in how it chooses to regulate immigration, even though "some states may inhibit migration altogether."[18] This echoes a certain habit of thinking about sovereignty that has come to be widely adopted over time. It is a habit that must be challenged.

For starters, we need to be careful not to take sovereign statehood to be the natural and inevitable model of political community. After all, it is historically quite novel. The idea of sovereignty—the idea that a political community should enjoy independence from external authorities and that the supreme authority within the community should have no internal rivals in making law or commanding allegiance—was constructed at a particular time

---

[15]This section draws on Luke Glanville, "Hypocritical Inhospitality: The Global Refugee Crisis in the Light of History," *Ethics & International Affairs* 33, no. 4 (2020): 3-12. Used with permission.

[16]US Mission to the UN, "Press Release: Ambassador Haley on the UN's Criticism of U.S. Immigration Policies," June 5, 2018.

[17]Mark R. Amstutz, *Just Immigration: American Policy in Christian Perspective* (Grand Rapids, MI: Eerdmans, 2017), 223.

[18]Amstutz, *Just Immigration*, 100.

and place, early modern Europe, gradually displacing the diverse and interwoven systems of social organization and political authority that had characterized the medieval period. For a long time, moreover, sovereign statehood was held to be a privilege enjoyed only by Europeans and those peoples beyond Europe that Europeans deigned to acknowledge as civilized members of the "family of nations." Indeed it was not until the second half of the twentieth century—only a generation or two ago—that Europe's widespread empires were finally dismantled, self-government was granted to formerly colonized peoples, and the institution of the territorially bounded sovereign state was finally spread across the globe. The distribution of humanity among 190 or so sovereign states is a recent phenomenon.[19]

More crucially, the meaning and implications of sovereignty have changed and continue to change over time. In the language of social scientists, sovereignty is a "social construct." We need to be careful, therefore, not to persuade ourselves that the particular constructions of the rights and responsibilities of sovereignty that happen to be widely accepted today are necessary, timeless, and immutable principles inherent to the concept. And we certainly should not accept them uncritically as just. After all, up until the nineteenth century, states accepted each other's sovereign right to participate in and benefit from the traffic of slaves, and until the twentieth century they maintained a sovereign right to wage war at their own choosing.[20] We therefore ought not to take for granted that the assumptions about the rights and responsibilities of sovereignty shared by states today regarding the treatment of refugees are either necessary or just.

This is particularly so given that a glance at history makes clear that rights and responsibilities pertaining to questions of asylum and hospitality have typically been constructed and reconstructed in ways that reflect the changing interests of powerful states. Consider this tragic irony: It is well known, even if often downplayed, that the wealth of many European powers was augmented and the territories of their settler colonies beyond Europe were acquired historically by means of the violent conquest, subjection, enslavement, displacement, and sometimes eradication of indigenous peoples. Less well known is a key justification for these practices proffered by European

---

[19]Daniel Philpott, *Revolutions in Sovereignty: How Ideas Shaped Modern International Relations* (Princeton, NJ: Princeton University Press, 2001); and Christian Reus-Smit, *Individual Rights and the Making of the International System* (Cambridge: Cambridge University Press, 2013).

[20]Luke Glanville, *Sovereignty and the Responsibility to Protect: A New History* (Chicago: University of Chicago Press, 2014); and Oona A. Hathaway and Scott J. Shapiro, *The Internationalists: How a Radical Plan to Outlaw War Remade the World* (New York: Penguin, 2017).

imperial powers, at least for a time: that the indigenous peoples violated a supposedly natural and enforceable duty of hospitality.

Contemplating the justice of the Spanish conquests in the New World in the sixteenth century, Spanish theologian Francisco de Vitoria asserted that the Spaniards would have had just cause for war if they had been unjustifiably denied the right to travel and dwell in the Native Americans' lands. "The Spaniards are the barbarians' neighbors, as shown by the parable of the Samaritan," he claimed, "and the barbarians are obliged to love their neighbors as themselves, and may not lawfully bar them from their homeland without due cause." The French could not lawfully prohibit Spaniards from living in France so long as they did no harm, he claimed, and so neither could the Native Americans bar them from the New World. He invoked Jesus' narrative of the sheep and goats: "'I was a stranger and you did not invite me in' (Mt 25:43), from which it is clear that, since it is a law of nature to welcome strangers, this judgment of Christ is to be decreed amongst all men."[21]

It should be noted that Vitoria doubted whether the Native Americans had in fact breached their duty of hospitality to the Spaniards, particularly since the Spaniards were strongly armed and gave the indigenous people good reasons to fear their intentions. Indeed, he worried that the Spaniards really had no other cause for war than "sheer robbery."[22] But his argument was enthusiastically taken up by European powers and their advocates to justify imperial expansion over subsequent decades. The Dutchman Hugo Grotius wrote of the "sacrosanct law of hospitality" and cited not only Vitoria but also Augustine's endorsement of Israel's war against the Amorites, a war said to be waged with justice since the Amorites had denied Israel the right of passage.[23] An anonymous tract commissioned by the Virginia Company even portrayed the colonizer as a peaceful seeker of sanctuary: "Is it not against the law of nations, to violate a peaceable stranger, or to deny him harbor?"[24]

This argument for an enforceable duty of hospitality was one item in an evolving grab bag of justifications utilized by colonial powers to justify the

---

[21]Francisco de Vitoria, "On the American Indians," in *Political Writings*, ed. Anthony Pagden and Jeremy Lawrance (Cambridge: Cambridge University Press, 1991), 231-92, at 278-79.

[22]Vitoria, "Letter to Miguel de Arcos, OP Salamanca, 8 November [1534]," in *Political Writings*, 332. See also Vitoria, "On the American Indians," 282.

[23]Hugo Grotius, *Commentary on the Law of Prize and Booty*, ed. Martine Julia van Ittersum (Indianapolis: Liberty Fund, 2006), 304-5, citing Augustine, *Questions on the Heptateuch* 4.44; Numbers 21:21-25.

[24]*A True Declaration of the Estate of Virginia* (1610), quoted in Andrew Fitzmaurice, "Sovereign Trusteeship and Empire," *Theoretical Inquiries in Law* 16, no. 2 (2015): 447-71, at 453.

mass killing of indigenous peoples, the extraction of wealth, the acquisition of territory, the mass migration of tens of millions of Europeans out of Europe, and the establishment of new sovereign authorities.[25] Put bluntly, not only are the wealth and territory enjoyed by many Western states today—both former centers of empire and former settler colonies—at least partially products of the violent subjection of indigenous peoples, which is appalling enough, but this violence was at times justified with appeals to a duty of hospitality that these same states now refuse to so many who desperately need it.

The powerful once demanded hospitality from the weak. They now deny it to them. We should be wary, therefore, of allowing the biblical imperative to welcome the stranger as kin to be trumped by mere appeals to sovereign prerogative.

PREFERENTIAL LOVE FOR ONE'S OWN PEOPLE?

Some readers may be thinking that, even if the mere desire to preserve national identity or mere recourse to Romans 13 or the principle of state sovereignty does not provide grounds for excluding vulnerable and displaced strangers, surely states are justified in strictly limiting the admission of outsiders on the plain grounds that governments are charged with caring for the safety and well-being of their own people. Sure, the sociological concerns underpinning arguments for national identity need to be made subject to the demands of justice. And, sure, appeals to Romans 13 and prevailing understandings of sovereignty are inadequate justifications for restricting the welcome of displaced people. But perhaps political communities have legitimate reasons for prioritizing the interests of their members and, in turn, carefully controlling and strictly limiting the admission of displaced outsiders.

This is an argument made by some Christian theorists. Amstutz makes the case particularly clearly. "Sovereign governments are responsible for maintaining social order, protecting human rights, and promoting prosperity," he claims.[26] This role is especially apparent to Christians "because they are aware of how greed, selfishness, and avarice can undermine the common good." In a world without sin, there would be nothing stopping "the pursuit of a just world order and equitable migration practices. . . . But because greed and selfishness predominate in communal life, sovereign governments must seek

---

[25] Achiume reports, "The European colonial project involved the out-migration of at least 62 million Europeans to colonies across the world between the nineteenth and the first half of the twentieth century alone." E. Tendayi Achiume, "Migration as Decolonization," *Stanford Law Review* 71, no. 6 (2019): 1509-74, at 1509.

[26] Amstutz, *Just Immigration*, 2.

to rectify offenses and advance proximate justice through the maintenance of order and the rule of law." Governments, therefore, must give "the interests of their citizens precedence over those of strangers. This does not mean that human beings are morally unequal or that states can disregard the wants and needs of noncitizens. Rather, a moral approach to migration must advance the interests of citizens while taking into account the wants and needs of others."[27] Amstutz repeatedly insists that, while people have a right to leave their communities, they do not have an inherent right to join other communities.[28] Rather, decisions on membership are the prerogative of the governing authorities of each community. While governments should take into account the needs of the stateless, they are fundamentally charged with caring for their own. Peter Meilaender puts it even more bluntly: "Immigration regulations are a way of embodying in policy a preferential love for our own fellow citizens and the way of life that we share."[29]

This idea that governments are responsible for the care of their own people was central to early modern justifications for sovereign statehood. Thomas Hobbes theorized how individuals escape the misery and brutality of the state of nature and secure their own peace and protection by covenanting with each other to transfer their rights to a sovereign authority. In turn, he claimed, the purpose for which a monarch or governing assembly is entrusted with sovereign power is "the procuration of *the safety of the people*."[30] John Locke theorized how people escape the violence and insecurity of the state of nature by binding themselves in "one Body Politick under one Supreme Government." The people establish for themselves "a Judge on Earth, with Authority to determine all the Controversies, and redress the Injuries, that may happen to any Member of the Commonwealth."[31] This government, the people's representatives, was therefore charged with securing the natural right of citizens to "Life, Health, Liberty, Happiness."[32] This argument had clear influence on the American founding fathers.

---

[27] Amstutz, *Just Immigration*, 102.

[28] Amstutz, *Just Immigration*, 99.

[29] Peter C. Meilaender, "Immigration: Citizens and Strangers," *First Things*, May 2007. An alternative argument that we will not explore here is one of democratic association. It holds that questions regarding the control of borders should be democratically decided by the citizens of each state. For a compelling response to this argument, which explains that, insofar as it is correct, potential immigrants ought also to have a democratic say in such matters since they too are affected by the decision, see Arash Abizadeh, "Democratic Theory and Border Coercion: No Right to Unilaterally Control Your Own Borders," *Political Theory* 36, no. 1 (2008): 37-65.

[30] Thomas Hobbes, *Leviathan*, ed. J. C. A. Gaskin (Oxford: Oxford University Press, 1996), 2.30.1.

[31] John Locke, *Two Treatises of Government*, edited by Peter Laslett (London: Mentor, 1960), 2.89.

[32] Locke, *Two Treatises of Government*, 2.6.

Neither Hobbes nor Locke concluded that their theories of sovereignty required the establishment of strictly controlled territorial boundaries. Indeed, they both accepted the permissibility of people migrating and settling in the lands of "countries not sufficiently inhabited" or in tracts of land that, while possessed by others, "lie waste"—arguments that would, of course, be put to use by European colonialists.[33] But it is easy to see how, over time, people came to deduce that the responsibility of governments for securing the safety and well-being of citizens must outweigh and override consideration of the needs of outsiders. And even if this didn't justify the closure or the tight regulation of borders in the early modern period, some might conclude that such an exclusionary approach is necessary in today's overpopulated and dangerous world.[34]

A writer for a Christian foreign policy journal puts it thus:

> We should distinguish between government policy and the obligations of the church. . . . The state, at least in the West, exists for the benefit and safety of its citizens. . . . Yes, the church should be on the frontlines taking care of refugees and displaced peoples, but it's not clear the American government faces a similar obligation to admit refugees because the American government is not a charity organization or the church and we should be glad that it is not.[35]

Now, there is much to be commended about the idea that governments are responsible for the care of their people. The care of fellow members of a community is a true and valuable implication of kinship at the level of the family, the city, and the "body politic." States should provide for the common good of citizens. Governments should pursue order and justice for the people. Scripture repeatedly commands authorities to extend relief and protection to the poor, the marginalized, the widow, and the orphan within a community. But we cannot forget that the biblical model of community is also relentlessly outward looking.[36]

Vattel on duties to citizens and strangers. The thoughts of another early theorist of sovereignty, Emer de Vattel, whose 1758 treatise on international

---

[33]Hobbes, *Leviathan*, 2.30.19; and Locke, *Two Treatises of Government*, 2.45.

[34]For a related history of the development of the concept "illegal alien," see Robert W. Heimburger, *God and the Illegal Alien: United States Immigration Law and a Theology of Politics* (Cambridge: Cambridge University Press, 2018), 25-44, 65-94, 149-78.

[35]Daniel Strand, "Throwing Caution to the Wind: Charity and the Dilemma of America's Syrian Immigration Policy," *Providence*, November 25, 2015.

[36]As Danny Carroll puts it, "Concern for the sojourners was part of an expansive ethical vision for the needy that included widows, orphans, and the poor. In the biblical view, one cannot isolate vulnerable groups that one does not want to engage from the comprehensive biblical call to incarnate God's presence and care for all in need." Carroll R., *Christians at the Border*, 97.

law was regarded as authoritative by the American founding fathers and for
several decades afterwards, are valuable here.[37] Vattel argued that, while individuals are free to unite with each other to form their own states for their
own benefit, they cannot thereby excuse themselves from their duties to all
of humankind. Rather, having united in community, "it thenceforth belongs
to that body, that state, and its rulers, to fulfil the duties of humanity towards
strangers."[38] While a state should certainly pay attention to the safety and
interests of its citizens, it should nevertheless be willing to bear some cost and
inconvenience for the sake of the vulnerable beyond its borders, Vattel
claimed. A state is under no obligation to contribute to the welfare of outsiders if this would require doing "an essential injury to herself."[39] But it
ought not to refuse to aid others out of fear of "a slight loss, or any little inconvenience: humanity forbids this; and the mutual love which men owe to
each other, requires greater sacrifices."[40]

Vattel applied this reasoning directly to the question of strangers who are
driven from their own country and seek asylum in another. If a state judges
that admission of a particular group of strangers "would be attended with too
great an inconvenience or danger," he said, it has "a right to refuse." But in
general, "every state ought, doubtless, to grant to so unfortunate a people every
aid and assistance which she can bestow without being wanting to herself."[41]

Vattel's account of responsibilities to strangers would today be described as a
"sufficientist" approach to global justice.[42] It accepts that political communities
have special responsibilities for the care of their members, for *instrumental*

---

[37]Vincent Chetail, "Vattel and the American Dream: An Inquiry into the Reception of the Law of
Nations in the United States," in *The Roots of International Law / Les fondements du droit international*, ed. Pierre-Marie Dupuy and Vincent Chetail (Leiden: Brill, 2013), 249-300.

[38]Emer de Vattel, *The Law of Nations*, ed. Béla Kapossy and Richard Whatmore (Indianapolis:
Liberty Fund, 2008), Preliminaries §11.

[39]Vattel, *Law of Nations*, Preliminaries §14.

[40]Vattel, *Law of Nations*, II.10.131. Vattel elaborated on this idea of sacrifice in a later passage:
A nation is under many obligations of duty towards herself, towards other nations, and
towards the great society of mankind. We know that the duties we owe to ourselves are,
generally speaking, paramount to those we owe to others; but this is to be understood only
of such duties as bear some proportion to each other. We cannot refuse, in some degree, to
forget ourselves with respect to interests that are not essential, and to make some sacrifices,
in order to assist other persons. (Vattel, *Law of Nations*, II.18.332)

[41]Vattel, *Law of Nations*, II.10.136. For further discussion, see Luke Glanville, "Responsibility to
Perfect: Vattel's Conception of Duties Beyond Borders," *ISQ* 61, no. 2 (2017): 385-95.

[42]For a classic defense of the sufficientist conception of global justice, see Henry Shue, *Basic Rights:
Subsistence, Affluence, and U.S. Foreign Policy*, 2nd ed. (Princeton, NJ: Princeton University Press,
1996). For a powerful recent argument that pushes further and insists on the need for global
equality, see Samuel Moyn, *Not Enough: Human Rights in an Unequal World* (Cambridge, MA:
Harvard University Press, 2018).

reasons of effectiveness and for *psychological* reasons of communal attachment. But it urges that, if there are strangers beyond borders who lack basic needs—who stand in need of community and of the security and subsistence that it can provide—a state should provide it insofar as it is able without being left "wanting to herself" and unable to provide for its own needs.[43]

This is a more demanding account of responsibilities than Western states tend to accept, to be sure. But when we look around the world, we find that it is actually the lived experience of many countries: 85 percent of refugees live in developing regions of the world. Twenty-seven percent are hosted by the world's least developed countries, countries like Uganda, Sudan, Ethiopia, and Bangladesh.[44] If these relatively poor countries can find a way to extend welcome to their neighbors in need, how can we in the West justifiably refuse to sacrifice more for the sake of the vulnerable? Yes, it is good for Western countries to promote the well-being and interests of their citizens. But as Pope John XXIII declared, the common good of the state "cannot be divorced from the common good of the entire human family."[45] And as Catholic theologian David Hollenbach adds, "The needs of the poor take priority over the wants of the rich. . . . The participation of marginalized groups takes priority over the preservation of an order which excludes them."[46]

The Meilaenders on prioritizing those with whom our lot has been cast. Christian ethicists Gilbert Meilaender and Peter Meilaender appeal to Paul's speech at the Areopagus to suggest the possibility of a providential, rather than instrumental, justification for the preferential love of one's own people: we should prioritize the care of those with whom our lot has been cast.[47] Paul

---

[43]See similarly, and more recently, Arash Abizadeh, "The Special-Obligations Challenge to More Open Borders," in *Migration in Political Theory: The Ethics of Movement and Membership*, ed. Sarah Fine and Lea Ypi (Oxford: Oxford University Press, 2016), 105-24.

[44]United Nations High Commissioner for Refugees (UNHCR), *Global Trends: Forced Displacement in 2019*, June 18, 2020, 2, 22, www.unhcr.org/en-au/statistics/unhcrstats/5ee200e37/unhcr-global-trends-2019.html.

[45]Pope John XXIII, *Pacem in Terris*, Librcria Editrice Vaticana, April 11, 1963. On the relationship between the national and the global common good, see David Hollenbach, "The Global Common Good," in *The Common Good and Christian Ethics* (Cambridge: Cambridge University Press, 2002), chap. 8.

[46]David Hollenbach, *Claims in Conflict: Retrieving and Renewing the Catholic Human Rights Tradition* (New York: Paulist Press, 1979), 204. Another Catholic theologian makes a similar point: "Even if borders of nation states have some proximate value in constructing identity, protecting values, securing rights, and administering resources, from a Christian perspective, sovereign rights are subject to a larger vision of human rights, the common good, the kingdom of God, and the gratuity of God." Daniel G. Groody, "Crossing the Divide: Foundations of a Theology of Migration and Refugees," *Theological Studies* 70, no. 3 (2009): 638-67, at 666.

[47]Peter C. Meilaender, "Loving Our Neighbors, Both Far and Near," in *Immigration* (Waco, TX: Center for Christian Ethics at Baylor University, 2008), 11-18; and Gilbert Meilaender and Peter C.

declared to the Athenians that God "made all nations to inhabit the whole earth, and he allotted the times of their existence and the boundaries of the places where they would live, so that they would search for God and perhaps grope for him and find him" (Acts 17:26-27). While their argument is nuanced, the Meilaenders ultimately suggest that this passage provides a warrant for giving special care to those with whom, by God's providence, we have been allotted. Peter Meilaender puts in bluntly:

> Because we share in a common life, involving a range of shared institutions and practices, we develop obligations towards one another that we do not have, or not to the same degree, towards outsiders—not because we do not love those outsiders, or because we think that our fellow citizens are somehow better than folks elsewhere, but simply because these are the people with whom our lot has been cast.[48]

But this argument will not do—or at least in light of the biblical ethic of kinship, it does not justify refusing to welcome displaced people. While we may find ourselves in political community with others by God's providence, might not our encounters with the forcibly displaced and our opportunity to welcome them as kin also be the result of providence?[49] To maintain otherwise, we suggest, is simply to sanctify unjust privilege. As philosopher Joseph Carens put it in a famous article, "Citizenship in Western liberal democracies is the modern equivalent of feudal privilege—an inherited status that greatly enhances one's life chances. Like feudal birthright privileges, restrictive citizenship is hard to justify when one thinks about it closely."[50] To confine the dispossessed, the oppressed, and the forcibly displaced to a particular station in life and to refuse them admission into our territory because that is their lot and this is ours is surely the opposite of Scripture's vision of community. When we consider also the unjust violence that has marked the acquisition of territory and the accrual of wealth and power by so many Western states, the idea that we may now seek to preserve our "lot," prioritizing the advantages of fellow citizens over the needs of strangers, begins to look absurd.

Meilaender, "Fences and Neighbors: A Theological Analysis of Immigration and Borders," *First Things*, August 2018.

[48]P. Meilaender, "Loving Our Neighbors," 14.

[49]See similarly Justin Ashworth, "Who Are Our People?: Toward a Christian Witness Against Borders," *Modern Theology* 34, no. 4 (2018): 495-518, at 501.

[50]Joseph H. Carens, "Aliens and Citizens: The Case for Open Borders," *Review of Politics* 49, no. 2 (1987): 251-73, at 252. See also, more recently, idem, *The Ethics of Immigration* (Oxford: Oxford University Press, 2013).

An Analogy with Private Property

We might fruitfully think of the territorially bounded sovereign state as Christians have historically thought of private property.[a] Most of the church fathers accepted that it was legitimate for people to own property, but they emphasized that it should be understood as a gift from God to be used for the benefit of others. In a sermon delivered in the mid-fourth century, for example, Basil of Caesarea instructed his listeners to be mindful of what things had been placed in their charge and from whom they had received them: "Do not imagine that all these fruits were prepared for your stomach. Regard what you hold within your own hands as though it belonged to others."[b] Basil chastised those who kept their possessions for themselves and failed to do justice: "Are you not a grasper of everything; are you not a robber? You who treat as absolutely yours what you received that you might dispense to others? . . . Whomsoever you could have helped and did not, to so many have you been unjust."[c]

Twelfth- and thirteenth-century medieval canonists sought to clarify the responsibilities that attended property ownership. If no one else is in need, they suggested, individuals are free to accrue and retain substantial wealth. However, in times of necessity, the superfluous wealth of individuals should be considered common property and shared with those in need.[d] Medieval theologian Thomas Aquinas said the same. Superfluous possessions should be given to succor the poor, he declared. Echoing some of the canonists, he even claimed that individuals in extreme need committed no sin in taking from the property of another, "for need has made it common." In cases of manifest and urgent need, he declared, "It is lawful for a man to succor his own need by means of another's property, by taking it either openly or secretly." To do so was not theft or robbery "because that which he takes for the support of his life becomes his own property by reason of that need."[e]

Perhaps we might think of the boundaries of sovereign states and the membership of political communities the same way. Esther Reed helpfully suggests that territorial borders might be considered "a relative, not absolute, right permitted within divine providence for the sake of humanity's need, potentially a way of ensuring a peaceable world and of managing the goods of the earth, . . . not recognized theologically for their own sake but for the social benefits they can bring."[f] Amidst the global crisis of displacement that we face today, communities might acknowledge that they possess their

territory, wealth, and security as a gift from God and that they
should share these material and social possessions with others insofar as they are able. They might also recognize that those in desperate need who, in a sense, take from the community's possessions by
entering their territory in search of asylum are merely taking what is
in a sense theirs, "by reason of that need."

ᵃFor a similar suggestion, see Esther D. Reed, "Refugee Rights and State Sovereignty: Theological Perspectives on the Ethics of Territorial Borders," *Journal of
the Society of Christian Ethics* 30, no. 2 (2010): 59-78, at 67.
ᵇBasil of Caesarea, "I Will Pull Down My Barns," in *The Sunday Sermons of the Great
Fathers*, trans. and ed. M. F. Toal (London: Longmans, Green, 1959), 3:327-28.
ᶜBasil of Caesarea, "I Will Pull Down My Barns," 3:331-32.
ᵈBrian Tierney, *Medieval Poor Law: A Sketch of Canonical Theory and Its Application in England* (Berkeley: University of California Press, 1959), 34-35.
ᵉThomas Aquinas, *Summa Theologica*, trans. Fathers of the English Dominican Province (repr., Westminster, MD: Christian Classics, 1981), 2-2.66.7.
ᶠReed, "Refugee Rights and State Sovereignty," 67.

LOVING OUR DISTANT NEIGHBORS

Scripture commends the care of vulnerable people with whom individuals
and communities come in contact. The good Samaritan loves the beaten man
that he happens upon. Israel is called to love the stranger that lives among
them. But, while we find nations being condemned for violent acts of injustice beyond their territories (Amos 1:3–2:5), we do not find them being
called to go in search of distant vulnerable people to whom they may offer
care and kinship. Are our responsibilities to refugees limited by considerations of proximity? Are nations called to welcome only the stranger in their
midst, the asylum seeker at their border?

There is a rich tradition of Christian theorizing that might be read as
pointing in this direction. Augustine wrote of the need to "order" one's love.
"All people should be loved equally," he declared. "But you cannot do good
to all people equally, so you should take particular thought for those who,
as if by lot, happen to be particularly close to you in terms of place, time, or
any other circumstances."[51] Aquinas drew from Augustine's reference to
"place" that "one is not bound to search throughout the world for the needy
that one may succor them; and it suffices to do works of mercy to those one
meets with."[52] We hear echoes of this kind of thinking today in the words of

[51] Augustine, *On Christian Teaching*, trans. R. P. H. Green (Oxford: Oxford University Press, 1997), I.28.
[52] Thomas Aquinas, *Summa Theologica*, trans. Fathers of the English Dominican Province (repr.,
Westminster, MD: Christian Classics, 1981), 2-2.71.1 a.1.

Christians who worry about the abstract nature of cosmopolitan arguments for the promotion of universal rights. Contemplating a caravan of people fleeing Central America in search of a new home in the United States in 2018, Rod Dreher asserts:

> The Bible tells Christians to love their neighbors as they love themselves. But who is their neighbor? The man next door? Yes. The people who live across town? Surely. Those who live in another part of their country? Okay. People from another country who want to settle in their country? Erm....
>
> If everybody is your neighbor, then nobody is.[53]

Oliver O'Donovan expresses the same point in more sophisticated terms, warning against "complacent forms of universalism . . . which may amount to not much more than universal indifference, for . . . to love everybody in the world equally is to love nobody very much." He takes from the parable of the good Samaritan a clear rebuke of "racial or class self-love" within any society, but he suggests that it also draws our attention to "an urgent form of contingent proximity." The priest, the Levite, and the Samaritan, after all, happened to be going down the road where the beaten man lay in need. It was this contingent proximity to the man that generated the obligation to help him. "Far from denying the significance of proximate relations, the parable discovers them where they are not looked for, nearer to us and under our very noses."[54]But considerations of proximity have less weight for us in a globalized world than they did in the times of Jesus or Aquinas. Today, we as individuals and certainly as communities are likely well aware of the suffering of many distant and vulnerable people and also capable of offering them much needed neighborly love. They may be geographically far from us, but they are nevertheless in an important sense "under our very noses." Certainly, we should be wary of the temptation to espouse an abstract love of humanity while neglecting to love those nearest to us. It would be concerning if we as individuals or communities were to occupy ourselves with championing the

---

[53]Rod Dreher, "How (Not) to Think About the Caravan," *American Conservative*, October 25, 2018.
[54]Oliver O'Donovan, "The Loss of a Sense of Place," in Oliver O'Donovan and Joan Lockwood O'Donovan, *Bonds of Imperfection: Christian Politics, Past and Present* (Grand Rapids, MI: Eerdmans, 2004), 296-320, at 316-17. For thoughtful deliberations on this theme of proximity, see Luke Bretherton, *Christianity and Contemporary Politics* (Oxford: Wiley-Blackwell, 2010), 146-48; idem, "The End of National Borders: Thinking Ethically in the Face of Mass Migration," *ABC Religion and Ethics*, May 20, 2015; Eric Gregory, "*Agape* and Special Relations in a Global Economy: Theological Sources," in *Global Neighbors: Christian Faith and Moral Obligation in Today's Economy*, ed. Douglas A. Hicks and Mark Valeri (Grand Rapids, MI: Eerdmans, 2008), 16-42; and Esther D. Reed, "Nation-States and Love of Neighbour: Impartiality and the *ordo amoris*," *SCE* 25, no. 3 (2012): 327-45.

plight of distant Rohingya people, displaced within or beyond Myanmar, while caring little for indigenous peoples dispossessed and dishonored among us, for example. But we cannot pretend that we do not know of the persecution and suffering of the Rohingya, or of Syrian or South Sudanese or Venezuelan civilians, internally displaced within their countries of origin or housed in refugee camps in neighboring countries or on the move in continued search for asylum. Many of us saw the heart-wrenching images of the drowned bodies of the three-year-old Syrian boy, Alan Kurdi, in 2015, and the Salvadoran migrants, Óscar Alberto Martinez and his twenty-three-month-old daughter Valeria, in 2019. And we all have an opportunity to offer welcome and kinship to some of the many millions who, like Alan, Óscar, and Valeria, so desperately need it.

On being the priest and the Levite. In his own treatment of the parable of the good Samaritan, legal philosopher Jeremy Waldron alerts us to the fact that the refusal of the priest and Levite to act as neighbor to the beaten man was not passive.

> Those who fail to help the man who fell among thieves are portrayed in the parable as *going out of their way* not to help, or *going out of their way* to avoid a decision about whether to help. . . . Their not helping is an intentional doing: a decision to cross the road, a choice to go out of their way to avoid the predicament.[55]

It is worth contemplating the many ways in which Western states do not merely passively disregard the plight of their distant neighbors but actually "*go out of their way*" to keep them at a distance and to avoid an encounter that may require them to provide protection and welcome. Consider, for example, how the European Union (EU) struck a multibillion-dollar deal with Turkey in 2016, according to which Turkey would accept the return of asylum seekers who reached Greece by sea, use its security forces to prevent others from getting to Greece, and improve conditions for refugees in Turkey. The deal was justified on the grounds that it would reduce deaths of those seeking passage across the Mediterranean but was actually accompanied by both an increase in deaths at sea (since asylum seekers now needed to take more dangerous routes to reach EU countries) and a deterioration of conditions for those who remained in Turkey.[56] The EU subsequently struck an even

---

[55]Jeremy Waldron, "Who Is My Neighbor?: Humanity and Proximity," *Monist* 86, no. 3 (2003): 333-54, at 343, cited and discussed in Gregory, "*Agape* and Special Relations in a Global Economy," 41.

[56]Katy Budge, "Refugees out of Sight, out of Mind Two Years on from EU-Turkey Deal," *Conversation*, March 19, 2018.

more problematic deal with Libya, funding, resourcing, and training the Libyan coast guard to intercept boats in the Mediterranean and return asylum seekers and other migrants to Libya, leaving them vulnerable to the well-documented possibility of arbitrary detention, torture, rape, enslavement, and murder.[57] European governments condemn and even seek to criminalize efforts by nongovernmental actors to rescue asylum seekers stranded at sea, insisting that they should defer to the Libyan coast guard, who will return them to Libya.

Australian authorities, meanwhile, run a multimillion-dollar advertising campaign aimed at dissuading refugees from seeking asylum by boat. They have sought to discourage Afghanis in particular from seeking asylum by distributing a graphic novel depicting people like them stuck in offshore detention centers and suffering from medical problems and depression.[58] Australia has also sought to keep vulnerable neighbors at a distance in a legal sense by excising the entirety of Australia's territory from its migration zone. This means that even if some asylum seekers manage to make it to the mainland, they can be legally removed to an "offshore" detention center in a third country such as Nauru or Papua New Guinea and made subject to the government's stated policy that none of them will ever be allowed into Australia.[59] Those that Australia holds in indefinite offshore detention suffer greatly. Médecins Sans Frontières (MSF) reports that the mental health suffering of asylum seekers on Nauru is "among the worst MSF has ever seen, including in projects providing care for victims of torture."[60]

On being the robbers. Consider further the many ways in which Western states act not merely as the priest and Levite but even as the robbers, not merely keeping vulnerable neighbors at a distance but also contributing to their vulnerability. We so often bear a measure of responsibility for the displacement of our distant neighbors. When defending his claim that governments are only responsible for those they represent (discussed in chap. 6), O'Donovan suggested that there are commonly injustices beyond one's

---

[57]United Nations Support Mission in Libya and Office of the High Commissioner for Human Rights, "Desperate and Dangerous: Report on the Human Rights Situation of Migrants and Refugees in Libya," December 20, 2018.

[58]Oliver Laughland, "Australian Government Targets Asylum Seekers with Graphic Campaign," *Guardian*, February 11, 2014.

[59]Karen Barlow, "Parliament Excises Mainland from Migration Zone," *ABC News*, May 16, 2013; and Gareth Hutchens, "Asylum Seekers Face Lifetime Ban from Entering Australia If They Arrive by Boat," *Guardian*, October 29, 2016.

[60]Médecins Sans Frontières, *Indefinite Despair: The Tragic Mental Health Consequences of Offshore Processing on Nauru*, December 2018, 4-5.

borders that cry out for redress but for which a government "could never responsibly take responsibility." He rhetorically asks, "Which of us, for example, was at fault in failing to put a stop to the Rwandan genocide?"[61] But it is actually quite easy to answer the question of who was at fault for failing to act in this example, and in many others like it.

Multiple bystander states were liable in one way or another for failing to halt the atrocities in Rwanda, which from April to July 1994 claimed the lives of eight hundred thousand people and displaced two million more. We can variously point to Belgium, who as the colonial power had accentuated and politicized the difference between Hutu and Tutsi people and sparked their antagonism for each other; to France, South Africa, Egypt, and China, who supplied a mountain of arms to the obviously troubled state in the lead-up to the genocide; or to the United States, the United Kingdom, and France, who impeded an effective international response once the atrocities began by intentionally misrepresenting the crisis and failing to share with other states their knowledge of its genocidal nature.[62] Each of these states surely bore special responsibilities to make amends by contributing to an international response to end the suffering and by offering relief and welcome to the displaced, in addition to the general responsibilities that they and all other states had to act by virtue of the imperative to love the Rwandans as themselves.

A similar story can be told of the responsibilities of bystander states regarding the Syrian refugee crisis today. Numerous states are culpable in one way or another for enabling the outbreak, prolonging the duration, and increasing the severity of the civil war that has raged in Syria since 2011, claiming the lives of at least 450,000 people and displacing thirteen million more. Consider the impact of the disastrous decision of the United States–led Coalition of the Willing to invade Iraq in 2003, for example. The Iraq war not only amplified sectarian tensions in the region but also led to an influx of one million Iraqis into Syria, straining resources and infrastructure and increasing social tensions in the country. These developments contributed to the outbreak of the Syrian civil war.[63] Consider the culpability of Russia and China,

---

[61]Oliver O'Donovan, "Deliberation, History and Reading: A Response to Schweiker and Wolterstorff," *SJT* 54, no. 1 (2001): 127-44, at 130-31.

[62]See Linda Melvern, *A People Betrayed: The Role of the West in Rwanda's Genocide*, 2nd ed. (London: Zed Books, 2009); and idem, *Conspiracy to Murder: The Rwandan Genocide*, 2nd ed.(New York: Penguin, 2006).

[63]Alise Coen, "Capable and Culpable?: The United States, RtoP, and Refugee Responsibility-Sharing," *EIA* 31, no. 1 (2017): 71-92, at 79-82.

who, once the war began, repeatedly exercised their veto power in the UN Security Council to impede the adoption of meaningful resolutions aimed at protecting civilians from violence. And consider the multitude of states that have supplied arms to either side or themselves intervened militarily, with the predictable effect of increasing the severity and duration of the violence.[64] None of these states can plausibly say that they are not implicated in the suffering of distant, displaced Syrians.

Finally, consider the ways in which powerful and wealthy states are responsible, both historically and also in ongoing ways, for contributing to and sustaining the poverty and weakness of others, leaving them vulnerable to displacement-generating crises. Think of the European colonial project, for example, with its brutal subjugation of colonized people and extraction of human and natural resources from colonized territories, which contributed to enduring global vulnerabilities and inequalities. With these historical injustices in mind, legal scholar Tendayi Achiume goes so far as to suggest that the migration of formerly colonized peoples to former imperial powers and their settler colonies, who benefitted from these historic wrongs, might be appropriately framed as part of an ongoing and necessary process of decolonization.[65]

Moreover, these former imperial powers and settler colonies, which remain some of the world's wealthiest and most powerful states, have in part sustained their wealth and power in the postcolonial era through the establishment and perpetuation of global practices, rules, and structures that contribute to sustaining the weakness and poverty of others. Exploitative economic bargaining practices, inequitable international trade agreements, restrictive intellectual property rights regimes, and the routine destruction of the global climate do harm to others in the present. While these may be less dramatic than past harms wrought by colonialism or by foolish wars and the reckless provision of arms and finance to abusive regimes, they still have the effect of perpetuating poverty and oppression and heightening the risk of suffering, violence, and forcible displacement in many parts of the world. The

---

[64]For research demonstrating the negative impact of supplying arms and intervening in the context of civil wars, Dursun Peksen, "Does Foreign Military Intervention Help Human Rights?" *Political Research Quarterly* 65, no. 3 (2011): 558-71; Idean Salehyan, David Siroky, and Reed M. Wood, "External Rebel Sponsorship and Civilian Abuse: A Principal-Agent Analysis of Wartime Atrocities," *IO* 68, no. 3 (2014): 633-61; and Katherine Sawyer, Kathleen Gallagher Cunningham, and William Reed, "The Role of External Support in Civil War Termination," *Journal of Conflict Resolution* 61, no. 6 (2017): 1174-1202.

[65]Achiume, "Migration as Decolonization."

affluence and security of some are inextricably connected to the poverty and vulnerability of others.[66]

Consider, for example, the World Trade Organization's treaty system, which, as philosopher Thomas Pogge summarizes, "permits the affluent countries to protect their markets against cheap imports (agricultural products, textiles and apparel, steel, and much else) through tariffs, anti-dumping duties, quotas, export credits, and huge subsidies to domestic producers." This system reduces the export opportunities for poor countries and enables producers from rich countries to undersell them. If this system were not in place, it has been estimated that poor countries would realize gains of more than US$100 billion annually. Global poverty would be radically reduced.[67] With the system left in place, many poor countries remain poor and thus more vulnerable to the kinds of instabilities, insecurities, and resource scarcities that are known to drive displacement.

Consider more specifically the contribution of global economic structures and practices to the outbreak of displacement-generating conflicts in recent decades. The structural adjustment programs of the International Monetary Fund in Sierra Leone in the late 1980s, for example, have been shown to have generated a collapse in state capacity that weakened the government's monopoly on the use of force and allowed a rebel group, the Revolutionary United Front (RUF), to recruit large numbers of disaffected people. Civil war broke out. Private capital and international markets, in turn, contributed to prolonging the conflict as demand for conflict diamonds provided the RUF with an ongoing source of revenue and an incentive to continue fighting for control of the country's mines. When the conflict finally ended in 1999, 75,000 people were dead and over half of the population was displaced.[68]

Consider finally the scientifically documented contribution of human-induced climate change—for which wealthy, developed states bear disproportionate responsibility—to the outbreak of the Syrian civil war in 2011, which, as noted, has generated the displacement of Syrian civilians on such a massive scale. A severe three-year drought coupled with poor water management led to "multiyear crop failures, economic deterioration, and consequently mass migration of rural families to urban areas," which in turn

[66]Richard W. Miller, *Globalizing Justice: The Ethics of Poverty and Power* (Oxford: Oxford University Press, 2010); Thomas Pogge, *World Poverty and Human Rights*, 2nd ed. (Cambridge, UK: Polity Press, 2008); and Iris Marion Young, *Responsibility for Justice* (Oxford: Oxford University Press, 2011).
[67]Thomas Pogge, *Politics as Usual: What Lies Behind the Pro-Poor Rhetoric* (Cambridge, UK: Polity Press, 2010), 20.
[68]Alexander Betts, *Forced Migration and Global Politics* (Oxford: Wiley-Blackwell, 2009), 139-41.

contributed to overcrowding, unemployment, and political unrest. These climate change–induced shifts, combined with other causal factors identified earlier, helped put the country on the path to civil war.[69]

Indian-born writer Suketu Mehta summarizes these many historic and ongoing injustices in powerful terms:

> This is how the game was rigged: First they colonized us and stole our treasure and prevented us from building our industries. After plundering us for centuries, they left, having drawn up maps in ways that ensured permanent strife between our communities. Then they brought us to their countries as "guest workers"—as if they knew what the word "guest" meant in our cultures—but discouraged us from bringing our families.
>
> Having built up their economies with our raw materials and our labor, they asked us to go back and were surprised when we did not. They stole our minerals and corrupted our governments so that their corporations could continue stealing our resources; they fouled the air above us and the waters around us, making our farms barren, our oceans lifeless; and they were aghast when the poorest among us arrived at their borders.[70]

Our purpose in highlighting these injustices is not to determine which state is most culpable for this or that crisis of displacement and therefore which state is most bound to provide assistance, protection, and refuge (though we will briefly consider such questions in chap. 10). Rather, it is simply to make clear that states are so often implicated in the suffering and displacement of distant strangers that they cannot claim to be responsible only for the care of those that they encounter directly. Nations are called to love the vulnerable stranger. In a globalized era, the distant stranger is not so distant, and the nation that claims a mandate to focus on the needs of its own is commonly more implicated in the vulnerability of others than it cares to admit.[71] Nations are to love vulnerable strangers, wherever they may be found.

The criterion of opportunity. To gain further specificity, let's return to the book of Deuteronomy. What was the scope of kinship responsibility there?

---

[69]Guy J. Abel, Michael Brottrager, Jesus Crespo Cuaresma, and Raya Muttarak, "Climate, Conflict and Forced Migration," *Global Environmental Change* 54 (2019): 239-49, at 239. A global agreement, signed by 181 countries in 2018, acknowledges that "climate, environmental degradation and natural disasters increasingly interact with the drivers of refugee movements." UNHCR, *Global Compact on Refugees, A/73/12 (Part II)*, September 13, 2018, 2, www.unhcr.org/gcr/GCR_English.pdf. We discuss this *Global Compact* further in chap. 10.

[70]Suketu Mehta, "This Land Is Their Land," *Foreign Policy*, September 12, 2017.

[71]Part of this chapter makes use of material presented in Luke Glanville, "The Refugee and the Sovereign State," *International Journal of Public Theology* 14, no. 4 (2020).

As we saw in chapter two, the bounds of kinship responsibility extended to wherever there was *opportunity* to share the good gifts of Yahweh with people who lacked protection and belonging (Deut 14:28-29). Kinship responsibility was found wherever interpersonal influence extended in the spheres of economics, debt, labor, kinship, and living arrangements. If there was *opportunity* to bless the widow, the orphan, and the stranger by leaving the gleanings of the field for them, then God's people were required to do so (Deut 24:19-22).

Modern readers might wonder why the Old Testament doesn't display greater sensitivity to *global* displacement—why so local? Certainly, the prophets *did* declare Yahweh's judgment on the brutality of kings of other nations, brutality that no doubt produced displacement (e.g., Ex 15:1; 1 Kings 21; Is 2:3-4; 13:11). However, the average ancient Israelite lived a very local agrarian existence. Apart from warfare and religious pilgrimage, there was little reason to leave the family estate—and to do so was perilous. For this reason, the sphere of social responsibility in Deuteronomy remained localized. In Deuteronomy, the key criterion for kinship responsibility was *opportunity*.

The scope of kinship responsibility in Deuteronomy can also be seen in negative terms—and this is particularly relevant for our contemporary scene. Wherever there was risk of oppressing or exploiting a vulnerable person or family, an Israelite was expected to instead protect and enfold them. For example, a landed person might be tempted to keep a stranger's outer garment in order to extract unceasing farm labor. Not only does Deuteronomy prohibit this injustice (Deut 24:17), but it also compels the landowning Israelite and the household to enfold the stranger as kin (Deut 16:11, 14). Deuteronomy as much as says, Draw a circle big enough to encompass all those people you could potentially benefit from, all those out of whom you might be tempted to squeeze what you can. That circle is your sphere of kinship responsibility.

So, whether viewed positively or negatively, the key criterion for defining the scope of kinship responsibility is *opportunity*. Wherever there was opportunity to bless displaced people, this was required; wherever there was opportunity to exploit vulnerable people, such exploitation was forbidden and blessing was required. The *criterion of opportunity* (viewed both positively and negatively) clearly implicates Western nations in their responsibility to extend kinship to people who are displaced globally.

Viewed positively, Western nations have the opportunity to enfold displaced people as these people are pleading to be allowed to make a home within our borders.

Viewed negatively, the circle that Western nations have drawn to siphon wealth from other communities encompasses the whole world. Western nations continue to presume that the world is their playground. How outrageous it is for Western nations to impose their greedy and destructive policies on vulnerable nations for their own economic and strategic benefit and then claim that these same people groups are outside of the scope of their kinship responsibility! There is no logic that can justify this behavior, except the twisted logics of selfishness and national conceit. Deuteronomy makes clear that Yahweh deplores such behavior and insists upon a better response. The scope of kinship responsibility is *opportunity*, and Western nations have every opportunity to respond with compassion and tenderness to displaced people globally, by dint of history, ongoing culpability, and capacity. To fail to do so is to come under the judgment of the God of gods and Lord of lords (Deut 10:17-19).

We have offered in chapters six and seven a political theology that invites, indeed urges, nation-states to welcome vulnerable outsiders and enfold them within the community as kin. This is God's desire and design for all communities. The arguments that are habitually invoked to justify diluting or circumscribing this biblical vision when applying it to political communities—arguments about national identity, sovereign statehood, citizen prioritization, and geographical proximity—do not stand up to scrutiny. They may remind us of the need to apply God's vision for community in ways that best fit our historical and social contexts, but they provide no grounds for abandoning this vision of protective kinship. Let us strive, then, to reimagine our countries as communities that humbly and joyfully seek to welcome strangers—repenting of past injustices against "the least of these" and seizing the opportunity to love them now. Such an appeal, of course, generates a range of practical questions about the limits, hazards, and possibilities of national communities adopting such a disposition of relentless inclusion. In chapters six and seven, we have sought to explain why nation-states should welcome the stranger as kin; in the next chapter we'll explain how.

7

RELINQUISHING FEAR, NURTURING COMPASSION, INSTITUTIONALIZING LOVE

"The hallmark of our times—in our politics, our social discourse, and increasingly, our faith—is fear," Stephan Bauman, former president of World Relief, declares. "Often subtle but also brazen at times, fear is becoming so commonplace we assume it's normal. We are more afraid than we realize."[1] Fear underpins the reluctance of many in the West, including many Christians, to welcome increased numbers of refugees. A 2016 survey of US Protestant pastors found that 44 percent believed there was a sense of fear within their congregation about refugees coming to the United States.[2]

Our fearful minds see refugees as security threats (inclined to terrorism and violent crime), economic threats (stealing jobs and straining resources), and cultural threats (weakening communal bonds and altering national identities).[3] In addition to these tangible concerns, our fearful minds simply

---

[1]Stephan Bauman, *Break Open the Sky: Saving Our Faith from a Culture of Fear* (New York: Multnomah, 2017), 5. For broader analyses of the historical and contemporary politics of fear, see Corey Robin, *Fear: The History of a Political Idea* (Oxford: Oxford University Press, 2004); and Martha C. Nussbaum, *The Monarchy of Fear: A Philosopher Looks at Our Political Crisis* (New York: Simon & Schuster, 2018).

[2]Bob Smietana, "Churches Twice as Likely to Fear Refugees Than to Help Them," Research, *Lifeway*, February 29, 2016.

[3]A 2016 survey of ten European countries found that a majority of people in eight of the countries

fear strangers. As Zygmunt Bauman puts it, "Strangers tend to cause anxiety precisely because of being 'strange'—and so fearsomely unpredictable, unlike the people with whom we interact daily and from whom we believe we know what to expect."[4] We as individuals and national communities have become so used to engaging with strangers from a posture of fear that we are hardly aware of it anymore. Fear has become the lens through which we view those beyond ourselves.[5] And this is no less the case when the strangers we encounter are in need, seeking asylum, and desiring community. Asylum seekers are "harbingers of a troubled world," Jonathan Rutherford notes.[6] They come from suffering and violence, and the fearful mind worries that they carry the portents and possibilities of such suffering and violence with them to their new homes.[7]

Our fears are actively cultivated and preyed upon by others.[8] Recent years have seen populist leaders across the world fostering and exploiting collective fears (and resentment and loathing) of outsiders in a manner that has facilitated the advance of xenophobic and exclusionary nationalisms. Over and over again, they have evoked and encouraged citizens' fears for their own security, economy, and culture: refugees and other migrants are portrayed as threats in all these areas.

US President Donald Trump has frequently spoken of an "invasion" of people crossing the US-Mexico border, warning that his political opponents "want illegal immigrants, no matter how bad they may be, to pour into and infest our Country." He warns that they are "going to flood your streets with criminal aliens."[9] Hungarian Prime Minister Viktor Orbán declares that "all terrorists are migrants" and then the following year amplifies his claim by

---

believed that the surge of refugees into Europe increased the likelihood of terrorism in their country and a majority in five of the countries believed refugees would take away jobs and social benefits. Richard Wike, Bruce Stokes, and Katie Simmons, "Europeans Fear Wave of Refugees Will Mean More Terrorism, Fewer Jobs," *Global Attitudes & Trends*, Pew Research Center, July 11, 2016.

[4] Zygmunt Bauman, *Strangers at Our Door* (Cambridge, UK: Polity Press, 2016), 8.

[5] S. Bauman, *Break Open the Sky*, 15.

[6] Quoted in Susanna Snyder, *Asylum Seeking, Migration and Church* (Surrey, UK: Ashgate, 2012), 101.

[7] See generally Snyder, *Asylum Seeking*, 85-126.

[8] And Christians have long been both purveyors and recipients of this politics of fear. See John Fea, *Believe Me: The Evangelical Road to Donald Trump* (Grand Rapids, MI: Eerdmans, 2018). See more generally Barry Glassner, *The Culture of Fear: Why Americans Are Afraid of the Wrong Things*, 2nd ed. (New York: Basic Books, 2018).

[9] Donald J. Trump on Twitter, June 24, 2018 (https://twitter.com/realdonaldtrump/status/10109008 65602019329?lang=en); June 19, 2018 (https://twitter.com/realdonaldtrump/status/1009071403918 864385?lang=en); Maggie Haberman, "At a Rally Looking Toward November, Trump Sets His Sights Two Years Beyond," *New York Times*, October 1, 2018.

inverting the connection: "Every single migrant poses a public security and terror risk."[10] US Attorney General Jeff Sessions asks, "What good does it do to bring in somebody who's illiterate in their own country, has no skills, and is going to struggle in our country and not be successful? That is not what a good nation should do, and we need to get away from it."[11] And Australian Minister for Immigration Peter Dutton confusingly warns that refugees will both take Australian jobs and languish in unemployment queues.[12]

Forced migration has been "securitized," to use a term of international relations theory, such that we are led to conceive of refugees not as vulnerable people with rights and needs but as threats to our physical, economic, and cultural well-being.[13] Tragically, we have allowed our thinking to be shaped such that we often consider immigration issues in terms of ensuring our protection *from* refugees rather than offering protection *to* refugees.

In this chapter, we begin by explaining not only that our fears of refugees are overblown but that they provoke us to unjustly harm so many who are already in desperate need. We then turn to consider a better way, seeking to explain in both emotional and institutional terms *how* nations might practically pursue the model that we have retrieved and defended in previous chapters, that of joyful and self-sacrificial welcome of vulnerable strangers into kinship.

INFLATED AND HARMFUL FEARS

The threats posed by refugees and other migrants tend to be smaller than many of us think, and certainly much smaller than certain political leaders and commentators would have us believe. Indeed, in many respects the admission of refugees tends to bring net material benefits. We mention some of these benefits not to make the case that we have a material self-interest in welcoming refugees. Such a claim risks dehumanizing displaced people in the

---

[10]Z. Bauman, *Strangers at Our Door*, 31; and Suketu Mehta, "This Land Is Their Land," *Foreign Policy*, September 12, 2017.

[11]Quoted by Fox News on Twitter, January 16, 2018, https://twitter.com/FoxNews/status/95344180 5873369089.

[12]Latika Bourke, "Peter Dutton Says 'Illiterate and Innumerate' Refugees Would Take Australian Jobs," Politics, *Sydney Morning Herald*, May 17, 2016.

[13]For the seminal work on securitization, see Barry Buzan, Ole Wæver, and Jaap de Wilde, *Security: A New Framework for Analysis* (Boulder, CO: Lynne Rienner, 1998). For its application to forced migration, see Anne Hammerstadt, "The Securitization of Forced Migration," in *The Oxford Handbook of Refugee and Forced Migration Studies*, ed. Elena Fiddian-Qasmiyeh, Gil Loescher, Katy Long, and Nando Sigona (Oxford: Oxford University Press, 2014), 265-77; and Jef Huysmans, *The Politics of Insecurity: Fear, Migration and Asylum in the EU* (New York: Routledge, 2006).

same way as the claim that they pose a burden and a threat. Rather, we merely wish to demonstrate that our fears of refugees are exaggerated and to note how these fears lead us to do harm to neighbors in need.

Security. The risk that refugees will engage in terrorist activities is very small. Western states apply rigorous background checks to those they admit. David Miliband summarizes that the US vetting process for screening refugees "takes an average of eighteen to twenty-four months . . . and involves twelve to fifteen government agencies conducting multiple checks, biometric tests, and in-person interviews to ensure that refugees are who they say they are and pose no threat to the United States."[14] And this vetting process works. The United States resettled 784,000 refugees in the fourteen years following September 11, 2001. During that time only three resettled refugees were arrested for planning terrorist activities, and two of those three planned to undertake their activities outside of the United States.[15] Indeed, not one of the more than three million refugees resettled in the United States since the Refugee Act of 1980 has committed a lethal terrorist attack on American soil.[16] A study of the period from 1975 to 2015 found that "the chance of an American being murdered in a terrorist attack caused by a refugee is 1 in 3.64 billion per year." This is almost a thousand times less than the (still very small) chance of being murdered by a foreigner on a common tourist visa.[17]

In contrast, amicus briefs filed by a nonpartisan group of twenty-six retired generals and admirals and a bipartisan group of fifty-two former national security, foreign policy, and intelligence officials assert that the decision of the Trump administration in 2017 to indefinitely bar the entry of nationals from six Muslim-majority countries actually *harms* US national security interests. It does so by reinforcing the perception that the United States is hostile to Muslims and Muslim-majority nations, thus undermining US activities abroad and "fuel[ing] the propaganda narrative spread by terrorists and others who seek to harm US interests." They note additionally that the travel ban has "a devastating humanitarian impact" as it "disrupts the travel of numerous men, women, and children who have themselves been

[14]David Miliband, *Rescue: Refugees and the Political Crisis of Our Time* (New York: TED Books, 2017), 97-98.

[15]Kathleen Newland, "The U.S. Record Shows Refugees Are Not a Threat," *Migration Policy Institute*, October 2015.

[16]Stephan Bauman, Matthew Soerens, and Issam Smeir, *Seeking Refuge: On the Shores of the Global Refugee Crisis* (Chicago: Moody Publishers, 2016), 78-80.

[17]Alex Nowrasteh, "Terrorism and Immigration: A Risk Analysis," *Cato Institute*, September 13, 2016, policy analysis no. 798.

victimized by terrorists."[18] The president of the National Association of Evangelicals, Leith Anderson, puts it well: "Of course we want to keep terrorists out of our country, but let's not punish the victims of ISIS for the sins of ISIS."[19]

Similarly, while 42 percent of Americans surveyed in a 2019 poll think that immigration worsens crime, the evidence points in the opposite direction.[20] A study of the period between 1970 and 2010 finds that increased numbers of immigrants in metropolitan areas is "consistently linked to decreases in violent (e.g., murder) and property (e.g., burglary) crime."[21] Another study finds that this holds true even in the case of undocumented immigrants.[22] Studies moreover consistently find that immigrants themselves commit crimes at lower rates and are less likely to be incarcerated than native-born Americans.[23]

But what about Germany, which opened its borders to welcome more than one million asylum seekers in 2015? Certainly, we should be troubled by the widely publicized sexual assaults perpetrated by asylum seekers against German women in the years since then, but we should take care not to generalize from these high-profile crimes. President Trump claimed in 2018 that the influx of asylum seekers had "violently changed" Germany and that crime in the country was "way up."[24] But a 2017 study showed that Chancellor Angela Merkel's decision to open Germany's borders led generally only to "very small increases in crime." This involved merely a rise in drug offenses and fare evasion in areas with bigger refugee reception centers. The crimes were committed not only by asylum seekers but also by German citizens, and

---

[18]Quoted in Patricia Stottlemyer, "Ex-Military, Intelligence, and Foreign Policy Officials: Travel Ban Harms National Security," *Just Security*, April 4, 2018. See similarly Benjamin Wittes, "In Defense of Refugees," *Lawfare* (blog), November 17, 2015.

[19]Quoted in Bauman, Soerens, and Smeir, *Seeking Refuge*, 77.

[20]Results of June 3-16, 2019, survey, "Immigration," *Gallup*, https://news.gallup.com/poll/1660/immigration.aspx.

[21]Robert Adelman, Lesley Williams Reid, Gail Markle, Saskia Weiss, and Charles Jaret, "Urban Crime Rates and the Changing Face of Immigration: Evidence Across Four Decades," *Journal of Ethnicity in Criminal Justice* 15, no. 1 (2017): 52-77, at 52.

[22]Michael T. Light and Ty Miller, "Does Undocumented Immigration Increase Violent Crime?," *Criminology* 56, no. 2 (2018): 370-401.

[23]Nazgol Ghandnoosh and Josh Rovner, "Immigration and Public Safety," *Sentencing Project*, March 16, 2017; Michelangelo Landgrave and Alex Nowrasteh, "Criminal Immigrants in 2017: Their Numbers, Demographics, and Countries of Origin," *Cato Institute*, March 15, 2017. See also Daniel Masterson and Vasil I. Yasenov, "Does Halting Refugee Resettlement Reduce Crime?: Evidence from the United States Refugee Ban," *Immigration Policy Lab* (IPL), December 20, 2018.

[24]Donald J. Trump, Twitter, June 18, 2018, https://twitter.com/realDonaldTrump/status/1008696508697513985.

the higher crime counts in these areas may have been simply a product of an increased police presence.[25] In 2018, Germany's internal ministry reported that, despite the inflow of asylum seekers, Germany's crime rate was at its lowest level in thirty years.[26]

Economics. What about the threat posed by refugees to national economies and individual economic well-being? Again, the evidence does not support the fears. A draft study by the US Department of Health and Human Services—a study that was rejected by Trump administration officials—found that, while refugees relied on the department's programs, particularly in their first four years, at a higher per person cost than the rest of the US population, refugees still had a positive net fiscal impact of $63 billion between 2005 and 2014.[27] A study of fifteen Western European countries between 1985 and 2015 draws a similar conclusion.[28]

Research suggests that immigration also tends to have a positive impact on employment and incomes for individual, native-born citizens. It can "create more and better employment" by filling labor shortages, raising productivity, generating new job opportunities and increasing labor-force participation of existing citizens, boosting innovation and growth, and increasing wages.[29] Certainly, immigration can "negatively affect employment for some groups during some periods," especially groups of people with similar skills and experience as new migrants.[30] But the evidence suggests that, if the labor market implications of immigration are handled well by policymakers, new arrivals can substantially benefit not only the national economy but the job opportunities and incomes of native-born individuals.[31] To use a simple metaphor, it

---

[25]Marcus Gehrsitz and Martin Ungerer, "Jobs, Crime, and Votes: A Short-Run Evaluation of the Refugee Crisis in Germany," *IZA*, January 22, 2017, discussion paper no. 10494.

[26]Latika Bourke, "Donald Trump Taunts Angela Merkel on Twitter over Immigration," *Sydney Morning Herald*, June 19, 2018.

[27]Julie Hirschfeld Davis and Somini Sengupta, "Trump Administration Rejects Study Showing Positive Impact of Refugees," *New York Times*, September 18, 2017; and related article: "Rejected Report Shows Revenue Brought In by Refugees," *New York Times*, September 19, 2017.

[28]Hippolyte d'Albis, Ekrame Boubtane, and Dramane Coulibaly, "Macroeconomic Evidence Suggests that Asylum Seekers Are Not a 'Burden' for Western European Countries," *Science Advances* 4, no. 6 (2018).

[29]Michael Clemens, Cindy Huang, Jimmy Graham, and Kate Gough, *Migration Is What You Make It: Seven Policy Decisions That Turned Challenges into Opportunities*, CDG Note (Washington, DC: Centre for Global Development, May 2018), 1.

[30]Clemens, et al., *Migration Is What You Make It*, 1.

[31]Clemens, et al., *Migration Is What You Make It*, 1-30. See similarly Ryan Nunn, Jimmy O'Donnell, and Jay Shambaugh, *A Dozen Facts About Immigration*, The Hamilton Project, Brookings, October 2018.

is a common mistake to think of a national economy as a pie of fixed size with a limited number of slices to go around. If this is the case, won't an influx of refugees result in less pie for everyone else? But economies don't work like that. The economic pie grows. Newcomers don't only assume jobs; they also consume, and bring skills, creativity, drive, and entrepreneurship. As the economic pie grows, there is more to go around.

While some readers may remain unconvinced, we think it is important to note that, in those instances in which immigration reduces employment opportunity and incomes for individual workers, blame should usually be assigned not to the migrants but to the governing authorities that left these existing workers in such a precarious position.[32] Populist leaders have found much success in pitting vulnerable citizens against vulnerable asylum seekers in recent years, convincing voters that excessive immigration is the cause of their poverty and unemployment. But the evidence consistently attests to the net economic benefits of immigration at national levels.[33] It is surely the responsibility of governments to ensure that these benefits are shared, particularly among poor and vulnerable citizens, rather than merely distributed to wealthy businesses in the form of cheap labor provided by new arrivals.[34]

That being said, we should be careful not to rely too much on the economic argument for welcoming refugees and other migrants. Such an argument risks tempting countries and their leaders to choose for resettlement those displaced people who can provide the most economic benefit rather than those who are most in need of safety and sustenance. Indeed, this already occurs. Western countries often refrain from picking sick and disabled refugees for resettlement due to economic concerns, even though such refugees are often the ones most in need.[35] So while we ought not to believe politicians

---

[32]See similarly Lea Ypi, "Borders of Class: Migration and Citizenship in the Capitalist State," *EIA* 32, no. 2 (2018): 151-74, at 144-46.

[33]Organisation for Economic Co-operation and Development (OECD), "Is Migration Good for the Economy?," *Migration Policy Debates*, May 2014.

[34]Some immigration skeptics point to the problem of "brain drain," arguing not that immigration harms host communities but that it harms the communities that migrants leave behind. In some instances, the remittances that migrants send home outweigh the brain drain experienced by sending states, but in others brain drain undeniably leaves poor sending states worse off. For a persuasive explanation of why the brain-drain argument is compelling in only a small minority of cases, see Kieran Oberman, "Can Brain Drain Justify Immigration Restrictions?" *Ethics* 123, no. 3 (2013): 427-55.

[35]William Maley, *What Is a Refugee?* (London: Hurst, 2016), 87.

and commentators who recklessly claim that existing levels of immigration are economically burdensome, we ought to ready ourselves and our communities to accept economic costs—perhaps *substantial* economic costs—as we call on our nations to welcome and enfold as kin larger numbers of displaced people, including the most marginalized, vulnerable, and needy—people who may bring an economic cost but who also bring opportunity for joyful cultivation of new kinship, for mutual enrichment and transformation, and for self-sacrificial love of vulnerable neighbors that can soften and renew national identities. We say more about such opportunities later in the chapter.

Culture. What about the fear that large influxes of refugees threaten the existing culture of a national community? We touched on this in our discussion of national identity in chapter six, arguing that national identities and cultures ought to be oriented to justice and that, whatever else they may be about, nations will ideally be marked by a desire to embrace and enfold vulnerable strangers as kin. A willingness to welcome strangers from beyond one's national community inevitably requires a willingness to welcome a diversity of cultures.

The idea of multiculturalism has been demeaned and rejected by many Western political leaders in recent years. But it turns out that, when multicultural policies are developed with due regard for considerations of justice and in contexts where refugees and other migrants are not falsely portrayed as security or economic threats, such policies have a reasonable record of success. Canadian political philosopher Will Kymlicka points to his own country as an example. He notes that, whereas in most countries "native-born citizens with a strong sense of national identity or national pride tend to be more xenophobic, intolerant, and distrusting of immigrants," strength of national identity among Canadian citizens is "positively correlated with support for immigration." He suggests that this is difficult to explain without reference to the fact that Canada officially defines itself as a multicultural nation. Thus, multiculturalism itself "serves as a source of shared national identity and pride for native-born citizens and immigrants alike."[36] Canada's embrace of multiculturalism has enabled

---

[36]Will Kymlicka, "Multiculturalism: Success, Failure, and the Future," *Migration Policy Institute*, February 2012, 11-12. See also Keith G. Banting, "Is There a Progressive's Dilemma in Canada?: Immigration, Multiculturalism and the Welfare State," *Canadian Journal of Political Science* 43, no. 4 (2010): 797-820; Keith Banting and Will Kymlicka, "Canadian Multiculturalism: Global Anxieties and Local Debates," *British Journal of Canadian Studies* 23, no. 1 (2010): 43-72; and Andrew Griffith, "Building a Mosaic: The Evolution of Canada's Approach to Immigrant Integration," *Migration Policy Institute*, November 1, 2017.

it to retain strong levels of communal trust and social capital despite increasing ethnic and religious diversity.[37]

But not all countries are like Canada. American political scientist Robert Putnam famously finds that, in the short run, immigration and ethnic diversity tends to reduce solidarity and trust in neighborhoods within the United States. In American neighborhoods with high levels of immigration, solidarity and trust tend to be lower not only between immigrant and native-born groups but even within each group.[38] Putnam is disturbed by his findings and seeks comfort from evidence that in the long run "immigration and diversity are likely to have important cultural, economic, fiscal, and developmental benefits."[39] He concludes that, while we ought not to "deny the reality of the challenge to social solidarity posed by diversity," we also ought not to "deny that addressing that challenge is both feasible and desirable."[40] Despite his optimism, Putnam's short-term findings alert us that the welcome of strangers can have real social and cultural costs in certain national contexts.

This difference between the Canadian and the American experience of multiculturalism prompts us to consider how inclusive national identities may be cultivated. For as Kymlicka reports, the kind of short-term loss of trust produced by increased diversity that Putnam finds in the United States has not been replicated in Canada, and it is especially absent among younger Canadians, who tend to take multiculturalism for granted.[41] This contrast raises the challenge of renarrating our national identities in ways that express the diversity already within them and create space for new arrivals. As we explained in chapter six, Western national identities tend to be narrated from the perspective of the dominant culture. The influence of minority cultures tends to be muted in these national stories. Western nations have the opportunity to celebrate the ways in which they are already a mosaic of cultures. This way nations can mature to consider their encounters with new arrivals from other cultures as an opportunity for cultural enrichment rather than as a threat to their communal identity and shared traditions.

---

[37]Kymlicka, "Multiculturalism," 12; and Marek Kohn, *Trust: Self-Interest and the Common Good* (Oxford: Oxford University Press, 2008), 127.

[38]Robert D. Putnam, "*E Pluribus Unum*: Diversity and Community in the Twenty-First Century," *Scandinavian Political Studies* 30, no. 2 (2007): 137-74.

[39]Putnam, "*E Pluribus Unum*," 137.

[40]Putnam, "*E Pluribus Unum*," 165.

[41]Kymlicka, "Multiculturalism," 12-13.

Perspective. Our fears of strangers in need begin to look not just inflated but positively myopic and selfish when we consider that relatively weak and poor states in developing regions of the world have much larger numbers of people approaching their borders in search of asylum in their territories than we do in the West, and they welcome these strangers into their communities in much larger numbers and at much greater risk and cost than we do. The United States, Canada, and Australia point to their willingness to admit tens of thousands of refugees each year as evidence of their generosity, and of course the welcome of each and every refugee should be celebrated. But let's not forget that Turkey hosts 3.6 million refugees, Colombia hosts 1.8 million, and Pakistan and Uganda each host 1.4 million. One in every six people in Aruba is a "Venezuelan displaced abroad." One in every seven people in Lebanon is a refugee.[42] As Bangladesh was confronted with an influx of 650,000 Rohingya Muslims fleeing Myanmar in 2017, Prime Minister Sheikh Hasina declared, "Bangladesh is not a rich country . . . but if we can feed 160 million people, another 500 or 700,000 people, we can do it."[43]

Certainly, the security, economic, and cultural threats faced by Western states would increase somewhat if they themselves started admitting similar numbers of refugees, but perhaps we can afford to. Recall that one Western state in particular, Germany, responded with uncommon generosity to the cries of asylum seekers fleeing the Syrian civil war in 2015, opening its borders to admit more than one million. Chancellor Angela Merkel declared at the time, "Germany is a strong country—we will manage."[44] And Germany has indeed managed. Whatever the risks and costs that have followed this act of welcome, and there have been many, Germany remains far from reaching the limits of what it can cope with.[45]

Harms. And yet we in the West continue to fear the security, economic, and cultural implications of welcoming refugees into our communities. Such fears can lead us to do great harm to vulnerable people. Reinhold Niebuhr famously observed how the fears and anxieties and, in turn, selfishness of individuals are amplified at the level of groups, and particularly the level of

---

[42]United Nations High Commissioner for Refugees (UNHCR), *Global Trends: Forced Displacement in 2019*, June 18, 2020, 3, www.unhcr.org/en-au/statistics/unhcrstats/5ee200e37/unhcr-global-trends-2019.html.

[43]Michelle Nichols, "Exclusive: Bangladesh PM Says Expects No Help from Trump on Refugees Fleeing Myanmar," World News, *Reuters*, September 18, 2017.

[44]BBC News, "Migrant Crisis: Merkel Warns EU of 'Failure,'" *BBC*, August 31, 2015.

[45]Nanette Funk, "A Spectre in Germany: Refugees, a 'Welcome Culture' and an 'Integration Politics,'" *Journal of Global Ethics* 12, no. 3 (2016): 289-99, at 293-97.

nations. "All human life is involved in the sin of seeking security at the expense of other life," he claimed.[46] And groups are more ruthless in their pursuit of such security than individuals: "The larger the group the more certainly will it express itself selfishly in the total human community. It will be more powerful and therefore more able to defy any social restraints which might be devised. It will also be less subject to internal moral restraints."[47] We see this play out in manifold ways as states encounter asylum seekers. By securitizing displaced peoples, states justify their exclusion and also enable and normalize the violence they do to them.

Consider the violence of our borders.[48] The increased efforts of Western states to secure their borders in recent years do not merely leave displaced people without a home. These efforts force them to pursue more treacherous journeys in search of a home. The International Organization for Migration recorded more than thirty-six thousand migrant fatalities worldwide between 2014 and 2019 and suggested that this was likely only a fraction of the real number of deaths on migratory routes during the period.[49]

Consider the violence of our containment and deterrence policies. The European Union pays Turkey and Libya billions of dollars to prevent people on the move from reaching Europe, where they would be legally entitled to claim asylum. It funds, resources, and trains the Libyan coast guard to intercept boats in the Mediterranean and return asylum seekers and other migrants to Libya, knowing full well the "unimaginable horrors" that await them.[50] "If someone escapes hell," Bamba, an asylum seeker fleeing the Ivory Coast justifiably asks, "how can you grab them and take them back to hell?"[51]

Consider the violence of our detention practices.[52] For much of this century, vulnerable people who have sought asylum in Australia by boat have

[46]Reinhold Niebuhr, *The Nature and Destiny of Man: A Christian Interpretation*, vol. 1, *Human Nature* (London: Nisbet, 1941), 194.

[47]Reinhold Niebuhr, *Moral Man and Immoral Society: A Study in Ethics and Politics* (New York: Charles Scribner's Sons, 1932), 48. See also Kristin E. Heyer, *Kinship Across Borders: A Christian Ethic of Immigration* (Washington, DC: Georgetown University Press, 2012), 14-17; and Niebuhr, *Nature and Destiny of Man*, 1:221-22.

[48]See also Reece Jones, *Violent Borders: Refugees and the Right to Move* (London: Verso, 2016).

[49]See International Organization for Migration (IOM), *Missing Migrants: Tracking Deaths Along Migratory Routes*, https://missingmigrants.iom.int.

[50]Office of the High Commissioner for Human Rights (OHCHR), *Desperate and Dangerous: Report on the Human Rights Situation of Migrants and Refugees in Libya*, December 20, 2018.

[51]Human Rights Watch, *No Escape from Hell: EU Policies Contribute to Abuse of Migrants in Libya*, January 21, 2019.

[52]Stephanie J. Silverman, "Detaining Immigrants and Asylum Seekers: A Normative Introduction," *Critical Review of International Social and Political Philosophy* 17, no. 5 (2014): 600-617.

been warehoused indefinitely in offshore processing centers in third countries such as Nauru and Papua New Guinea under conditions that, according to the United Nations' special rapporteur on torture, violate their right "to be free from torture or cruel, inhuman or degrading treatment."[53] Numerous children detained in Nauru have been diagnosed with "resignation syndrome," a rare psychiatric condition in which patients withdraw from reality; stop eating, drinking, and talking; and require medical care to keep them alive.[54] "Yesterday I cut my hand," said eight-year-old Sajeenthana, a Sri Lankan refugee who had been on Nauru since she was three. "One day I will kill myself. Wait and see, when I find the knife. I don't care about my body."[55]

Strict border controls are cast by some as a compassionate means of protecting vulnerable people.[56] US President Donald Trump frames his policy of building a wall along the US-Mexico border as a necessary response to a "national security crisis" and to a "humanitarian crisis" at the border.[57] The EU Commission's high representative and vice president, Federica Mogherini, has justified the EU's "cooperation with countries of origin and transit" as necessary "to save lives, clamp down on smuggling networks, and protect those in need."[58] Australian politicians have long insisted that their border policies are necessary to put nefarious people smugglers out of business and prevent tragic deaths at sea. As the former Australian prime minister, Tony Abbott, puts it, "Stopping the boats and restoring border security is the only truly compassionate thing to do."[59]

But such policies of containment, deterrence, and detainment either consign displaced people to insecure and impoverished lives or compel them to take even more dangerous journeys elsewhere in search of asylum. So long

---

[53]Josh Butler, "All the Times the UN Has Slammed Australia's Asylum Seeker Policy," *Huffington Post*, July 25, 2017. See also Bianca Hall and Jonathan Swan, "Rudd Slams the Door on Refugees," *Sydney Morning Herald*, July 20, 2013.

[54]Médecins Sans Frontières, *Indefinite Despair: The Tragic Mental Health Consequences of Offshore Processing on Nauru*, December 2018, 4-5.

[55]Mridula Amin and Isabella Kwai, "The Nauru Experience: Zero-Tolerance Immigration and Suicidal Children," *New York Times*, November 5, 2018.

[56]For a sophisticated critique of the deployment of notions of "compassionate borderwork" to justify practices of exclusion, see Adrian Little and Nick Vaughan-Williams, "Stopping Boats, Saving Lives, Securing Subjects: Humanitarian Borders in Europe and Australia," *EJIR* 23, no. 3 (2017): 533-56.

[57]Donald J. Trump, "Remarks by President Trump on the National Security and Humanitarian Crisis on Our Southern Border," news conference, White House, March 15, 2019.

[58]Quoted in Little and Vaughan-Williams, "Stopping Boats, Saving Lives," 535.

[59]Tony Abbott, "Transcript: Tony Abbott's Controversial Speech at the Margaret Thatcher Lecture," *Sydney Morning Herald*, October 28, 2015.

as wealthy countries continue to offer resettlement to less than 1 percent of the world's forcibly displaced people each year and continue to impede asylum seekers from claiming protection in their territories, desperate and vulnerable people will continue to seek asylum someway and somehow, and there will continue to be a market for people smugglers. Preventing access to asylum and stopping people smuggling in one place does not protect the vulnerable. It is not compassionate. Rather, to borrow a line from refugee scholar William Maley, it sends vulnerable people a clear message: "Go and die somewhere else."[60]

Consider, moreover, how refugees, even when granted asylum, are so often demonized by Western politicians, scapegoated for preexisting societal problems, and subjected to hate crimes, all of which can have the perverse effect of producing the very social ills among migrants that we fear, by creating suspicion, isolation, shame, and resentment. And consider, finally, how our fearful pursuit of absolute security and economic advantage leads us to engage in or support foolish wars, maintain structural injustices, and perpetuate the climate destruction that helps ensure that people will continue to be forcibly displaced and in urgent need of protection and relief, in larger and larger numbers, into the future.

Habits. "Fear is not a Christian habit of mind," novelist Marilynne Robinson helpfully reminds us.[61] "The fear of others lays a snare," Proverbs 29:25 declares, "but one who trusts in the LORD is secure." We say with the psalmist,

> Even though I walk through the darkest valley,
> I fear no evil;
> for you are with me. (Ps 23:4)

Certainly, individuals and nations are at times confronted with real dangers, and it is right that we guard ourselves against them. A measure of caution and self-care may even be appropriate when confronted with strangers in need, in some circumstances. But we ought not to cling fearfully to "treasures on earth" (Mt 6:19), seeking anxiously more and more security against physical, economic, and cultural threats.

Our fears blind us to the needs of others and paralyze us in the face of their desperate cries for help. Our anxieties lead us to compromise our faith as we

---

[60]William Maley, "'Die Somewhere Else,'" *Sydney Morning Herald*, July 27, 2013. See also Maley, *What Is a Refugee?*, 94-100; and Peter Tinti and Tuesday Reitano, *Migrant, Refugee, Smuggler, Savior* (Oxford: Oxford University Press, 2017).

[61]Marilynne Robinson, "Fear," *New York Review of Books*, September 24, 2015.

grasp every marginal increase in real or felt security at the expense of loving our neighbors as ourselves.[62] Warning against President Barack Obama's decision to admit ten thousand Syrian refugees into the United States in 2015, a writer for a Christian foreign policy journal declared, "It is foolish and theologically irresponsible to imagine the gospel requires us to have an immigration policy that would invite potential terrorists into our borders. We are called to love our enemies, but that does not mean the American government should offer up American citizens on a platter to the wolves."[63] Such dehumanizing responses to encounters with displaced people abound in our fearful societies today.

How wonderful it would be if Western Christians rejected this culture of anxiety and, as Sarah Quezada puts it, recognized the value of "risking trust in a fearful world."[64] What a powerful witness this could be to Western nations that are convinced that they must secure themselves against the rest of humanity. What a profound opportunity we have to encourage each other to let go of our fears and seek both the emotional and institutional transformations necessary to pursue the biblical vision of compassionate communities that enfold the displaced as kin. Let's consider now what this might look like.

Nurturing Collective Compassion

Emotions are contagious. Rather than being confined to individuals, they can be transmitted and exchanged through social interaction. Summarizing recent findings of sociology and neuroscience, Andrew Ross reports that, while people may not exactly replicate the emotions of others, social interactions tend to "intensify, harmonize, and blend the emotional responses of those who participate in them."[65] Through such processes of "emotional contagion," emotions can come to be collectively felt.[66] Such collective feeling can extend to the level of large groups such as states.[67] Emma Hutchison describes this in terms of the generation of "emotional cultures" that can "genuinely transform national and transnational communities."[68]

---

[62]As Robinson puts it in "Fear," "Fear operates as an addiction. You can never be safe enough."

[63]Daniel Strand, "Throwing Caution to the Wind: Charity and the Dilemma of America's Syrian Immigration Policy," *Providence*, November 25, 2015.

[64]Sarah Quezada, *Love Undocumented: Risking Trust in a Fearful World* (Harrisonburg, VA: Herald Press, 2018). See similarly Fea, *Believe Me*.

[65]Andrew A. G. Ross, *Mixed Emotions: Beyond Fear and Hatred in International Conflict* (Chicago: University of Chicago Press, 2014), 1.

[66]Ross, *Mixed Emotions*, 1-38.

[67]Brent E. Sasley, "Theorizing States' Emotions," *International Studies Review* 13, no. 3 (2011): 452-76.

[68]Emma Hutchison, *Affective Communities in World Politics: Collective Emotions After Trauma* (Cambridge: Cambridge University Press, 2016), xi.

Such contagions can be purposefully cultivated by individuals and groups and channeled toward particular ends. We have seen this through history as political and religious leaders have provoked the perpetration of atrocities by those under their influence by cultivating and preying upon collective fear, resentment, and hatred of others.[69] We are seeing it again today in less horrific but still deeply damaging ways as populist leaders foster and exploit these same emotions to justify xenophobic and exclusionary approaches to displaced people seeking a home.

What hope is there for the cultivation of more positive emotional contagions and emotional cultures whereby national communities come to joyfully welcome displaced strangers? Some like Niebuhr might argue that there is little ground for hope. Niebuhr acknowledged that individuals are "endowed by nature with a measure of sympathy and consideration" for others and so may at times be capable of "preferring the advantages of others to their own." But he insisted that the generation of such other-regarding sentiments is "more difficult, if not impossible, for human societies and social groups," and particularly so for large groups such as states.[70] Historians of emotions, however, have repeatedly demonstrated how increased awareness, personal narratives, and surrogate experiences of the suffering of strangers have produced contagions of compassion for vulnerable foreigners.[71] In the nineteenth century, for example, these contagions helped motivate the abolition of the slave trade across the Atlantic world,[72] European interventions to rescue persecuted Christians in the Ottoman Empire,[73] the provision of humanitarian relief to foreigners in crisis,[74] and the promotion of more humane governance of colonized peoples.[75] These projects have tended to produce complex outcomes and leave complex

---

[69]For a classic study, see Ervin Staub, *The Roots of Evil: The Origins of Genocide and Other Group Violence* (Cambridge: Cambridge University Press, 1989). For more recent analysis, see Thomas Brudholm and Johannes Lang, eds., *Emotions and Mass Atrocity: Philosophical and Theoretical Explorations* (Cambridge: Cambridge University Press, 2018).

[70]Niebuhr, *Moral Man and Immoral Society*, xi.

[71]See generally Lynn Hunt, *Inventing Human Rights: A History* (New York: Norton, 2007); and Richard Ashby Wilson and Richard D. Brown, eds., *Humanitarianism and Suffering: The Mobilization of Empathy* (Cambridge: Cambridge University Press, 2009).

[72]Margaret Abruzzo, *Polemical Pain: Slavery, Cruelty, and the Rise of Humanitarianism* (Baltimore: Johns Hopkins University Press, 2011).

[73]Gary J. Bass, *Freedom's Battle: The Origins of Humanitarian Intervention* (New York: Knopf, 2008).

[74]Michael Barnett, *Empire of Humanity: A History of Humanitarianism* (Ithaca, NY: Cornell University Press, 2011).

[75]Adam Hochschild, *King Leopold's Ghost: A Story of Greed, Terror, and Heroism in Colonial Africa* (New York: Mariner, 1998).

legacies. At times, moral sensibilities have motivated the care only of certain groups of strangers, they have been marked by troubling sensationalism and paternalism and devastating hypocrisy, and they have motivated reckless actions that have done more harm than good. But at the very least they confirm the possibility of emotional contagions pushing states to care for vulnerable strangers.

Avenues to collective compassion. If nations are "imagined communities," as Benedict Anderson famously observed,[76] then nations have a wonderful opportunity to reimagine themselves and to cultivate a disposition toward displaced strangers that accords with the biblical imperative to enfold the vulnerable, the marginalized, and the displaced as kin. Churches and other Christian organizations and individuals have a key role to play in this, as do other civil society actors and political leaders. Let's briefly consider three avenues by which compassionate concern for vulnerable strangers can be effectively nurtured at the level of the national community.

First, collective compassion can be nurtured through the use of narratives, images, and personal testimonies of distant suffering.[77] For better or worse, the depiction of suffering is often crucial to the successful channeling of compassion toward meaningful action. Psychologist Paul Slovic shows that raw statistics of mass suffering, no matter how large the numbers, "fail to spark emotion or feeling and thus fail to motivate action."[78] Much more effective are images and stories of individual victims. But the short-lived and shallow character of the global response to the heart-wrenching images of the drowned body of the three-year-old Syrian boy, Alan Kurdi, points to the limits of this means of nurturing compassion.[79] The question that remains, therefore, is how producing empathy might spur communities to

---

[76]Benedict Anderson, *Imagined Communities: Reflections on the Origin and Spread of Nationalism* (London: Verso, 1983).

[77]On the value of novels not only for cultivating empathetic responses to suffering, but for generating appreciation of the ethical complexities of caring for refugees, see Erin Goheen Glanville, "R2P and the Novel: The Trope of the Abandoned Refugee Child in Stella Leventoyannis Harvey's *The Brink of Freedom*," *Global Responsibility to Protect* 10 (2018): 143-61. On the value of encouraging people to put themselves in the shoes of refugees themselves, see Claire L. Adida, Adeline Lo, and Melina R. Platas, "Perspective Taking Can Promote Short-Term Inclusionary Behavior Toward Syrian Refugees," *PNAS* 115, no. 38 (2018): 9521-26.

[78]Paul Slovic, "'If I Look at the Mass I Will Never Act': Psychic Numbing and Genocide," *Judgment and Decision Making* 2, no. 2 (2007): 79-95, at 79.

[79]Bauman likewise worries about the "notoriously short-lived carnivalesque explosions of solidarity and care that are triggered by media images of successive spectacular tragedies in the migrants' unending saga." Z. Bauman, *Strangers at Our Door*, 80.

share resources and power more equitably. The way narratives, images, and testimonies are framed is thus an important question to consider.[80]

Alternatively, individuals can seek to nurture compassion within their communities by evoking their own compassion in front of others, thus making use of the possibilities of emotional contagion. This was the approach taken by Merkel when courageously opening Germany's borders to more than one million asylum seekers in 2015. The chancellor declared her happiness that "Germany has become a country that many people abroad associate with hope." She encouraged Germans to embrace the opportunity to make sacrifices for the sake of vulnerable strangers. And she celebrated that those who responded positively and worked to support new arrivals had "painted a picture of Germany which can make us proud of our country."[81] Merkel's decision was enthusiastically received by large parts of the German population, many of whom volunteered to fill the state's administrative and resource gaps so as to help realize the "welcome culture" that Merkel envisaged. One observer summarizes, "Civil society's efforts were vast, polyphonic and everywhere—in small towns and large cities, urban and suburban, in eastern and western Germany, by Christian and Muslim, students and professors, old and young, retired and working people, overwhelmingly, but not only, by women." German people everywhere welcomed asylum seekers, made them feel safe and accepted, and assisted them with "everything from A to Z."[82]

Certainly, there was a fragility to the emotional culture that emerged, and opposition to Merkel's policy swelled in the face of reports of sexual assaults by asylum seekers in Cologne on New Year's Eve 2015 and some further high-profile assaults by migrants on German women in subsequent years.[83] Nevertheless, while Merkel paid a political cost for her decision, she managed to cling to power even through a 2017 federal election. And what better way to spend one's political capital than to strive to care for the vulnerable?

---

[80]For more, see Erin Goheen Glanville, "What Happens to a Story? Encountering Imaginative Humanitarian Ethnography in the Classroom," in *Opening Up the University: Teaching and Learning with Refugees*, eds. Ian Cook, Celine Cantat, and Prem Kumar Rajaram (Oxford: Berghahn Books, forthcoming).

[81]Mihret Yohannes, "Angela Merkel Welcomes Refugees to Germany Despite Rising Anti-Immigration Movement," *Washington Times*, September 10, 2015; BBC News, "Migrant Crisis: Merkel Warns of EU 'Failure,'" *BBC News*, August 31, 2015; and "Germany to Spend Extra €6bn to Fund Record Influx of 800,000 Refugees," *Guardian*, September 7, 2015.

[82]Funk, "Spectre in Germany," 292.

[83]"Almost One Year After the Cologne Attacks, Germany Still Struggles with Refugee Integration," *TheJournal.ie*, December 17, 2016; and Katrin Bennhold and Melissa Eddy, "Merkel, to Survive, Agrees to Border Camps for Migrants," *New York Times*, July 2, 2018.

In the years following the 2015 decision, Merkel has made some lamentable concessions to her opponents, leading the European Union's efforts to reduce the number of asylum seekers entering its territories via disturbing deals with Turkey (2016) and Libya (2017) and then agreeing to build "transit centers" on Germany's borders in order to screen asylum seekers and exclude from admission those who have applied for asylum elsewhere (2018).[84] But the fact that Merkel has clung to power for several years while Germany continues to host almost one million asylum seekers reveals the great potential for nurturing a collective willingness to offer costly and risky generosity to strangers.

A third way to spark compassion in others is by acting compassionately oneself. This is where individual Christians and church communities can be particularly effective, witnessing to the broader national community a compassionate desire to embrace the vulnerable stranger. Social psychologist Jonathan Haidt gives the name "elevation" to the moral feeling that is generated by witnessing or hearing of "acts of virtue or moral beauty." This moral feeling, he explains, "causes warm, open feelings . . . in the chest; and it motivates people to behave more virtuously themselves."[85] How wonderful it is when we see church communities and other groups pursuing compassionate care for the forcibly displaced. How pleasing it is when this witness sparks transformative change in the dispositions and desires of national communities. How beautiful it would be if a wind of Christian compassion were to prompt spirals of compassion and generosity as a counter to the spirals of fear and anxiety that have so gripped Western societies in recent years.

Embracing vulnerability, making sacrifices, and celebrating mutual transformation. To really embrace the vulnerable stranger, we need to embrace for ourselves a measure of vulnerability. Replacing fear with compassion requires that we give up the pursuit of absolute security, place our trust in those that we welcome, and accept the risks entailed.[86] Philosopher Onora O'Neill explains the necessity of trusting others:

---

[84]Bennhold and Eddy, "Merkel, to Survive."

[85]Jonathan Haidt, "Elevation and the Positive Psychology of Morality," in *Flourishing: Positive Psychology and the Life Well Lived*, ed. Corey L. M. Keyes and Jonathan Haidt (Washington, DC: American Psychological Association, 2003), 275-89, at 275.

[86]A recent study by international relations scholar Burcu Bayram demonstrates the importance of a disposition of trust in facilitating the care of strangers. Bayram finds that "trusting individuals are substantially more willing to aid strangers even when this help requires personal or national sacrifice. . . . The bonds of trust expand the boundaries of global justice." A. Burcu Bayram, "Aiding Strangers: Generalized Trust and the Moral Basis of Public Support for Foreign Development Aid," *Foreign Policy Analysis* 13, no. 1 (2017): 133-53, at 135.

In placing trust we don't simply assume that others are reliable and predictable.
... All trust risks disappointment. The risk of disappointment, even of betrayal,
cannot be written out of our lives. As Samuel Johnson put it "it is happier to
be sometimes cheated than not to trust." Trust is needed not because everything is wholly predictable, let alone wholly guaranteed, but on the contrary
because life has to be led without guarantees.[87]

Certainly, we ought to exercise prudence. Neither individuals nor nations
are called to incautiously trust and embrace those whose intentions they have
good reasons to fear. But we noted earlier that Western states have very good
vetting processes in place for refugees. These processes are typically much
more rigorous than the processes for any other category of migrant or vis-
itor.[88] Recall that immigrants tend to commit crimes at lower rates than
native-born citizens. Recall that the risk of terrorist attacks by people resettled as refugees is close to zero. The decision of a state to welcome and
place trust in refugees is hardly akin to offering up its citizens "on a platter to
the wolves," as some would have it.[89] Nevertheless, our security can never be
guaranteed. In choosing to welcome vulnerable strangers, we take certain
risks and accept certain costs. We make sacrifices. The good Samaritan did
the same for the man by the side of the road. Jesus did the same for us. There
is vast potential for creative witness, bold advocacy, and moral leadership that
might cultivate a sense of joyful celebration of the opportunities we have to
bear risks and costs for the sake of those in need.[90]

We saw such joy manifest in Germany in 2015. Here the mobilization of
risky and costly compassion generated a range of positive emotions: the joy
of having chosen to care *for* strangers rather than seek security *from* them,
the feeling of connection and purpose in doing so in community with others,
and the sense of pride in a nation making amends for past injustices.[91] Such
positive feelings can be long lasting. Consider how, more than seventy years
after the event, the people of Denmark continue to take pride in their risky
and costly efforts to protect Jews from the Nazis during World War II.[92]

---

[87]Onora O'Neill, *A Question of Trust* (Cambridge: Cambridge University Press, 2002), 24.

[88]Bauman, Soerens, and Smeir, *Seeking Refuge*, 77-78.

[89]Strand, "Throwing Caution to the Wind."

[90]On risk, see Gemma Tulud Cruz, "Toward an Ethic of Risk: Catholic Social Teaching and Immigration Reform," *SCE* 24, no. 3 (2011): 294-310; and Sharon D. Welch, *A Feminist Ethic of Risk*,
rev. ed. (Minneapolis: Augsburg Fortress, 2000).

[91]For discussion, see Luke Glanville, "Self-Interest and the Distant Vulnerable," *EIA* 30, no. 3 (2016):
335-53.

[92]Emmy E. Werner, *A Conspiracy of Decency: The Rescue of the Danish Jews During World War II*
(Boulder, CO: Westview, 2002).

Research shows that compassion is good for our happiness and even for our health.[93] At a time when our nations seem sick with fear as they increasingly exclude and, in turn, harm vulnerable strangers in the impossible pursuit of absolute security, we might point out a better, happier, healthier way.

Just as we need to accept a degree of vulnerability and welcome a measure of sacrifice instead of selfishly and relentlessly pursuing absolute security, so too do we need to embrace the possibility of mutual transformation rather than clinging to fearful isolation and social stagnation. Miroslav Volf suggests that the very act of welcoming others involves being willing "to readjust our identities to make space for them."[94] Pope Francis speaks of the importance of promoting a "culture of encounter, in which we are not only prepared to give, but also to receive from others."[95] He applies this to nations, encouraging them to embrace "opportunities for intercultural enrichment brought about by the presence of migrants and refugees."[96] To truly embrace new arrivals, we must accept the need for adjustment and the possibility of losing some of what is familiar and comfortable. We may grieve this loss for a time, but we can also celebrate that which is new: new friendships, new communal traditions, and new national stories.

INSTITUTIONALIZING LOVE

Emotions are not only collectively felt. They are institutionalized. They are made concrete in the form of national policies and bureaucratic procedures. Our fears of vulnerable strangers are reflected not only in how we talk about them but also in how we aggressively engage them at our borders, how we indefinitely detain them while slowly processing their claims, how we exacerbate their traumas by demanding that they "perform their fearfulness" as we interrogate their claims so forcefully, and how we impose inflexible requirements for integration on those that we choose to welcome.[97] Our fears lead us to institutionalize unjust "solutions" to the refugee "problem."

---

[93]Stephen G. Post, "Altruism, Happiness, and Health: It's Good to Be Good," *International Journal of Behavioral Medicine* 12, no. 2 (2005): 66-77. The same is true of trust. See Kohn, *Trust*, 85-86, 123.

[94]Miroslav Volf, *Exclusion and Embrace: A Theological Exploration of Identity, Otherness, and Reconciliation* (Nashville: Abingdon, 1996), 29.

[95]Pope Francis, *Message of His Holiness Pope Francis for the World Day of Migrants and Refugees,* Libreria Editrice Vaticana, January 17, 2016.

[96]Pope Francis, *Message of His Holiness Pope Francis for the 104th World Day of Migrants and Refugees 2018,* Libreria Editrice Vaticana, January 14, 2018.

[97]Lyndsey Stonebridge notes that asylum seekers are increasingly required to "perform their fearfulness" in order to satisfy "ever more baroque" legal and administrative criteria for admission to Western countries. Lyndsey Stonebridge, *Placeless People: Writings, Rights, and Refugees* (Oxford: Oxford University Press, 2018), 169.

If we hope for our nations to relinquish their fears of strangers, it is vital that we not only strive to nurture collective compassion but seek to lock it in, in a sense, and make it manifest in practice by pursuing the institutionalization of love in place of our entrenched structures of fear.[98] What this ideally looks like will vary from context to context, but it will necessarily involve a hospitality that welcomes and embraces and that also gives time and space to those who have fled their homes so that they may continue to grieve and begin to adjust. It will seek to replace detention with stable housing arrangements for those seeking asylum. It will give assistance in making refugee claims, language training, vocational retraining, and support in finding work. Religious groups and other community groups will be mobilized to provide support for newcomers for the first number of years. Far from exacerbating physical and emotional suffering, it will include the provision of generous treatment for the traumas that so many refugees carry with them.[99] And rather than providing welcome with an expectation of gratitude and reciprocity, communities will simply care for newcomers, offering to enfold them as kin and inviting them to participate in life together.[100]

We described in chapter five some of the ways in which Kinbrace has worked alongside Canadian authorities to make the process of claiming refuge less adversarial and less traumatizing. Christian organizations and individuals involved in welcoming displaced people have a profound role to play in advocating on their behalf, urging the concretization of love, rather than fear, in the many bureaucratic regulations and practices that refugees encounter.

Embracing diversity. Perhaps the most delicate aspect of the process of institutionalizing love for new arrivals is the cultivation of policies that

---

[98]See similarly Neta C. Crawford, "Institutionalizing Passion in World Politics: Fear and Empathy," *International Theory* 6, no. 3 (2014): 535-57; and idem, "No Borders, No Bystanders: Developing Individual and Institutional Capacities for Global Moral Responsibility," in *Global Basic Rights*, ed. Charles R. Beitz and Robert E. Goodin (Oxford: Oxford University Press, 2009), 131-55.

[99]For discussion of the difficulties of "helping without hurting" in this context, see Bauman, Soerens, and Smeir, *Seeking Refuge*, 131-51.

[100]Augustine puts it well:

Once you have bestowed gifts on the unfortunate, you may easily yield to the temptation to exalt yourself over him, to assume superiority over the object of your benefaction. He fell into need, and you supplied him: you feel yourself as the giver to be a bigger man than the receiver of the gift. You should want him to be your equal, that both may be subject to the one on whom no favor can be bestowed.

Augustine, *Homilies on the First Epistle of John* 8.5, quoted in Eric Gregory, "*Agape* and Special Relations in a Global Economy: Theological Sources," in *Global Neighbors: Christian Faith and Moral Obligation in Today's Economy*, ed. Douglas A. Hicks and Mark Valeri (Grand Rapids, MI: Eerdmans, 2008), 16-42, at 34.

uphold justice amidst increased cultural diversity. Christians in the Dutch Reformed tradition have thankfully given much attention to the ways in which diverse cultures and even diverse religions might be treated equitably and justly within a single political community, developing models of "principled pluralism," "confessional pluralism," and "Christian pluralism," each of which aims at ensuring "public justice" in a context of diversity.[101] The task of a state should not be to protect a homogenous culture and enforce the assimilation of newcomers into that culture. The approach of Denmark, for example, in which children born in low-income and heavily Muslim neighborhoods have been separated from their families from the age of one for at least twenty-five hours a week for mandatory instruction in "Danish values," is to be deplored.[102] Genuine embrace of new arrivals involves embracing the possibility of mutual transformation. And remember that Western societies are not homogenous anyway; we should be wary of the motives of those claiming that they are. The rightful task of a state confronting increased diversity is to establish just laws and public policies that balance the many legitimate interests within the community, including the interests of those from diverse backgrounds who have only recently joined.[103]

Why? Why should Christians put at risk the cultural dominance that they have long enjoyed and encourage their political communities to make room and ensure justice for newcomers with different cultures, traditions, and beliefs? Matthew Kaemingk answers this well in his book *Christian Hospitality and Muslim Immigration in an Age of Fear*. Kaemingk reminds us that Christ is "a sovereign king who demanded justice for all religions and ideologies under his sovereign rule—even those who denied Christ's very kingship."[104] We saw in chapter four how Jesus loved as kin the dishonored, the marginalized, and the vulnerable that he encountered, even as some rejected his Lordship. And indeed, does not the call of the gospel for every person to come

---

[101]See for example James W. Skillen, *In Pursuit of Justice: Christian Democratic Explorations* (Lanham, MD: Rowman & Littlefield, 2004); Jonathan Chaplin, "Beyond Multiculturalism—But to Where?: Public Justice and Cultural Diversity," *Philosophia Reformata* 73, no. 2 (2008): 190-209; and Matthew Kaemingk, *Christian Hospitality and Muslim Immigration in an Age of Fear* (Grand Rapids, MI: Eerdmans, 2018). On the parallels between these reformed models of pluralism and liberal models of multiculturalism, see Will Kymlicka, "Is There a Christian Pluralist Approach to Immigration?" *Comment*, April 19, 2018.

[102]Ellen Barry and Martin Selsoe Sorensen, "In Denmark, Harsh New Laws for Immigrant 'Ghettos,'" *New York Times*, July 1, 2018.

[103]Chaplin, "Beyond Multiculturalism," 197. And the task of Christians and others within the state is to nurture virtues—not least hospitality—that make space for diversity within community. Kaemingk, *Christian Hospitality*.

[104]Kaemingk, *Christian Hospitality*, 24.

to Christ as Lord also assume a *plurality* of religious beliefs? In this light, Christians should likewise seek justice for diverse peoples, and especially those in need, within their political communities. Kaemingk calls on American evangelicals in particular to "lay down their dreams of American cultural domination" and "pick up the more humble—and, frankly, more interesting— dream of American pluralism, justice, and respectful contestation."[105]

How? How should political communities go about institutionalizing public justice amidst diversity? Jonathan Chaplin neatly summarizes the Reformed answer: "The state establishes societal space and infrastructural conditions within which individuals, associations, institutions and other agents can freely and responsibly pursue their own distinctive callings and pursuits, and also restrains acts which violate or damage the capacity of such agents to do these things."[106] States will appropriately place certain minimal demands on recent immigrants in order to maintain social order and stability. This will of course include a duty to abide by the law and to pay taxes. States will also seek to nurture—though not enforce—societal participation and integration by providing or funding opportunities to learn the language and to understand the community and its institutions. But states will also seek to ensure that newcomers are allowed to enjoy cultural and religious freedoms as individuals and as groups, placing limits on these freedoms only where necessary to protect people from harm or to prevent serious civil disorder. As Abraham Kuyper put it in his own defense of pluralism more than a century ago, "That freedom which we want for ourselves we must not withhold from others."[107]

Building capacity. The task of institutionalizing love is by no means easy. It requires not merely the careful development of compassionate and just policies and procedures but also a conscious effort to build national capacities so that a disposition of self-sacrifice for the neighbor in need might be sustained over time. The example of Germany in 2015 is again useful here. In addition to the wonderful efforts of many German citizens to welcome hundreds of thousands of asylum seekers, the German state worked hard to provide basic needs, such as housing, medical care, and living expenses, and also to offer language courses and job training to facilitate integration into society and the labor market. It created 100,000 workfare jobs for those living

---

[105]Kaemingk, *Christian Hospitality*, 290.

[106]Chaplin, "Beyond Multiculturalism," 197. And the task of Christians and others within the state is to nurture habits, virtues, and practices—not least of hospitality—that make space for diversity within community. Kaemingk, *Christian Hospitality*.

[107]Abraham Kuyper, *Pro rege: of, Het koningschap van Christus* 3.181-82, quoted in Kaemingk, *Christian Hospitality*, 289.

in collective housing and adjusted labor laws to make it easier for potential employers to hire refugees for regular jobs. Germany spent as much as €20 billion on these programs in the first year. But still Germany's institutions struggled to cope with the influx of so many new people.[108] Significantly, one year on from her decision to open Germany's borders, and amidst a growing domestic backlash, Merkel did not back away from her choice. She merely expressed regret that Germany's institutions were unprepared for the mass movement of people fleeing the violence in the Middle East: "If I was able to, I would turn back time by many, many years, so that I could have prepared the whole government and the authorities for the situation which hit us out of the blue in the late summer of 2015."[109]

Such capacity building among wealthy countries will become more and more necessary over the coming decades as climate change amplifies the frequency and severity of civil wars and generalized violence, food and water scarcity, and natural disasters, driving levels of displacement higher and higher. How wonderful it would be to institutionalize our love for the stranger to the extent that we might choose to welcome displaced people and be in a position to welcome them well. How beautiful it would be to conceive part of our national purpose to be the development of institutional capacity to embrace and enfold as kin as many as we can of the tens of millions of desperate people around the world forcibly displaced from their homes.

But, you may be thinking, any single country can only do so much. No one country can solve the global refugee crisis. So we must leave it up to each country to choose to be more generous, more welcoming, and to take up the opportunity of embracing and enfolding as kin a larger number of dispossessed, dishonored, and displaced people than they currently do. Existing Christian treatments of how countries should respond to suffering beyond their borders often leave the argument here. They offer reasons why individual countries should do more—perhaps much more. But they refrain from engaging with the opportunities and possibilities (and also limits) of international cooperation that aims at not merely providing safety and community for some displaced people but genuinely addressing the global crisis of displacement itself. We take up this neglected task in chapters nine and ten.

---

[108]Funk, "Spectre in Germany," 291-92. For a recent and excellent overview of the impact of Merkel's decision, see Philip Oltermann, "How Angela Merkel's Great Migrant Gamble Paid Off," *Guardian*, August 30, 2020.

[109]Quoted in Philip Oltermann and Kate Connolly, "Angela Merkel Admits Mistakes over Asylum Seekers After Disastrous Election," *Guardian*, September 19, 2016.

PART FOUR

THE WORLD

8

HOPE FOR GLOBAL KINSHIP

IN JULY 2013, POPE FRANCIS visited refugees and other migrants from North Africa who had recently arrived on the island of Lampedusa, the southernmost part of Italy, seeking a home in Europe. Here he prayed for the many who had drowned attempting the same journey. In his homily, he lamented what he described as "the globalization of indifference" toward our brother and sister migrants, our kin. Just as God asked Cain, "Where is your brother?," Francis observed that the question has to be asked today, "Who is responsible for the blood of these brothers and sisters of ours?" We reply, "It isn't I; I don't have anything to do with it; it must be someone else, but it is certainly not I." Francis continued:

> Today no one in our world feels responsible. We have lost a sense of responsibility for our brothers and sisters. We have fallen into the hypocrisy of the priest and the Levite whom Jesus described in the parable of the Good Samaritan: we see our brother half dead on the side of the road and perhaps we say to ourselves, "poor soul . . . !" and then we go on our way. It's not our responsibility, we think, and with that we feel reassured, assuaged. The culture of comfort, which makes us think only of ourselves, makes us insensitive to the cries of other people, makes us live in soap bubbles which, however lovely, are insubstantial; they offer a fleeting and empty illusion that results in indifference to others; indeed, it even leads to the globalization of indifference. In this globalized world, we have fallen into globalized indifference. We have become used to the suffering of others: it doesn't affect me; it doesn't concern me; it's none of my business![1]

---

[1]Pope Francis, *A Stranger and You Welcomed Me: A Call to Mercy and Solidarity with Migrants and Refugees* (Maryknoll, NY: Orbis, 2018), 5.

Genesis: Human Dignity

The book of Genesis asserts the essential unity of all of humanity and the dignity of every human being and of every people group.[a] Genesis teaches that every human bears the image of God (Gen 1:27). In the creation event, all of humanity is blessed (Gen 1:28). Following the flood, God makes a covenant with all of humanity and with every living creature (Gen 9:9-10).

Another way that Genesis communicates an essential unity among humankind is through a series of genealogies.[b] One highly unusual aspect of the Genesis genealogies when compared with other ancient genealogies is that they encompass the nations of the world. Following the flood narrative, the whole world is depicted as descending from Noah. In describing the various people groupings, there is no reference to differences between groups. Rather, the common descent of humanity is emphasized (Gen 10).[c] The dignity and unity of humankind communicated via these texts pave the way for non-Israelites to be grafted into Israel's family tree (e.g., Gen 41:50-52).

This globalized indifference has only worsened in the years since Francis spoke these words. In 2013, the United Nations' refugee agency, UNHCR, reported that 51.2 million people were forcibly displaced by persecution, conflict, or generalized violence. By the end of 2019, the number had risen to 79.5 million. 15.7 million refugees have been displaced for more than five years.[2] But, in a global climate of rising nationalist populism and international antagonism, we increasingly refuse responsibility for our vulnerable brothers and sisters. As the number of forcibly displaced people rises year by year, the number of people being welcomed and resettled by countries has begun to decline at an alarming rate—from 189,300 in 2016 to 107,800 in 2019[3]—and efforts to secure global commitment to a broad program of action to address the crisis of displacement are being rejected by some countries as incompatible with their "sovereign interests."[4] This is a crisis of kinship.

So far in this book, we have highlighted the biblical mandate for a thick form of kinship with the displaced, a kinship that embraces and enfolds

---

[2] United Nations High Commissioner for Refugees (UNHCR), *Global Trends 2013: War's Human Cost*, June 20, 2014, 2, www.unhcr.org/statistics/country/5399a14f9/unhcr-global-trends-2013.html; and UNHCR, *Global Trends: Forced Displacement in 2019*, June 18, 2020, 2, 24, www.unhcr.org/en-au/statistics/unhcrstats/5ee200e37/unhcr-global-trends-2019.html.

[3] UNHCR, *Global Trends: Forced Displacement in 2017*, June 25, 2018, 30, www.unhcr.org/5b27be547.pdf; UNHCR, *Global Trends: Forced Displacement in 2019*, 2.

[4] US Ambassador Kelley Currie, "Explanation of Vote in a Meeting of the Third Committee on a UNHCR Omnibus Resolution," United States Mission to the United Nations, November 13, 2018.

The book of Genesis, then, has a universal emphasis, which high-lights God's ongoing care for every nation, locating Israel as a peo-ple whom God chose for a particular calling, within a larger commu-nity of nations. An ancient Jewish document, the Mishnah, puts it this way: "Why did God create only one human being? To promote peace among the creation, so that no-one can say to a fellow human being: 'my father was better than yours.'"[d]

---

[a]See further, Frank Crüsemann, "Human Solidarity and Ethnic Identity: Israel's Self-Definition in the Genealogical System of Genesis," in *Ethnicity and the Bible*, ed. Mark G. Brett (Leiden: Brill, 2002), 57-76, at 72.

[b]Genealogy-like material is found in Genesis 4:17-26; 5:3-32; 10:1-32; 11:10-32; 22:20-24; 25:1-26; 29–30; 35:16-29; 36:1-43; 46:8-27.

[c]The unity—indeed kinship—of humanity is noted even in the context of animosity between nations. When nations such as Moab and Ammon are denigrated, they are depicted as arising from incest (Gen 19:30-38). Even Israel's traditional enemy, the Amalekites, are represented as close kin (Gen 36:12; cf. Ex 17:14-16; Deut 25:17-19; Crüsemann, "Human Solidarity and Ethnic Identity," 71).

[d]Sanhedrin 4:5.

---

vulnerable strangers into church communities and national communities, a deeply relational kinship. The cultivation of such kinship by communities engaged in welcoming strangers is certainly a vital aspect of a comprehensive global response to the issue of forced displacement. But a comprehensive response requires that individual countries also work together, cooperating and collaborating, sharing responsibilities and opportunities, to ensure that those who are displaced internally within their home countries or seeking temporary asylum in other countries are given protection and assistance, that those who wish to return to their home countries and towns after a period of displacement are able to do so with safety and dignity, and that those who seek permanent resettlement in other countries are able to secure it within a reasonable period of time and without further trauma.

Such a comprehensive response is appropriately grounded in a broader understanding of kinship: a kinship with all humanity. We noted in our in-troduction how UN Secretary-General Kofi Annan, reflecting on the 1994 Rwandan genocide, spoke of the need for the international community to move "from dehumanization and toward a stronger sense of global kinship."[5]

---

[5]Kofi Annan, "Rwanda Genocide 'Must Always Leave Us with a Sense of Bitter Regret and Abiding Sorrow,' Says Secretary General to New York Memorial Conference," *Meetings Coverage and Press Releases*, SG/SM/9223-AFR/870-HQ/631, United Nations, March 26, 2004.

Only on such a notion of "global kinship" can we begin to build a comprehensive global response to the present crisis.

There is of course a biblical mandate for a globalized understanding of kinship, as Pope Francis's words made clear. God created each of us in God's own image and calls us all into relationship with Jesus Christ. Perhaps we might not all be rightly described as "in Christ" in the full sense of the phrase, but we are all called to such a relationship and thus are called to unity with each other. Gendered language aside, Martin Luther King Jr. put it well in his powerful 1967 speech at Riverside Church against the Vietnam War: "I share with all men the calling to be a son of the living God. Beyond the calling of race or nation or creed is this vocation of sonship and brotherhood. . . . We are called to speak for the weak, for the voiceless, for the victims of our nation, for those it calls 'enemy,' for no document from human hands can make these humans any less our brothers."[6] Recall the insight of Kinbrace's cofounder, Loren Balisky: "Refugees are the you and me of another place." Such notions of global kinship surely challenge some common habits of thinking about global affairs.

In this chapter and the next, we shift our focus from the individual nation to the global community of nations. We begin by wrestling with a dominant approach to thinking about global affairs taken by many today: Christian realism. This approach, in its simplest and most influential form, assumes that countries will behave selfishly in their relations with those beyond their borders. And it insists that it is necessary and right for them to do so in a dangerous and unpredictable world. We find this approach wanting on both descriptive and theological grounds; it offers an unjustifiably fearful description of international reality and an unjustifiably selfish ethic for how states should respond. In its place, we offer a renewed vision for international relations, grounding it in a biblical ethic of global kinship with the vulnerable and drawing inspiration from the global effort in the nineteenth century to abolish the slave trade. This will set us up for the next chapter, in which we pursue the possibility of a creative, feasible, and comprehensive response to our global crisis of forced displacement.

WRESTLING WITH CHRISTIAN REALISM

Since the mid-twentieth century, the clearest and most thoroughly developed model for Christians—indeed for anyone—wanting to think about

---

[6]Martin Luther King Jr., *A Call to Conscience: The Landmark Speeches of Dr. Martin Luther King, Jr.*, ed. Clayborne Carson and Kris Shepard (New York: Warner Books, 2001), 145-46.

and contribute to global politics has been a tradition called Christian realism.[7] A wide range of public figures, from George W. Bush and John McCain to Barack Obama and Hillary Clinton, have cited it as influential in their thinking about international affairs.[8] This tradition emphasizes the reality of human sin, the perils of idealistic projects, the inevitability of international competition and conflict, and the virtue of each state carefully pursuing its national interest. It is an approach that has seeped into the Christian imagination today to such effect that, when confronted with the plight of the forcibly displaced, many feel that it would be imprudent, reckless, and even immoral for their country to make substantial sacrifices for the sake of strangers. To concerns about threats to national identity and state sovereignty and fears of domestic insecurity and economic decline that we considered in previous chapters, Christian realists add worries about global threats, the obstacles to international cooperation, and the dangers of neglecting one's own national interests. It is vital, therefore, that we briefly wrestle with the Christian realist approach, focusing on the arguments of its most influential proponent, Reinhold Niebuhr, before offering an alternative vision for global politics that can form the basis of a more just and compassionate global response to the plight of the displaced.

Christian realists begin with a number of assumptions about the "reality" of international life. As we saw in chapter eight, Niebuhr observed in the mid-twentieth century that the fallen nature of individuals expresses itself in fears and anxieties, which motivate acts of selfishness and ruthlessness, and this is intensified at the collective level and particularly the level of the nation. When contemplating global affairs, Christian realists like Niebuhr add to this problem of national selfishness the problem of international anarchy. By this they mean that, whereas the harmful impacts of individual selfishness can be mitigated to a degree by domestic authorities, there is no equivalent authority at the global level that can compel or constrain the behavior of states. "Try as he will," Niebuhr observed, "man seems incapable

---

[7]For some beautiful alternative Christian approaches that place greater emphasis than realists do on the possibilities of peaceful, just, and compassionate global relations, see Lisa Sowle Cahill, *Global Justice, Christology and Christian Ethics* (Cambridge: Cambridge University Press, 2013); Daniel Philpott, *Just and Unjust Peace: An Ethic of Political Reconciliation* (Oxford: Oxford University Press, 2012); and Glen H. Stassen, ed., *Just Peacemaking: The New Paradigm for the Ethics of Peace and War* (Cleveland: Pilgrim Press, 2008).

[8]Peter B. Josephson and R. Ward Holder, *Reinhold Niebuhr in Theory and Practice: Christian Realism and Democracy in America in the Twenty-First Century* (Lanham, MD: Rowman & Littlefield, 2018).

of forming an international community, with power and prestige great enough to bring social restraint upon collective egoism."[9]

From this bleak description of international life, Christian realists derive a "realistic" ethic for how states ought to behave. The realities of international relations, they insist, excuse and indeed require in relations between states a degree of selfishness that is not acceptable in relations between individuals: since the selfishness of other states is unrestrained, our own states need to be selfish too.

"Group relations can never be as ethical as those which characterize individual relations," Niebuhr claimed. The reality of global politics "justifies and necessitates political policies which a purely individualistic ethic must always find embarrassing."[10] He warned against a "saintly abnegation of interest" that might "encourage the ruthless aggrandizement of the strong and the unscrupulous"[11] and cautioned against idealistic scheming that fails to account for humanity's corruption. Instead, he recommended prudent care of one's own interests and solemn recognition of the limits of political possibility.[12]

When we look at the world today, it is easy to see the attraction of Christian realism and to understand why it remains persuasive to so many. The international community is riven with hypocrisy and mistrust, rivalry and conflict. The global crisis of forced displacement is itself a product of this anarchical condition. Tens of thousands of vulnerable people are forced to flee war, conflict, and persecution every day. Many more are compelled to leave their homes and communities to escape conditions of grave poverty and vulnerability produced in part by the selfish and aggressive trade policies of powerful states. And so long as states continue to refuse to cooperate meaningfully to address the escalating destruction of the global climate, this crisis of survival migration is only going to get worse.

At its best, Christian realism offers vital insights. It reminds us of our fallen nature and the temptations of power, the limits of human understanding, and the dangers of seeking to remake the world in our image. It calls us to humility. Christian realists have been particularly quick to call out the imprudence and injustice of foolish and reckless wars. Niebuhr expressed his dismay over the Vietnam War, declaring it "an example of the illusion of

---

[9]Reinhold Niebuhr, *Moral Man and Immoral Society: A Study in Ethics and Politics* (New York: Charles Scribner's Sons, 1932), 48.

[10]Niebuhr, *Moral Man and Immoral Society*, 83, xi.

[11]Quoted in Nicholas Wolterstorff, *Justice in Love* (Grand Rapids, MI: Eerdmans, 2011), 66.

[12]Reinhold Niebuhr, *The Children of Light and the Children of Darkness* (1944; repr., Chicago: University of Chicago Press, 2011).

American omnipotence."[13] Many of Niebuhr's realist descendants were likewise vocal critics of the 2003 invasion of Iraq.[14]

When thinking about the global dynamics of forced displacement, Christian realism usefully reminds us of the challenges before us: states tend to protect their own sovereignty and prioritize their own national interests, competition and conflict between states impedes cooperation, and international laws and institutions struggle to constrain the most powerful from behaving as they wish.[15]

But Christian realism risks encouraging complacency and moral compromise. To be sure, while emphasizing the effects of sin, Niebuhr still sought a more just world. He worried about narrow constructions of national interests that obscure "the residual capacity for justice and devotion to the larger good."[16] He even expressed hope for the future realization of a form of global kinship: "There are no limits to be set in history for the achievement of more universal brotherhood, for the development of more perfect and more inclusive mutual relations. . . . The *agape* of the Kingdom of God [is] a resource for infinite developments towards a more perfect brotherhood in history."[17] But ultimately, for Niebuhr, humanity's "residual capacity for justice" could not be relied on. The possibilities for pursuing what he termed "the law of love" were severely circumscribed. He was criticized in his day by black liberation theologians and feminist theologians for being too comfortable with the status quo, too cautious about the pursuit of justice, and too pessimistic about the possibilities of change.[18] Niebuhr indicated that the most we can realize is a moderated approximation of justice, which seeks balance among the interests of competing powerful groups. But, as liberation theologian James Cone rightly responded, "What about groups without power?"[19]

---

[13]Quoted in Michael Joseph Smith, *Realist Thought from Weber to Kissinger* (Baton Rouge: Louisiana State University Press, 1986), 128.

[14]See for example the advertisement placed by thirty-three international relations scholars, including many who identify as realists, in the *New York Times* on September 26, 2002, declaring "War with Iraq Is Not in America's National Interest."

[15]See similarly Duncan Bell, "Security and Poverty: On Realism and Global Justice," in *Politics Recovered: Realist Thought in Theory and Practice*, ed. Matt Sleat (New York: Columbia University Press, 2018), 296-319, at 306.

[16]Reinhold Niebuhr, *Man's Nature and His Communities: Essays on the Dynamics and Enigmas of Man's Personal and Social Existence* (New York: Charles Scribner's Sons, 1965), 71, quoted in William E. Scheuerman, *The Realist Case for Global Reform* (Cambridge, UK: Polity Press, 2011), 29.

[17]Reinhold Niebuhr, *The Nature and Destiny of Man: A Christian Interpretation*, vol. 2, *Human Destiny* (London: Nisbet, 1943), 89.

[18]Robin W. Lovin, *Reinhold Niebuhr* (Nashville: Abingdon, 2007), 63-66.

[19]James H. Cone, *The Cross and the Lynching Tree* (Maryknoll, NY: Orbis, 2011), 71.

These dangers of complacency and compromise are evident in the arguments of those who see the global refugee crisis through a realist lens today.
Some observers draw from realism a belief that states cannot afford to sacrifice
their interests and be more generous to refugees in a competitive and unco-
operative world. Others take the insights of realism even further to argue that
generosity toward the displaced can actually *worsen* the global crisis.

Leading refugee scholars Alexander Betts and Paul Collier, for example,
criticize Chancellor Angela Merkel's decision to open Germany's borders to
asylum seekers in 2015, lamenting that this decision triggered a flood of Syrian
refugees into Europe from Turkey, Lebanon, and Jordan.[20] This is a troubling
lamentation since it implies that the tragedy was not that millions of people
were forcibly displaced but that a portion of them made their way to Europe.
In any event, as we explain in chapter ten, the claim that Merkel's decision led
to increased movement of Syrians into Europe is not even correct.

Similarly, Australian Minister for Home Affairs Peter Dutton warns that
Australia's "hard-won success" in deterring people smugglers "could be
undone overnight by a single act of compassion" toward refugees and asylum
seekers denied entry to Australia and held in indefinite offshore detention.[21]
This is a disturbing claim, not least because it ignores the reality that deterring
people smuggling in one part of the world does little to protect vulnerable
people. Indeed, it commonly compels them to undertake more dangerous
journeys in search of asylum in more dangerous parts of the world.[22]

We might try to put the Christian realist way of thinking to work in the
pursuit of just ends, articulating interest-based reasons for states to be more
generous to displaced people and more cooperative with each other in addressing the global crisis. Niebuhr himself noted that national interests can
at times be "inextricably related" to "a web of mutual and universal or general
interests," such that a state best advances its own interests through activities
that also advance the interests of the global community.[23] A Christian realist
case for caring for the displaced would be grounded in the observation that
the world is interconnected. Conflict and instability in one part of the world

---

[20]Alexander Betts and Paul Collier, *Refuge: Rethinking Refugee Policy in a Changing World* (Oxford:
   Oxford University Press, 2017).
[21]"Compassion Can Undo Efforts Against People-Smugglers: Dutton," *SBS News*, June 23, 2018.
[22]Our argument here rests not on the claim that Betts, Collier, or Dutton identifies as a Christian
   realist but that their (problematic) arguments accord with a realist approach.
[23]Reinhold Niebuhr, *Man's Nature and His Communities*, 79, quoted in Scheuerman, *Realist Case for
   Global Reform*, 28. See similarly Robin W. Lovin, *Christian Realism and the New Realities* (Cambridge: Cambridge University Press, 2008).

very often generates conflict and instability elsewhere. Refugee flows and situations of protracted displacement are both produced by and contribute to such conflict and instability. Consider, for example, how the flows of refugees from Iraq after the United States–led invasion in 2003 strained resources and increased tensions in Syria, contributing to the outbreak of civil war. This war in turn paved the way for the rise of ISIS and led to a broader war that engulfed the region, drew in most of the world's major powers, and generated the forcible displacement of millions more, triggering further local, regional, and global instability. It is arguably in every state's strategic interest both to address the causes of displacement and to care for the displaced.

This is a valuable point to remember. Yet, the realist approach remains a self-centered way of thinking about the plight of the displaced. The risk with such an approach is that, while states may perceive an interest in responding to certain situations of displacement for the sake of their own security and economic well-being, they will perceive little interest in addressing other situations that are more distant and less strategically important. And even in those instances where states perceive a strategic interest in engaging with displacement beyond their borders, they may conclude that their interests are best served by closing their borders and seeking to contain the problem elsewhere, rather than caring for the vulnerable. What's more, insofar as this realist approach relies on casting the displacement of strangers as a threat to one's own security, it risks being co-opted by those who wish to gain from the xenophobic and exclusionary politics of fear that we grappled with in chapter eight.

PURSUING A RENEWED VISION FOR GLOBAL RELATIONS

We urgently need a renewed vision for global engagement with the plight of the displaced. Christian realism will not do. Thankfully, it turns out that the relentlessly fearful description of international reality that Christian realists present is inaccurate. States do not inevitably and ruthlessly pursue their own strategic and economic interests. Consider, among countless examples, the United States' effort to provide mass famine relief to Soviet Russia in 1921 or Denmark's willingness to risk national suicide in protecting Jews from the Nazis during World War II, or, again, Germany's decision to open its borders to asylum seekers in 2015.[24]

---

[24]On the Soviet famine relief effort, see Robert W. McElroy, *Morality and American Foreign Policy* (Princeton, NJ: Princeton University Press, 1992). On the rescue of Danish Jews, see Emmy E. Werner, *A Conspiracy of Decency: The Rescue of the Danish Jews During World War II* (Boulder, CO: Westview, 2002).

Such moral action, moreover, is sometimes witnessed not only at the level of individual states but collectively, even globally, in ways that realists cannot explain. Consider the successful cooperative effort of the United States and the Soviet Union to eradicate smallpox in the 1960s and 1970s—at the height of the Cold War—or the global outpouring of generosity in response to the Indian Ocean tsunami of 2004.[25] Consider more broadly the many examples of sustained change generated by shifts in shared values rather than strategic interests, such as the emergence of global norms prohibiting slavery, colonialism, and apartheid; chemical weapons, land mines, and cluster munitions.[26]

The possibilities for neighbor-loving behavior in global affairs are far greater than Christian realists tell us. As one international relations (IR) theorist rightly declares, "Realists regularly, sometimes spectacularly, overstate the nature and significance of the 'facts' that constrain the pursuit of moral objectives in (international) politics."[27] Another plainly concludes: "Anarchy is what states make of it."[28] States are free to seek cooperation over conflict and shared moral projects over self-interested pursuits, if they choose to do so.

The selfish ethic that Christian realists advance, therefore, is unjustifiable. The relentless pursuit of security and economic gain that we so often see in international relations is a choice made by political leaders. It is not a moral necessity. It is not a requirement of statecraft in an anarchic world. And we should not justify it as such.

There is nothing, therefore, about the nature of international relations that renders naive or problematic the arguments made in earlier chapters for why states should pursue justice both for those within their borders and for those beyond. Certainly, state leaders should think and act with humility. They

---

[25]For the smallpox example, see D. A. Henderson, *Smallpox: The Death of a Disease* (Amherst, NY: Prometheus, 2009).

[26]Neta C. Crawford, *Argument and Change in World Politics: Ethics, Decolonization, and Humanitarian Intervention* (Cambridge: Cambridge University Press, 2002); Audie Klotz, *Norms in International Relations: The Struggle Against Apartheid* (Ithaca, NY: Cornell University Press, 1995); Ethan A. Nadelmann, "Global Prohibition Regimes: The Evolution of Norms in International Society," *IO* 44, no. 4 (1990): 479-526; Margarita H. Petrova, "Rhetorical Entrapment and Normative Enticement: How the United Kingdom Turned from Spoiler into Champion of the Cluster Munition Ban," *ISQ* 60, no. 3 (2016): 387-99; Richard M. Price, *The Chemical Weapons Taboo* (Ithaca, NY: Cornell University Press, 1997); and idem, "Reversing the Gun Sights: Transnational Civil Society Targets Land Mines," *IO* 52, no. 3 (1998): 613-44.

[27]Jack Donnelly, "The Ethics of Realism," in *The Oxford Handbook of International Relations*, ed. Christian Reus-Smit and Duncan Snidal (Oxford: Oxford University Press, 2008), 153.

[28]Alexander Wendt, "Anarchy Is What States Makes of It: The Social Construction of Power Politics," *IO* 46, no. 2 (1992): 391-425.

should be wary of pride and arrogance—within their own hearts and in the hearts of their nations—and resist the temptations of hypocritical and destructive moral crusades. But they should also recognize that the choice to pursue exclusively their own national interests, rather than also the love of vulnerable neighbors—a choice too often rationalized with an emaciated notion of justice that is all too comfortable with global injustice—is sadly unimaginative. The decision to respond to fears and anxieties by striving for *absolute security*, and to justify such a response as realistic and necessary, is tragically uncreative. It is also ultimately self-defeating since the relentless pursuit of security fuels global cycles of fear and suspicion, antagonism and aggression—in a word, insecurity.

The enormous efforts of powerful and wealthy Western states to deter vulnerable asylum seekers from reaching their borders and to contain the global crisis of forced displacement to the Global South comes at an absurd cost. Many of these Western states expend significantly more resources keeping displaced people at a distance than they do contributing to international efforts to care for them. The effect of this is to leave the vulnerable in conditions of vulnerability, passing the risks and costs of care onto others, forgoing the opportunity of welcoming and creating kinship with strangers, and exacerbating already existing animosities toward the West.[29]

How much better would it be if states were willing to embrace a measure of vulnerability in their global relations rather than seeking ever greater measures of security? How much more beautiful would it be if states were willing to accept risks and costs for the sake of vulnerable strangers rather than constantly obsessing about their own vulnerability? As IR theorist Debra DeLaet suggests, states have an opportunity to embrace vulnerability "as a universal, shared condition that can generate an openness to an expanded sense of community that, in turn, undergirds a broadened sense of ethical responsibility towards others."[30] Accepting a degree of vulnerability, mutuality *with* others, and dependency *on* others is surely more biblical than the selfish pursuit of security and advantage *over* others, even at the level of global affairs. Recall Paul's words: "Each of you should look not only to your own interests but also to the interests of others" (Phil 2:4).

---

[29]In chap. 10, we detail how the Australian government spent more than US$700 million keeping 1,140 refugees and asylum seekers in offshore detention in the 2016–2017 financial year.

[30]Debra L. DeLaet, "The Ethics of Vulnerability in International Relations," in Brent J. Steele and Eric A. Heinze (eds.), *Routledge Handbook of Ethics and International Relations* (London: Routledge, 2018), 361. See also Caron E. Gentry, "Anxiety Politics: Creativity and Feminist Christian Realism," *Journal of International Relations and Development* 22, no. 2 (2018): 389-412.

Christian realists do a good job of *explaining* the selfishness of states. States do commonly prioritize the pursuit of their security and economic interests.[31] But we know that this selfishness is not inevitable, we ought not to be comfortable with it, and wherever possible we should challenge it and point to a better way.

The church can play a vital role here. Individual Christian citizens and politicians, church communities and denominations, and faith-based domestic and transnational advocacy movements have a strong record of acting as "norm entrepreneurs," to use a term from IR theory, throughout history encouraging and shaping not only national but also global change—often, though sadly not always, in the direction of justice.[32] While we may be tempted to think of foreign policy and international relations as realms over which the church can have little impact, it turns out that the church, as well as other grassroots and global movements, can and often does make a profound contribution. These entities can make a difference, IR scholars explain, by framing issues in particular ways and generating increased attention; bringing new ideas, information, and testimonies to public debates; challenging prevailing understandings of national identities, interests, and preferences; advocating the adoption of new policies; demanding implementation; and monitoring compliance.[33] Margaret Keck and Kathryn Sikkink go so far as to say that, when they are successful, effective advocacy networks "can break the cycles of history."[34] Thus the church has a profound opportunity to faithfully and creatively seek renewed engagement with the plight of the displaced both at the national level and at the global level.

We seek to describe what such change might look like in the next chapter. However, let us first draw some inspiration from a historical Christian-led

---

[31]Even this realist claim, however, is problematic insofar as the interpretation of these interests by states is not naturally given but shaped and reconstructed over time.

[32]The notion of "norm entrepreneur" is developed in Martha Finnemore and Kathryn Sikkink, "International Norm Dynamics and Political Change," *IO* 52, no. 4 (1998): 887-917. For a powerful study of successful global advocacy by Christians in defense of vulnerable people, from the sixteenth to the nineteenth century, see Peter Stamatov, *The Origins of Global Humanitarianism: Religion, Empires, and Advocacy* (Cambridge: Cambridge University Press, 2013). For more troubling examples of successful global advocacy by Christians opposing gun control and supporting oppressive regimes, see Clifford Bob, *The Global Right Wing and the Clash of World Politics* (Cambridge: Cambridge University Press, 2012); and Lauren Frances Turek, *To Bring the Good News to All Nations: Evangelical Influence on Human Rights and U.S. Foreign Relations* (Ithaca, NY: Cornell University Press, 2020).

[33]Margaret E. Keck and Kathryn Sikkink, *Activists Beyond Borders: Advocacy Networks in International Politics* (Ithaca, NY: Cornell University Press, 1998), 2-3.

[34]Keck and Sikkink, *Activists Beyond Borders*, x. See also Joshua W. Busby, *Moral Movements and Foreign Policy* (Cambridge: Cambridge University Press, 2010).

movement that generated profound moral change at the global level: the effort by nineteenth-century abolitionists to end the transatlantic slave trade.

DRAWING INSPIRATION FROM THE ABOLITION OF THE SLAVE TRADE

The central role of Quakers and evangelicals in the advocacy campaign that led Britain to abolish the slave trade within its own empire in 1807 is well known.[35] Christ had died for Africans just as he had died for Britons, they claimed, and the enslavement of Africans was detestable in the sight of God. It is noteworthy that the cause of emancipation was commonly articulated in terms of global kinship. Think, for example, of the famous image used by the Abolitionist Society depicting an African man on his knee, in chains, pleading "Am I Not a Man and a Brother?"

Perhaps it is less well known that Britain's subsequent effort to extend abolition across the Western hemisphere was also prompted by the advocacy of Christians and other abolitionists. Having abolished the lucrative trade in her own empire, Britain arguably had a strategic interest in compelling others to do the same.[36] But it seems unlikely that it would have done so had it not been for the continuing pressure applied by the Abolitionist Society.

Britain's foreign secretary during the pivotal years from 1812 to 1822, Lord Castlereagh, did not believe at first that Britain should pursue abolition internationally. It was wrong, he claimed, "to force it upon nations, at the expense of their honor and of the tranquility of the world."[37] But the abolitionists pressured Castlereagh relentlessly. One historian reports that they were "a continuous charge upon his time and energy" and "never ceased to exercise a formidable pressure upon the Government."[38] The Abolitionist Society lobbied foreign leaders as well, targeting Russian Tsar Alexander I and French statesman Talleyrand among others, seeking both to break down their resistance and to increase the pressure on the British government. Leading abolitionist William Wilberforce put the case unusually bluntly in a

---

[35]Christopher Leslie Brown, *Moral Capital: Foundations of British Abolitionism* (Chapel Hill: University of North Carolina Press, 2006); and Adam Hochschild, *Bury the Chains: Prophets and Rebels in the Fight to Free an Empire's Slaves* (New York: Houghton Mifflin Harcourt, 2005).

[36]Lauren Benton and Lisa Ford, *Rage for Order: The British Empire and the Origins of International Law, 1800–1850* (Cambridge, MA: Harvard University Press, 2016), 117-31.

[37]Quoted in Jenny S. Martinez, *The Slave Trade and the Origins of International Human Rights Law* (Oxford: Oxford University Press, 2012), 29.

[38]Charles K. Webster, *The Foreign Policy of Castlereagh, 1815–1822: Britain and the European Alliance* (London: G. Bell and Sons, 1925), 454, quoted in Ian Clark, *International Legitimacy and World Society* (Oxford: Oxford University Press, 2007), 48.

letter to the tsar, warning that "we should have no favorable opinion of his Majesty's religious and moral character if he did not honestly exert his powers on our behalf."[39]

When a peace treaty negotiated in 1814, near the end of the Napoleonic Wars between France and the other European powers, included a provision allowing France to renew its participation in the slave trade for five more years, the abolitionists were quick to respond. Wilberforce decried the provision as "the death warrant of a multitude of innocent victims, men, women, and children." Three-quarters of a million Britons, of a population of merely twelve million, signed a petition denouncing it.[40]

The British government could take the pressure no longer. At the Congress of Vienna of 1815, Lord Castlereagh persuaded the other European powers to declare the slave trade "repugnant to the principles of humanity and universal morality" and to acknowledge that "at length the public voice, in all civilized countries, calls aloud for its prompt suppression." The powers proclaimed "their wish of putting an end to a scourge, which has so long desolated Africa, degraded Europe, and afflicted humanity," and they acknowledged "the duty and necessity of abolishing it."[41]

The agreement at Vienna was not legally binding and set no deadline for abolition. Nevertheless, it was understood to provide a mandate for international action. Over the next few years, amidst ongoing pressure from the abolitionists, Britain negotiated numerous bilateral treaties that banned the slave trade and provided for enforcement through "courts of mixed commission." These were courts with judges from more than one country—a novel development in the history of international law.[42] By the 1840s, all the Atlantic maritime powers had signed international treaties committing them to abolish the trade. Britain deployed the Royal Navy to ensure their enforcement. The effort was remarkably successful. Whereas in the first decade of the nineteenth century an estimated 609,000 slaves had been transported across the Atlantic, by the late 1860s the trade had been reduced to a few hundred per year. By the century's close, every state in the Western Hemisphere had outlawed not only the slave trade but slavery itself.[43]

---

[39]Clark, *International Legitimacy*, 49-51; quotation at p. 50.
[40]Martinez, *Slave Trade*, 28-29; quotation at p. 28.
[41]Great Britain, Parliament, "Declaration of the Powers, on the Abolition of the Slave Trade (1815)," in *The Parliamentary Debates: From the Year 1803 to the Present Time* (London: T. C. Hansard, 1816), 32:200-201.
[42]Martinez, *Slave Trade*.
[43]Martinez, *Slave Trade*, 12-13.

Of course, rather than a selfless act of generosity, abolition entailed merely the termination of a horrific evil that Western Christians had participated in for far too long. And abolition, like all human endeavors, was far from perfect. The care and protection of liberated slaves was often either insufficiently prioritized or invoked to justify European colonialism. Also, slavery and other coercive systems of labor and indentured servitude were not completely eradicated. Tens of millions of people remain ensnared in one or another form of slavery today. Displaced people are particularly vulnerable to the evils of human trafficking and modern slavery.

Nevertheless, nineteenth-century abolitionism is an example that shows that profound global change is possible, that the church can play a profound role in advocating for it, and that states can be willing to accept substantial risks and costs to pursue it. Abolition has been described as the "most expensive international moral effort in modern world history."[44] All told, the Royal Navy's effort to suppress the trade cost about five thousand British lives (mostly due to disease) and an average of 1.8 percent of British national income annually from 1808 to 1867.[45]

We can begin to conceive how much more we might do to care for the vulnerable today when we compare this 1.8 percent figure to the 0.19 percent (United States), 0.23 percent (Australia), and 0.26 percent (Canada) of national income that some wealthy states currently spend on international aid (including their contributions to assisting displaced people abroad and the costs of the first year of welcoming refugees at home).[46] Let us turn now to imagine what a more generous, just, cooperative, and comprehensive global response to the issue of forced displacement might look like.

---

[44]Chaim D. Kaufmann and Robert Pape, "Explaining Costly International Moral Action: Britain's Sixty-Year Campaign Against the Atlantic Slave Trade," *IO* 53, no. 4 (1999): 631-68, at 633.

[45]Kaufmann and Pape, "Explaining Costly International Moral Action," 634-36.

[46]Organisation for Economic Co-operation and Development (OECD), "Development Aid Stable in 2017 with More Sent to Poorest Countries," *Development*, September 4, 2018, www.oecd.org /development/development-aid-stable-in-2017-with-more-sent-to-poorest-countries.htm.

9

GLOBAL KINSHIP
WITH REFUGEES

ENVISAGING A COMPREHENSIVE global framework for the care of refugees is not an easy task. Some aspects are simple enough. Every country in the world is already bound by international law to comply with the duty of non-refoulement. According to this fundamental provision of the 1951 Refugee Convention, countries must refrain from returning refugees to other countries where they face a well-founded fear of persecution.[1] In addition to this *negative* duty to *refrain* from returning refugees to the dangers from which they have fled, a comprehensive global response to forced displacement needs also to involve states discharging *positive* duties to *give* assistance, to *provide* protection, to *offer* kinship. This is where things become complicated.

Which country in particular is bound to assist and protect the child internally displaced by violence in Colombia, to help the overwhelmed Kingdom of Jordan to provide temporary shelter and aid to the elderly Syrian displaced by war and awaiting the opportunity to return home safely, or to offer welcome and kinship to the Rohingya family forcibly displaced from Myanmar, waiting in a refugee camp in Bangladesh and liable to be persecuted should they ever return home?

---

[1] This principle is arguably legally binding even for states that are not signatories to the 1951 Refugee Convention. See Jean Allain, "The *jus cogens* Nature of *non-refoulement*," *IJRL* 13, no. 4 (2001): 533-58.

The absence of clear and settled answers to such questions gives rise to what is known as a "collective action problem": while all states would benefit from the greater international order and stability that would result from a collective global effort to care for the displaced, each individual state is tempted to sit back and let others take the lead.[2]

It is a particularly perverse example of a collective action problem because the default outcome overwhelmingly advantages the world's wealthiest countries. How so? Well, on the one hand, states that are neighbors to war, conflict, and persecution are inevitably the initial providers of asylum to the vast majority of the world's refugees. The duty of non-refoulement prohibits them from returning displaced people against their will to situations of danger and persecution. But these "countries of first asylum" tend to be relatively poor. Developing regions host 85 percent of the world's refugees. One-third of the world's refugees are hosted by some of the world's least developed countries, including Uganda, Sudan, Ethiopia, and Bangladesh.[3] On the other hand, those developed and wealthy states that have significant capacity to contribute to the care of refugees and other displaced people are at liberty do so at their own discretion (so long as the displaced do not reach their territory, in which case the negative duty of non-refoulement kicks in). The Refugee Convention does not assign particular positive duties to particular countries. It merely recognizes in its preamble the need for international cooperation: "The grant of asylum may place unduly heavy burdens on certain countries, and a satisfactory solution . . . cannot therefore be achieved without international co-operation." Countries have always been reluctant to agree to anything more concrete than that.

This gives rise to the problem of "free riding." Refugee protection benefits everyone. But while countries that are neighbors to conflict and suffering are required to welcome forcibly displaced people in extraordinarily large numbers, others free ride and refuse to carry out their duty to cooperate and help share the load. Certainly, some wealthy, developed countries do chip in. Some of them welcome a few thousand—even tens of thousands—of refugees each year. But they collectively welcome less 1 percent of the global refugee

---

[2]For two ground-breaking studies of this phenomenon, see Alexander Betts, *Protection by Persuasion: International Cooperation in the Refugee Regime* (Ithaca, NY: Cornell University Press, 2009); and Astri Suhrke, "Burden-Sharing During Refugee Emergencies: The Logic of Collective Versus National Action," *JRefS* 11, no. 4 (1998): 396-415.

[3]United Nations High Commissioner for Refugees (UNHCR), *Global Trends: Forced Displacement in 2019*, June 18, 2020, 2, 22, www.unhcr.org/en-au/statistics/unhcrstats/5ee200e37/unhcr-global -trends-2019.html.

population each year, and that is less than 10 percent of those that the United Nations' refugee agency, UNHCR, identify as being in urgent need of resettlement each year.[4] They contribute millions of dollars to partially fund UNHCR's efforts to help assist and protect refugees and internally displaced people in distant countries. But UNHCR usually receives less than 60 percent of what it requires to do its work in a given year.[5] In short, the situation is grossly unfair. Countries with the least capacity to care for strangers are the ones that do most of the caring.

This situation heightens the vulnerability and worsens the suffering of displaced people. Developing countries that have welcomed large numbers of refugees are overwhelmed, are unable to provide sufficient care on their own, and are given insufficient help to do so from others. And yet, as wealthy countries refuse to increase their intake of refugees, these developing countries become the default, long-term hosts of people consigned to situations of protracted displacement.[6] Recall that, at the close of 2019, more than three-quarters of people designated by UNHCR as refugees had been displaced for more than five years.

Unsurprisingly, overwhelmed as they are by the enormous numbers of refugees in their territories, exasperated by the shortfall in international assistance, and goaded by the examples of wealthy Western countries going to such great lengths to deter those who might approach their own territories in search of asylum, countries of first asylum in the developing world are increasingly closing their borders to newly displaced people and seeking to return asylum seekers to home countries still wracked with war and violence.[7]

This is a horrific situation. There is a clear and urgent need for the global community of states—particularly its wealthiest and most capable members—to more meaningfully cooperate and do much more to care for the displaced.

[4]UNHCR, "UNHCR Projected Global Resettlement Needs: 2021," 26th Annual Tripartite Consultations on Resettlement, Geneva, June 2020, 13, https://reliefweb.int/sites/reliefweb.int/files/resources/5ef34bfb7.pdf.

[5]Babar Baloch, "Refugees Bear Cost of Massive Underfunding," UNHCR, Geneva, October 9, 2018; and UNHCR, *Funding Update: 2019*, December 31, 2019, https://reporting.unhcr.org/sites/default/files/Global%20Funding%20Overview%2031%20December%202019.pdf.

[6]James Milner, "Protracted Refugee Situations," in *The Oxford Handbook of Refugee and Forced Migration Studies*, ed. Elena Fiddian-Qasmiyeh, Gil Loescher, Katy Long, and Nando Sigona (Oxford: Oxford University Press, 2014), 154.

[7]See for example the following reports by Human Rights Watch: "Pakistan Coercion, UN Complicity: The Mass Forced Return of Afghan Refugees," February 13, 2017; "'They Forced Us onto Trucks Like Animals': Cameroon's Massed Forced Return and Abuse of Nigerian Refugees," September 27, 2017; and "'I Have No Idea Why They Sent Us Back': Jordanian Deportations and Expulsions of Syrian Refugees," October 2, 2017.

This is commonly framed as a need for greater "burden-sharing" among states. But the notion that refugees are a burden is troubling. In its place, many suggest the label "responsibility-sharing." This is certainly better. But we prefer an alternative phrase that has been occasionally proposed by UN officials and diplomats in recent years: "opportunity-sharing." By this, we do not mean to highlight the economic and strategic benefits that accrue to states that extend protection to refugees, as those who have used the phrase tend to do (though it is certainly helpful to note these benefits). Rather, we want to emphasize that the chance to love our neighbors as ourselves, to welcome Christ in welcoming the stranger, and to enfold the displaced as kin should always be understood as an opportunity, not a burden. What would a creative, comprehensive, and feasible global approach to opportunity-sharing for the sake of the displaced look like?

TEMPORARY CARE FOR OUR GLOBAL KIN

This book has largely focused on one means of caring for displaced people: welcoming and enfolding the displaced into one's own community as kin. There are important things to be said about the hope and possibility for greater opportunity-sharing in this regard. We will say these things shortly. But welcoming the stranger into one's own community is only one component of what is needed for a comprehensive global response to the displacement of our global kin. In many cases, what is needed, particularly from wealthy, Western countries, is finances, material goods, and technical expertise for the temporary care of people displaced in developing regions. For many displaced people, resettlement in the West is not the preferred outcome. What they prefer is repatriation—the opportunity to return home. What they need while they await an opportunity to return home with safety and dignity— or until it becomes tragically clear that return will never be an option and they instead need a new home—is temporary care and protection.

The global community, including wealthy, Western countries, has a vital role to play in ensuring the provision of such temporary care and protection to displaced people, including those 45 million internally displaced persons (IDPs) within their own countries, those 26 million refugees, most of whom are displaced in neighboring countries in the developing world, and those millions more who, while neither IDPs nor refugees under the Refugee Convention's definition, are displaced—in many instances by sudden natural disasters or gradual processes of environmental change—and in need of international protection and assistance.

Humanitarian assistance. The task of caring for temporarily displaced people is substantial, not least because so many remain in this "temporary" situation for a decade or more while they await an opportunity to safely return home or permanently resettle elsewhere. Tens of millions of temporarily displaced people need protection, shelter, water, food, sanitation, and health care. Unaccompanied children, elderly people, people with disabilities, persecuted minorities, victims of trafficking and trauma, and survivors of sexual- and gender-based violence each have specific needs. UNHCR estimated that it would need $8.6 billion to do its work supporting host countries in caring for forcibly displaced people in 2019. It received from donor countries and other contributors only 56 percent of that amount.[8] This funding shortfall is sadly typical. UNHCR summed up the effects of such lack of funding in 2018:

> In situation after situation we are seeing increases in malnutrition, health facilities being overcrowded, housing and shelters becoming increasingly dilapidated, children either in overcrowded classrooms or doing without school altogether, and growing protection risks because of shortages of personnel to deal with unaccompanied children or victims of sexual violence.[9]

Women and girls in particular need protection from sexual violence, abuse, exploitation, and forced marriage. Small, practical measures can make an enormous difference. Women and girls are safer, for instance, when refugee camps have adequate lighting, toilets have locks, and food can be safely accessed. One study in the Dadaab refugee camp in Kenya found that, when houses were fully stocked with firewood and women and girls did not need to collect it from isolated areas, rapes decreased by 45 percent.[10]

An estimated 30-34 million forcibly displaced persons are children, and children need education.[11] We saw in chapter three that there are more Syrian school-aged children in Lebanon than there are Lebanese school-aged children, and hundreds of Lebanese schools have taken to operating a second shift each day to provide schooling for 220,000 Syrian children. But another 270,000 are not in school. They and many other displaced children elsewhere

---

[8]UNHCR, "Financials: Budget," https://reporting.unhcr.org/financial#_ga=2.155116344.1666374325 .1594089748-726568310.1577831459.

[9]Baloch, "Refugees Bear Cost of Massive Underfunding."

[10]David Miliband, *Rescue: Refugees and the Political Crisis of Our Time* (London: TED Books, 2017), 81, 83. See also Lucy Hall, "WPS, Migration, and Displacement," in *The Oxford Handbook of Women, Peace, and Security,* ed. Sara E. Davies and Jacqui True (Oxford: Oxford University Press, 2019), 643-56.

[11]UNHCR, *Global Trends: Forced Displacement in 2019*, 2.

are falling behind others their age and are vulnerable to child labor or alienation and radicalization.[12]

Wealthy countries have an opportunity to reach deeper into their pockets to ensure more comprehensive care of the temporarily displaced in the developing world.[13] UNHCR is chronically underfunded. So too is the United Nations' migration agency, International Organization for Migration (IOM). And other regional organizations and nongovernmental organizations, including faith-based organizations like World Vision, World Renew, and World Relief, are held back by limited funding from doing more to provide temporary care for the displaced. Some countries contribute much more to these organizations than others. The United States is well ahead of all others in contributing funds to UNHCR, both in raw terms and when controlled for gross domestic product (GDP) per capita. The United Kingdom, Canada, and Australia also feature in the world's top twenty.[14] But the global community—including these wealthy, Western countries—can do much more to ensure that the humanitarian needs of displaced people are met. We noted that UNHCR received only 56 percent of the $8.6 billion that it needed to do its work in 2019. In the same year, the United States alone spent $732 billion on its military.[15]

Development solutions. One of the most creative efforts to improve the global care of temporarily displaced people in recent years has been the attempt of scholars and practitioners to conceive and implement "development solutions" to the problem. The two leading refugee scholars championing this move, Oxford University's Alexander Betts and Paul Collier, urge countries and international organizations to move beyond the current focus on humanitarian assistance to a model that prioritizes the economic empowerment of refugees. Global actors, they suggest, should collaborate to help displaced people not only to survive but also to thrive in developing countries of first asylum, providing "autonomy and dignity" via opportunities to participate in the labor market. This, they argue, will bring economic benefits to these developing countries providing a temporary home to these refugees.

---

[12]See Miliband, *Rescue*, 77-80; Rima Cherri and Houssam Hariri, "Lebanon Puts in an Extra Shift to Get Syrian Refugees into School," UNHCR, June 26, 2018, www.unhcr.org/news/stories/2018/6/5b321c864/lebanon-puts-extra-shift-syrian-refugees-school.html.

[13]That is not to say that humanitarian assistance can always be easily provided. For example, international aid agencies are too often prevented from caring for internally displaced people due to the refusal of governments or armed groups to allow international access. We note the need to address the root causes of suffering such as this later in the chapter.

[14]UNHCR, *Funding Update: 2019*, December 31, 2019, https://reporting.unhcr.org/sites/default/files/Global%20Funding%20Overview%2031%20December%202019.pdf.

[15]Nan Tian et al., "Trends in World Military Expenditure, 2019," *SIPRI*, April 2020.

While acknowledging that different approaches will suit different countries, Betts and Collier propose a general model of "creating development areas in peripheral parts of the country in which both refugees and the host state and society can benefit from the creation of new jobs, new markets, and improved public services."[16] Developed countries ought to establish "a solid system of international financing," including the establishment of trade concessions and the transfer of funds to countries of first asylum willing to implement these solutions. They should also encourage private-sector investments in these new development areas. In return, countries in the developing world should agree to keep their borders open to refugees fleeing war, violence, and persecution and also to discourage onward movement to the developed world and to combat people smuggling.[17]

Betts and Collier highlight two contrasting examples of development solutions to displacement: Uganda and Jordan. Since the early 1990s, Uganda has adopted a "Self-Reliance Strategy," granting refugees freedom of movement, access to land, and the right to work. This has produced positive economic outcomes with refugees establishing businesses that have created jobs for each other and also for Ugandan nationals. By 2014, only 1 percent of refugees in Uganda were fully reliant on aid. In 2016, Jordan agreed to offer 200,000 permits to Syrian refugees to work in special economic zones. In return, wealthy states pledged US$11 billion, including US$1.7 billion in grants to support infrastructure projects, and the European Union agreed to remove tariff barriers for goods manufactured in these zones in order to encourage external investment and to generate jobs.[18] Similar models have since been established in Kenya, Ethiopia, Lebanon, and elsewhere.[19]

The results of these efforts have varied. While the Ugandan model has proved quite successful, job creation in Jordan has been negligible. Jordanian officials have had difficulty convincing Syrian refugees to make the long commute to factories in the special economic zones, particularly since many Syrians have already found informal, better paid, and closer work in construction or service industries.[20] Nevertheless, many scholars and practitioners

---

[16]Alexander Betts and Paul Collier, *Refuge: Rethinking Refugee Policy in a Changing World* (Oxford: Oxford University Press, 2017), 127, 205.
[17]Betts and Collier, *Refuge*, 135, 175, 230.
[18]Betts and Collier, *Refuge*, 156-81; Miliband, *Rescue*, 75-76.
[19]See, for example, Alexander Betts, "Refuge, Reformed," *Foreign Policy*, November 22, 2018.
[20]Daniel Howden, Hannah Patchett, and Charlotte Alfred, "The Compact Experiment: Push for Refugee Jobs Confronts Reality of Jordan and Lebanon," *Refugees Deeply: Quarterly*, December 2017.

are hopeful that lessons can be learned from these pilot programs so that the potential of development solutions can be realized over time.[21]

Those seeking to imagine and implement these development solutions are certainly to be applauded for their creativity. However, we ought to be wary of these solutions insofar as they become yet another means for wealthy, Western countries to contain displaced people within the developing world. It is telling that it wasn't until displaced people began to find their way to Europe in large numbers in 2015 that Western countries and international organizations developed a reinvigorated interest in these kinds of solutions. And it is troubling that Betts and Collier suggest that an ideal development-oriented response to the millions of refugees fleeing the Syrian civil war since 2011 would have required only a "symbolic minimum" number of Syrians being resettled in the developed world.[22] Such a claim is morally disconcerting as it seems to endorse wealthy countries buying out their obligations to welcome refugees by funding poorer countries to do it for them. It is also unrealistic. After all, the authors insist that development solutions need to be replaced by "durable solutions" such as resettlement if displacement continues for more than five years. The Syrian civil war is now in its tenth year.

Development solutions have potential to greatly improve the lives of many temporarily displaced people. But, at minimum, we need to pay close attention to the following. First, many displaced people, including some elderly people, traumatized people, refugees with disabilities, and refugees with primary responsibilities for the care of others will not be able to work. We need to make sure that they are not disadvantaged by any shift in priorities from humanitarianism to development. Second, we should also ensure that development solutions include provisions for the protection of labor rights, lest they simply add to the already widespread problem of migrant-labor

---

[21]For critiques and suggestions for improving the Ugandan and Jordan models, see Howden, Patchett, and Alfred, "Compact Experiment"; Lucy Hovil, "Uganda's Refugee Policies: The History, the Politics, the Way Forward," International Refugee Rights Initiative, Rights in Exile Policy Paper, October 2018; and Katharina Lenner and Lewis Turner, "Making Refugees Work? The Politics of Integrating Syrian Refugees into the Labor Market in Jordan," *Middle East Critique* 28, no. 1 (2019): 65-95. For a powerful general critique of the increasing emphasis on refugee "self-reliance," see Evan Easton-Calabria and Naohiko Omata, "Panacea for the Refugee Crisis? Rethinking the Promotion of 'Self-Reliance' for Refugees," *Third World Quarterly* 39, no. 8 (2018): 1458-74.

[22]Betts and Collier, *Refuge*, 230. Elsewhere, they recommend that some money currently spent on resettlement ought instead to be spent on development solutions (Betts and Collier, *Refuge*, 145). If implemented, this would presumably result in even fewer refugees being welcomed by developed countries than the shamefully small number that we see at present.

abuse.[23] And third, if it turns out that these solutions are ultimately being pushed by wealthy countries simply to justify denying the right of vulnerable, displaced people to seek a home beyond often impoverished and often unstable countries of first asylum, they are not solutions that we should embrace.

Voluntary, Safe, and Dignified Repatriation

In addition to caring for the temporarily displaced, the global community must strive to ensure that displacement does not become protracted. Durable solutions need to be made available so that displaced people can find a place, a community, and an opportunity to rebuild their lives.

One such durable solution is repatriation—the opportunity to return to one's country and community of origin safely and with dignity.

We in the West often tell each other that repatriation is what the vast majority of refugees desire. In 2017, US Ambassador to the United Nations Nikki Haley insisted that all the Syrian refugees she had spoken to wished to return home rather than come to the United States.[24] UNHCR's chief spokesperson, Melissa Fleming, went further the same year, declaring, "All refugees want to go home someday."[25] Repatriation is the preferred durable solution of wealthy Western countries, which are disinclined to welcome large numbers of displaced people into their own communities. It is also the preferred solution of UNHCR, which is so reliant on the funding of wealthy Western countries. But we should be wary of accepting too quickly the narrative that it is the preferred solution for *all* displaced people.

Certainly, the majority of refugees desire the opportunity to safely return home and reintegrate into their community. There is much that the global community can do to help make this possible, including working to help bring war, violence, and persecution to an end and to contribute to building a peaceful society that can sustain the return of displaced people. Peace building involves reestablishing law and order, creating stable and accountable institutions, revitalizing civil society, and promoting reconciliation and societal healing. The global community can also aid individuals to return to their countries of origin by providing reintegration and rehabilitation support, legal and financial assistance, and property restitution or compensation.

---

[23]Gillian Brock, "How Should We Assist Refugees?," paper delivered at Workshop: Feasibility and Immigration, Australian National University, April 23, 2018.

[24]Joel Gehrke, "Nikki Haley: Syrian Refugees Want to Go Home, Not to US," *Washington Examiner*, June 22, 2017.

[25]"'All Refugees Want to Go Home Someday'—UNHCR Spokesperson and Author Melissa Fleming," *UN News*, May 26, 2017.

But the task of establishing conditions for safe and dignified return is notoriously difficult, and international efforts to help end violence and rebuild societies can at times do more harm than good. Consider, for example, the ongoing displacement of Afghans, Iraqis, Libyans, and Syrians today despite—and in some instances because of—international efforts to end tyranny and restore peace. For many displaced people, safe and dignified repatriation within a reasonable period of time is simply not possible.

For many other refugees, the idea of repatriation, even if safe, is abhorrent. They may be traumatized by the idea of returning to a regime that persecuted them and to a town whose residents killed their relatives. They may have been displaced for so long that they have become more attached to their new "temporary" homes than their old. Some may have been displaced at such a young age that they have no memory of "home," aside from their new host country, and no desire to return to a country that rejected them and their parents.[26]

We in the West need to listen to the voices of displaced people themselves rather than assuming that they all crave the opportunity to return home.[27] We ought to be conscious of our privileged position in the world, a position that we enjoy in part due to historical and ongoing injustices that have left many non-Western countries impoverished, unstable, and vulnerable to displacement-triggering crises. We should be wary of imposing our preferred solutions on displaced people. They are our global kin whom God loves, just as he loves us, vulnerable people for whom Christ died, just as he died for us. We need to resist the temptation to think that the future of displaced people is for us to decide.

While the global community tends to agree that refugees should only be repatriated with their consent, states that are unwilling hosts of refugees often try to manipulate such consent.[28] In some instances, they fail to provide reliable information about the insecure and impoverished conditions to which refugees might return. In others, they seek to provoke consent by withdrawing aid from refugee camps. Sometimes, states go so far as to pay refugees to repatriate. States in developing regions of the world are encouraged

---

[26]Lena Kainz and Rebecca Buxton, "All Refugees Want to Go Home. Right?" *OpenDemocracy*, October 18, 2017.

[27]For perspectives of Syrian refugees about how they weigh the pros and cons of returning home and what, if anything, might make them willing to undertake a safe and dignified return, see Maha Yahya with Jean Kassir and Khalil el-Hariri, *Unheard Voices: What Syrian Refugees Need to Return Home* (Washington, DC: Carnegie Endowment for International Peace, 2018).

[28]For a detailed study, see Mollie Gerver, *The Ethics and Practice of Refugee Repatriation* (Edinburgh: Edinburgh University Press, 2018).

to do so by the fact that Western states do it too. In 2017, for example, the Australian government offered Rohingya refugees held in offshore detention facilities AU$25,000 to return to Myanmar, even while Myanmar's armed forces and police were waging a campaign of violence against other Rohingya that the United Nations' leading human rights official described as "a textbook example of ethnic cleansing."[29] Denmark has likewise offered to pay Iraqi, Iranian, and Somali refugees to return home. Germany has offered the same to all asylum applicants.[30] Refugee scholars note with regret that this practice of paying refugees to return home "amounts to using their destitution against them."[31] What a shameful message we give our vulnerable global kin when we tell them just how much we are willing to pay to ensure that we do not have to live with them!

But perhaps most troubling of all is that states sometimes ignore the principle of consent and instead coerce repatriation. It was alarming, for example, to see Bangladesh reach an agreement to return Rohingya refugees to Myanmar in 2018 without the refugees' consent and only one year after they had fled Myanmar's ethnic-cleansing campaign. As a UNICEF spokesperson noted, "For many, the trauma they witnessed during their exodus . . . is still fresh in their minds." We should be thankful that these plans were abandoned in the wake of widespread protests by Rohingya in Bangladeshi refugee camps.[32]

The preference of Western states for refugee repatriation arguably enhances the risks of such manipulative and coercive measures by host states in developing regions. Western states limit opportunities for resettlement, close their borders, and systematically deter displaced people from seeking asylum in their territories in the hope that they will remain in developing regions and ultimately choose to return to their countries of origin. US Senator Jeff Sessions (who subsequently became attorney general) stated this position clearly in 2015: "Our policy should be to keep the refugees as close to home as possible and then we need to be working to try to create the kind of stability [so] they could return to their home as soon as possible."[33]

---

[29]Oliver Holmes and Ben Doherty, "Australia Offers to Pay Rohingya Refugees to Return to Myanmar," *Guardian*, September 18, 2017.

[30]Mollie Gerver, "Paying Refugees to Leave," *Political Studies* 65, no. 3 (2017): 631-45, 631; and "Program Paying Asylum Applicants to Leave Germany Voluntarily Begins," *DW*, February 1, 2017.

[31]Theophilus Kwek and Rebecca Buxton, "Between Home and a Hard Place: Paying Refugees to Return," *Diplomat*, October 27, 2017.

[32]Helen Bush, "Stalled Repatriation Brings Relief but Not a Solution for Rohingya Refugees," *Globe Post*, November 16, 2018.

[33]Quoted in Gehrke, "Nikki Haley: Syrian Refugees Want to Go Home."

In such a context, overwhelmed and exhausted host states in the developing world see no other option but to incentivize and pressure unsafe and undignified repatriation.

Sadly, this strategy often works. As a result, vulnerable people suffer. Substantial numbers of displaced people decide to return home each year to conditions of violence and persecution. Indeed, the majority of refugees who returned to their home countries in 2017 did so to countries with ongoing armed conflicts and unresolved displacement crises.[34] Many refugees who have begun returning to Syria in recent years—often with encouragement, inducement, or pressure from host states—have been harassed, killed, or conscripted into military service.[35]

But even in this context of host states seeking to cajole vulnerable people to return home, the number of people who are repatriated each year remains much lower than the number of people newly displaced. In 2019, the number of refugee returns (317,200) was less than one-eighth of the number of people forced to flee their countries in search of protection (2.8 million).[36] Repatriation, then, while an important component of a comprehensive approach to caring for displaced people and one to which Western states should certainly devote much attention, ought not to be framed as the panacea, as *the* solution to our global crisis of forced displacement.

But what of the *naturalization* of refugees in countries of first asylum in developing regions (and by naturalization here we mean not only freedom of movement and the right to work but also permanent legal status and a pathway to citizenship)? The global number of naturalizations each year tends to be no more than 1 or 2 percent of the world's refugees. And we should hardly expect developing countries to agree to naturalize more, given the enormous contribution they already make to the care of the temporarily displaced. No, confronted with the forced displacement of millions of our global kin, we in the West urgently need to stop shifting the "burden" onto others, stop seeking to contain the "problem" elsewhere, and instead embrace the opportunity to care for our global kin by cooperating with each other and radically increasing our own contributions to a third solution: resettlement.

---

[34]Internal Displacement Monitoring Centre, *Global Report on Internal Displacement*, Norwegian Refugee Council, May 2018, 13.

[35]Patrick Wintour, "Syria's Neighbors Press for Help to Return Refugees," *Guardian*, March 11, 2019.

[36]UNHCR, *Global Trends: Forced Displacement in 2019*, 8.

Sharing the Opportunity to Resettle Our Global Kin

In 2018, UNHCR forecast that 1.4 million of the world's refugees would need resettlement in 2019.[37] UNHCR's resettlement requests tend to be conservative, derived from its understanding of which refugees are in specific or urgent need of protection at a particular time. The number of displaced people who may not be in immediate need of resettlement but who nevertheless are unlikely to be able to return safely to their homes and communities within a few years and thus stand in need of new homes and new communities is undoubtedly much higher. Nevertheless, the global community resettled only 107,800 refugees under UNHCR's mandate in 2019—less than 10 percent of UNHCR's requested amount and less than half of 1 percent of the global refugee population.[38]

And things are getting worse. As the number of people forecast by UNHCR to be in need of resettlement increases (increasing by 80 percent between 2011 and 2019), global resettlement offerings are declining.[39] The 2019 global resettlement figure of 107,800 was significantly lower than 2016's figure of 189,000, and country-level figures suggest that global figure for 2020 will be lower again.[40]

Much of the decline in resettlement globally can be attributed to a drastic reduction in resettlement by the United States in recent years. For several decades, the United States reliably contributed between one-third and one-half of the global refugee resettlement total. In 1980, the United States set its yearly resettlement ceiling as high as 230,000. In subsequent years it ranged between 67,000 and 142,000. President Barack Obama set the ceiling for 2017 at 110,000. But President Donald Trump lowered it to 45,000 for 2018, then 30,000 for 2019, and then a mere 18,000 for 2020. These are America's three lowest resettlement ceilings in four decades, and they have been set during the world's worst refugee crisis since World War II.[41] Worse, actual resettlement in some of these years was less than half the stated ceiling. Whereas

---

[37]UNHCR, "UNHCR Projected Global Resettlement Needs: 2019," 24th Annual Tripartite Consultations, June 25-26, 2018, 13, www.unhcr.org/5b28a7df4.pdf.

[38]UNHCR, *Global Trends: Forced Displacement in 2019*, 2. For a useful overview of the resettlement preferences and practices of both UNHCR and key countries, see Adèle Garnier, Liliana Lyra Jubilut, and Kristin Bergtora Sandvik, eds., *Refugee Resettlement: Power, Politics, and Humanitarian Governance* (New York: Berghahn, 2018).

[39]UNHCR, *Global Trends: Forced Displacement in 2019*, 51.

[40]United Nations High Commissioner for Refugees (UNHCR), *Global Trends: Forced Displacement in 2017*, June 25, 2018, 30, www.unhcr.org/5b27be547.pdf.

[41]Dara Lind, "The Trump Administration Doesn't Believe in the Global Refugee Crisis," *Vox*, December 4, 2017.

84,994 refugees were resettled in the United States in 2016, only 53,716 were resettled in 2017, and only 22,491 in 2018—America's lowest figure since 1977.[42]

But the fault is far from America's alone. After all, only twenty-nine countries provided resettlement for refugees in 2019. And of these, only the United States, Canada (30,100), and Australia (18,200) accepted more than 10,000.[43] The United Kingdom, France, and Sweden resettled around 5,000 each; and the numbers drop off further from there. Many countries, of course, lack the economic capacity or political stability to resettle refugees, and several such states already contribute much more than their fair share by "temporarily" hosting millions of people displaced from neighboring countries. But there is a clear need for more countries to step up and either begin to resettle refugees or increase their annual intake.

At minimum, it seems to us, countries should immediately aim to collectively increase resettlement at least ten times over so as to resettle the full number of refugees that UNHCR deems to be in urgent or specific need of protection each year. Anything short of that surely constitutes a grave moral failure of the global community. We simply cannot justify dividing the entirety of the earth's surface into a couple of hundred territorially bounded sovereign states, as we do, if we exclude so many of our global kin from membership in any of these states.[44] If they are displaced from their countries of origin and unable to return home in a reasonable amount of time, other countries need to welcome them. And even more so because, as we discussed in previous chapters, the wealth and comfort of so many countries with capacity to resettle larger numbers of refugees has been built on aggressive, exploitative, and climate-destructive policies that have contributed to our present global crisis of mass displacement.

It also seems to us that, once the global community has increased resettlement tenfold and ensures that it resettles all refugees that UNHCR identifies as being in acute need of resettlement each year, it must press on and continue to increase capacity for resettlement until all those in need of a home can find a home. None of the major displacement-inducing crises around the world—in places like Syria, Afghanistan, Myanmar, and

---

[42]Jennifer Hansler, "US Admits Lowest Number of Refugees in More Than 40 Years," *CNN*, October 3, 2018.

[43]UNHCR, *Global Trends: Forced Displacement in 2019*, 52.

[44]As Lyndsey Stonebridge observes, given that the division of humanity into territorially bounded sovereign states is accompanied by the mass displacement of so many "placeless people," we who do have a place need urgently to consider the global cost of our citizenships. Lyndsey Stonebridge, *Placeless People: Writings, Rights, and Refugees* (Oxford: Oxford University Press, 2018), 169.

Venezuela—appear likely to be resolved soon. Repatriation to such places over the next few years may be possible only for a few. None of the major countries of first asylum—countries like Turkey, Colombia, Pakistan, and Uganda—can reasonably be expected to naturalize more than a few of the millions of people now under their care. Nor can we in the West continue to justify consigning those millions of people to situations of protracted displacement in those countries. We must cooperate globally to increase resettlement.

Drawing hope from the resettlement of Indochinese refugees. Such international cooperation has worked in the past. Perhaps the best known and most successful initiative was the Comprehensive Plan of Action (CPA) for Indochinese Refugees, which brought together countries of first asylum, donor countries, and resettlement countries to respond to the large-scale movement of refugees in Southeast Asia in the aftermath of the Vietnam War. At an international conference convened in 1979, Southeast Asian countries agreed to provide temporary refuge to displaced people arriving at their borders in exchange for commitments from the United States, Canada, Australia, New Zealand, and several European countries to offer resettlement. An "orderly departure" program was also established, enabling people at risk of persecution to be settled directly from Vietnam without the need to undertake dangerous journeys.

Ten years later, as resettlement offerings in the West were failing to keep up with the numbers of Vietnamese people seeking asylum, and countries of first asylum were beginning to close their borders to the vulnerable, a second conference was convened. Here neighboring countries renewed their commitment to providing temporary refuge, Western countries renewed their commitment to resettlement, and new policies were put in place to voluntarily repatriate those able to return home safely. Neither the implementation nor the long-term outcomes of the CPA were without fault, but by the time the program closed in 1997, 1.95 million Indochinese people had been resettled directly from Vietnam or from refugee camps in neighboring countries; 1.29 million of them resettled in the United States.[45]

This was a time-limited cooperative response to a regional crisis. What we need today is an enduring cooperative response to a global crisis—a crisis

---

[45]W. Courtland Robinson, *Terms of Refuge: The Indochinese Exodus and the International Response* (London: Zed Books, 1998), 295; and Volker Türk and Madeline Garlick, "From Burdens and Responsibilities to Opportunities: The Comprehensive Refugee Response Framework and a Global Compact on Refugees," *IJRL* 28, no. 4 (2016): 656-78, at 667-68.

likely to keep worsening as ongoing climate change and environmental degradation further amplify the instability of countries and the vulnerability of people. Examples such as the Indochinese CPA show that cooperative solutions to large-scale displacement are possible. But the numbers of displaced people in urgent need of resettlement today are much, much larger.

How should the opportunity be shared? We have some mathematical models that can help as we try to determine how a tenfold increase in resettlement might be shared globally. Responding to the influx of asylum seekers into Europe in 2015, for example, the European Union (EU) agreed upon a formula for sharing resettlement among its members based on four criteria: population, GDP, unemployment, and past refugee intakes. This model, unfortunately, was never implemented.[46] Other models give different weighting to these four criteria or suggest alternative criteria for inclusion.[47]

It is sometimes suggested that the resettlement quotas produced by these criteria should be tradable, allowing one state to pay another to resettle its assigned number of refugees.[48] But this is a troubling suggestion. Refugee scholar B. S. Chimni notes that it "turns the refugee into a commodity which can be 'traded' on the world market."[49] Matthew Gibney likewise notes that it treats refugees "as if they possess negative value," like toxic waste. There is something particularly disturbing about providing refugees with "a monetary measure of how unwanted they are."[50] No, wealthy states need to embrace the responsibility and opportunity to welcome the vulnerable into their *own* communities.

In order for the global community to increase resettlement tenfold, states would ideally work quickly toward agreement on a model that would offer a guide for the minimum annual number of people that they each should resettle. (While they are at it, they should develop an equivalent model to ensure that the work of UNHCR in caring for displaced people, discussed earlier, is fully funded each year.) Each year this broad model will need to be reapplied and sometimes recalibrated to respond to developments both in

---

[46]Michael W. Doyle, "Responsibility Sharing: From Principle to Policy," *IJRL* 31, no. 4 (2018): 618-22.
[47]Penelope Mathew and Tristan Harley, *Refugees, Regionalism and Responsibility* (Cheltenham, UK: Edward Elgar, 2016), 94-138; and Alexander Betts, Cathryn Costello and Natascha Zaun, *A Fair Share: Refugees and Responsibility-Sharing*, Delmi Report 2017:10 (Stockholm: Delmi, 2017).
[48]Peter H. Schuck, "Refugee Burden-Sharing: A Modest Proposal," *Yale Journal of International Law* 22, no. 2 (1997): 243-97.
[49]B. S. Chimni, "The Geopolitics of Refugee Studies: A View from the South," *JRefS* 11, no. 4 (1998): 350-74, at 362.
[50]Matthew J. Gibney, quoted in Mathew and Harley, *Refugees, Regionalism and Responsibility*, 114.

the many existing and emerging situations of mass displacement and also in the countries engaging in resettlement across the world.

Gaining agreement on responsibilities for resettlement will be an enormously challenging task. Previous efforts at establishing concrete and widespread agreement dating all the way back to the negotiations for the 1951 Refugee Convention have failed. Regional agreements, such as that negotiated but not implemented by the EU in 2015, may be easier to achieve.[51] Nevertheless, a global agreement is not unimaginable. After all, states have long agreed to formulas that dictate their respective financial contributions to United Nations peacekeeping operations each year, generating an annual budget of several billion dollars. And the commitment of numerous Western states to share the task of resettling Indochinese refugees after the Vietnam War shows that such agreements need not be restricted to financial contributions but can also include the welcome of strangers.

To any model for sharing resettlement numbers that might be based on the varying capacity of states to welcome and enfold new members, however, we would add two considerations. First, in addition to *capacity*, we should bear in mind *culpability*.[52] As we explained in chapter seven, powerful and wealthy states are typically implicated in the displacement of particular groups of distant strangers. The coordinated decision of Western states to resettle large numbers of Indochinese refugees, for example, was partly produced by feelings of guilt about the Vietnam War and recognition of responsibility for the mass displacement that followed. The extension of welcome to almost two million Indochinese people was at least partly an act of restitution, perhaps even a form of repentance.

As we look at today's global refugee crisis, we in the West need to acknowledge that we are again implicated in the displacement of strangers due to our foolish wars, our reckless support of abusive regimes, our perverse pursuit of global arms sales, our exploitative trade practices, and our selfish destruction of the global climate. More than that, we are implicated in the global inequalities that enable us to exploit and exacerbate the vulnerabilities of strangers in these ways because of our past practices of colonialism, subjugation, and wealth

[51]Mathew and Harley, *Refugees, Regionalism and Responsibility*.
[52]For a range of arguments pointing in this direction, see Chimni, "The Geopolitics of Refugee Studies"; Maureen H. O'Connell, *Compassion: Loving Our Neighbor in an Age of Globalization* (Maryknoll, NY: Orbis, 2009); Tisha M. Rajendra, *Migrants and Citizens: Justice and Responsibility in the Ethics of Immigration* (Grand Rapids, MI: Eerdmans, 2017); and James Souter, "Towards a Theory of Asylum as Reparation for Past Injustice," *Political Studies* 62, no. 2 (2014): 326-42.

extraction.[53] Precisely apportioning blame for such injustices and accurately calculating their contributions to displacement is perhaps impossible. But at the very least, recognition that we are implicated in the displacement of strangers should prevent us from ever declining to contribute more than our "fair share" to global resettlement. Recognition of culpability should prevent us from conceiving of resettlement as a discretionary act of charity for which we can pat ourselves on the back. It is a matter of justice, of repentance and restitution for wrongs done to strangers, of restoration of relationship with our global kin.

Second, in pursuing a global program of resettlement, we need to ensure that we keep central the interests and choices of displaced people themselves. States should give particular weight to the preservation of family unity and the achievement of family reunification. Refugees may also prefer to be resettled in countries and communities with whom they have ideological, ethnic, or religious affinity, and the global community should do what it can to facilitate that.[54]

In short, our displaced kin are suffering from a drastic shortfall in global resettlement offerings. States need urgently to coordinate with each other to increase the global intake of displaced people tenfold and then set about welcoming even more. This will require a conscious effort to build national capacities to embrace and enfold large numbers of strangers. It sounds demanding, and it is. But what a wonderful opportunity it is too. We have the chance—and should find within ourselves the motivation—to reshape our national identities as people who count a cost on behalf of the stranger, a dynamic that we observed in the book of Deuteronomy. What a wonderful opportunity for cultivating solidarity as we cooperate and share with other nations this goal of loving our distant, vulnerable neighbors. And what a wonderful opportunity to humbly repent of our injustices and to joyfully work toward making amends for the sake of our global kin.

PROVIDING ASYLUM TO PEOPLE ON THE MOVE

Of course, many displaced people will not wait in their countries of origin or in countries of first asylum in the hope that a durable solution will be made

---

[53]On climate change, see Robyn Eckersley, "The Common but Differentiated Responsibilities of States to Assist and Receive 'Climate Refugees,'" *European Journal of Political Theory* 14, no. 4 (2015): 481-500. On colonialism, see E. Tendayi Achiume, "Reimagining International Law for Global Migration: Migration as Decolonization?," *American Journal of International Law* 111, no. 1 (2017): 142-46.

[54]For discussion, see Matthew J. Gibney, "Refugees and Justice Between States," *EJPT* 14, no. 4 (2015): 448-63.

available to them. They recognize that they have little chance of returning home with safety and dignity in the foreseeable future, they understand that less than 1 percent of refugees are chosen for resettlement each year, and they are unwilling to remain in limbo, in a situation of temporary displacement that can continue for decades. And so they move onward in search of asylum.

To do so takes courage. In 2018, the United Nations issued a report detailing "unimaginable horrors" suffered by people seeking passage through Libya across the Mediterranean Sea to Europe, from unlawful killings, torture, and arbitrary detention to rape, slavery, and human trafficking. Those seeking safety and a better life in Europe often find themselves "at the mercy of countless predators" in Libya—including government officials, armed gangs, people smugglers, and human traffickers—who view people on the move as "commodities to be exploited and extorted," the United Nations observed. "The overwhelming majority of women and older teenage girls interviewed [by UN officials] reported being gang raped by smugglers or traffickers or witnessing others being taken out of collective accommodations to be abused. . . . Across Libya, unidentified bodies of migrants and refugees bearing gunshot wounds, torture marks and burns are frequently uncovered in rubbish bins, dry river beds, farms and the desert."[55]

While the situation in Libya is particularly dire, similar stories are commonly heard elsewhere. Displaced people risk their lives and endure horrific traumas undertaking treacherous journeys along migratory routes, not only from eastern and western Africa through to Libya and then across the Mediterranean, but also from Myanmar and Bangladesh through to Thailand and Malaysia, from Central and South America through Mexico to the United States, and so on. Médecins Sans Frontières (MSF) finds that more than two-thirds of surveyed asylum seekers and other migrants fleeing Central America's Northern Triangle—Guatemala, Honduras, and El Salvador—claim to have experienced violence en route to the United States and almost a third of women report being sexually abused on their journey.[56] IOM has recorded more than four thousand fatalities on global migratory routes every year since it began counting in 2014 and notes that this is likely only a fraction of the real number of deaths.[57] How desperate people must be to take such risks and endure such suffering in search of asylum.

[55]Office of the High Commissioner for Human Rights, *Desperate and Dangerous: Report on the Human Rights Situation of Migrants and Refugees in Libya*, December 20, 2018, 4-6.

[56]Médecins Sans Frontières, *Forced to Flee Central America's Northern Triangle: A Neglected Humanitarian Crisis*, May 2017, 5.

[57]See International Organization for Migration (IOM), *Missing Migrants: Tracking Deaths Along Migratory Routes*, https://missingmigrants.iom.int.

Certainly, if the global community did a better job of ensuring the care of people in countries of first asylum, facilitating safe and dignified repatriation, and resettling greater numbers of refugees, fewer people would feel the need to take these dangerous journeys. But many still would do so. Many know that repatriation within a reasonable period of time to home countries wracked by ongoing armed conflicts and unresolved displacement crises will simply not be possible. And even if the global community increased resettlement tenfold overnight, this would still account for less than 10 percent of the global refugee population, and it would still be fewer than the number of new refugees fleeing countries of origin each year.[58] And there are many millions more people on the move today who have been compelled to leave their homes in search of safety but are not formally recognized as refugees under the 1951 convention.

Should we hope that asylum seekers stay where they are? We in the West are tempted to hope that displaced peoples will, nevertheless, choose to remain in countries of first asylum in developing regions of the world. Sure, we acknowledge, they do not have a permanent home. But they are safe enough. Can't they just stay where they are? Why should we have to deal with them? Writing about the Syrian refugee crisis in *First Things*, Marc LiVecche suggests:

> Were we certain that these Syrian refugees had no place else on earth to go then it would be incumbent upon us to accept some risk to help them. But this doesn't seem to be the case.
>
> The refugees coming to America are already in camps in countries outside Syria. To say these are not ideal locations for the flourishing of its inhabitants is surely a gross understatement. But neither are they quite the war-torn chaos the inhabitants have successfully fled. Moreover, America can help provide resources to make them more secure.[59]

Certainly, many refugees find themselves in situations that are preferable to the conditions from which they have fled. Often, they find safety, sustenance, opportunities for work, and schooling for their children. But too often they don't. Turkey, for example, welcomed refugees fleeing the Syrian civil war with open arms at first. But, struggling with its own challenges, Turkey could afford to do only so much, and shortfalls in global funding for humanitarian agencies such as UNHCR left more than 80 percent of Syrian

---

[58]In 2019, 11 million people were newly displaced, including 8.6 million IDPs and 2.4 million seeking protection outside their country. UNHCR, *Global Trends: Forced Displacement in 2019*, 8.
[59]Marc LiVecche, "Compassion, Yes, but Prudence, Too," *First Things*, November 23, 2015.

families in Turkey below the local poverty line and only half of Syrian children in school.[60] While we saw in chapter nine that influential voices such as Betts and Collier claim that the influx of Syrians into Europe from Turkey, Lebanon, and Jordan was a product of Angela Merkel's decision in 2015 to open Germany's borders, the evidence indicates that the sharp increase in the number of Syrians seeking asylum in Europe preceded Merkel's decision and can in fact be attributed in large part to the poverty and insecurity experienced by the shortfall in international humanitarian assistance in these Middle Eastern countries of first asylum.[61]

Moreover, as the Syrian civil war has dragged on, the Turkish public has grown increasingly hostile toward Syrian refugees, and violence between the two has grown.[62] The Turkish government is increasingly pressuring and in some instances forcing Syrians to return home to civil war.[63] No wonder some Syrians continue to move in search of a better life in the West.

Again we ask the question, Should we insist that asylum seekers stay where they are? In fact, Turkey is far from the worst place to be a refugee. In Libya, as noted earlier, the situation for displaced people tends to be more violent and more traumatic. Reflecting on the horrifying detention centers in which most displaced people who enter Libya are placed without trial, the United Nations' High Commissioner for Refugees, Filippo Grandi, sympathized with those who seek to flee across the Mediterranean: "If I was a refugee or a migrant or anybody going into this centre I would opt for anything to get out of there, even if I knew the risk of death was very high."[64]

Western states can only do so much to protect refugees in a country verging on dictatorship such as Turkey or a failed state such as Libya. And even if these refugees were protected in these countries, they would still remain displaced, without a permanent home, without a durable solution. Where is the justice in insisting that they be content with their lot rather than

---

[60]William Maley, *What Is a Refugee?* (London: Hurst, 2016), 73-74.

[61]Maley, *What Is a Refugee?*; Thomas Spijkerboer, "Fact Check: Did 'Wir Schaffen Das' Lead to Uncontrolled Mass Migration?," guest post at *Border Criminologies* (blog), September 28, 2016, www.law.ox.ac.uk/research-subject-groups/centre-criminology/centreborder-criminologies/blog/2016/09/fact-check-did-; and Ludger Pries, "'We Will Manage It'—Did Chancellor Merkel's Dictum Increase or Even Cause the Refugee Movement in 2015?" *International Migration* (Early View, December 30, 2019).

[62]International Crisis Group, *Turkey's Syrian Refugees: Defusing Metropolitan Tensions*, Europe and Central Asia Report no. 248, January 29, 2018, i.

[63]Shawn Carrié and Asmaa Al Omar, "'It's Against the Law: Syrian Refugees Deported from Turkey Back to War," *Guardian*, October 16, 2018.

[64]Peter Beaumont, "UN Refugee Chief: I Would Risk Death to Escape a Squalid Migrant Camp," *Guardian*, January 15, 2019.

continue to move in search of greater safety, opportunity, and permanency for themselves and their families? They are people for whom Christ was willing to die. How can we insist that they remain where they are for the sake of our own convenience and comfort?

Refugee scholars observe a troubling tendency of Western politicians and commentators to distinguish between "good" refugees and "bad" refugees. Good refugees are vulnerable victims who wait patiently where they are, in refugee camps or urban centers in impoverished countries, until they are rescued by benevolent Western saviors. Bad refugees are those who take matters into their own hands, pursuing their own strategies for survival, paying people smugglers, crossing borders, and taking advantage of all-too-generous laws that allow them to claim asylum in—and thus impose themselves on—the West. They come in "swarms," they "flood" into Western countries, they are "queue jumpers." (Never mind, that in most instances, there are no queues for them to jump!) When they die en route, it is a tragedy, but it is their fault for not staying put.[65]

People undertake dangerous journeys in search of asylum in the West because they perceive no other options. They can no longer wait for others to provide solutions for them. They need safety from violence and persecution, a way out of intractable poverty, an opportunity to send their kids to school. They need a home. Even if wealthy and powerful countries do a better job of caring for people temporarily displaced in the Global South, facilitating safe and dignified repatriation for as many as possible, and providing resettlement for many more, there will always be some displaced people who feel the need to continue to move in search of asylum. Not only do we in the West fail to care for them "over there," but we actively impede their efforts to claim and attain asylum "over here," via policies of containment, deterrence, and detention.

Containing, deterring, and detaining asylum seekers. We noted in chapters seven and eight the efforts of the EU and Australia to contain, deter, and detain asylum seekers, and the enormous harms done by such practices. Let us here briefly consider the efforts of the United States. The Trump administration

[65]Erin K. Wilson and Luca Mavelli, "The Refugee Crisis and Religion: Beyond Conceptual and Physical Boundaries," in *The Refugee Crisis and Religion: Secularism, Security and Hospitality in Question,* ed. Luca Mavelli and Erin K. Wilson (London: Rowman & Littlefield, 2017), 1-22, at 6-9; and Elena Fiddian-Qasmiyeh, "The Faith-Gender-Asylum Nexus: An Intersectionalist Analysis of Representation of the 'Refugee Crisis,'" in Mavelli and Wilson, *Refugee Crisis and Religion,* 207-22, at 209-11. Fiddian-Qasmiyeh notes the contrast with the Cold War in which asylum seekers from Eastern Europe and Vietnam were cast as courageous opponents of communism and welcomed by Western states.

seeks to drastically reduce the opportunities for people fleeing violence in Central America to claim and attain asylum in the United States. To this end, the administration has pursued an evolving set of strategies, targeting both those seeking legal entry and those who enter without documentation. In 2018, those wishing to present themselves at legal ports of entry at the US-Mexico border to apply for asylum were subjected to a practice of "metering," waiting weeks or months near the border. Only a few were granted the opportunity each day to present themselves for asylum.[66] Those who chose instead to cross the border without documentation, present themselves to a border agent, and ask for asylum—which they are entitled to do under both domestic and international law—were made the subject of a presidential order prohibiting them from securing permanent legal status in the United States. Fortunately, the US Supreme Court upheld a federal judge's finding that Trump's order violated US law allowing people to seek asylum whether or not they arrive at an official point of entry.[67] But other strategies of deterrence were constructed in its place. An increasing proportion of asylum seekers were placed in detention within the United States, often for many months, while their applications were processed. In 2019, the administration instituted a "Remain in Mexico" policy, sending tens of thousands of asylum seekers back to Mexico to await for their legal proceedings to be conducted.[68] It then pressured Guatemala, El Salvador, and Honduras to sign "safe third country" agreements, according to which asylum seekers must request asylum in the first "safe country" that they enter and, if they do not do this and instead proceed onwards to the United States, they can be returned to the "safe country." These "safe countries," it should be noted, have some of the highest rates of murder and gender-based violence in the world. The combination of the "Remain in Mexico" policy and the "safe country agreements" have made it incredibly difficult for people fleeing persecution and violence in Central America to request and receive asylum at the US-Mexico border.

At the time of writing, in 2020, while some of these more recent developments are being challenged in the US courts, the administration has used the COVID-19 pandemic to justify tightening border controls and putting the

[66]Dara Lind, "The US Has Made Migrants at the Border Wait for Months to Apply for Asylum. Now the Dam Is Breaking," *Vox*, November 28, 2018.

[67]Dara Lind, "Trump Signs a 90-Day Asylum Ban for Border Crossers," *Vox*, November 9, 2018; and BBC News, "Supreme Court Rejects Trump Asylum Ban on Illegal Migrants," *BBC*, December 21, 2018.

[68]Richard Gonzales, "U.S. Plans to Enforce 'Remain in Mexico' Policy on Central American Asylum-Seekers," *NPR*, January 24, 2019.

possibility of asylum for forcibly displaced people even further out of reach. Among numerous policy changes, Customs and Border Protection has been using special powers under the public health emergency to remove immediately all asylum seekers and unaccompanied minors seeking protection at the southern border, and the administration has proposed redefining the requirements for asylum in a manner that would restrict its availability to many vulnerable people—especially victims of gang violence and gender-based violence.[69]

President Trump has sought to develop a narrative of a "crisis" of undocumented immigration. In reality, total numbers of illegal crossings of the US-Mexico border remain lower than they were two decades ago, falling from a high of over 1.6 million in 2000 to around five hundred thousand per year more recently.[70] While numbers of illegal crossings increased in 2019, they still added up to less than one million for the year, which is far short of the numbers seen in 2000, and they have declined again in 2020.[71] The more significant shift in undocumented immigration in the United States in recent years is the shift in the kinds of people crossing the border. In recent decades, the majority of illegal border crossers were single men, mostly from Mexico, seeking work. Today, the majority are Central American families and unaccompanied children, fleeing violence and poverty, and in many instances turning themselves in to authorities as soon as possible in order to apply for asylum.[72] Indeed, Central American asylum seekers compose a growing proportion of both illegal and legal border crossings. The greater crisis is surely not undocumented immigration in the United States but mass displacement in and from Central America—a crisis that is only made worse by US efforts to deter rather than welcome the stranger.

We in the West should also consider the absurd financial costs of our policies of containment, deterrence, and detainment and the enormous good that could be done if these resources were redirected toward caring for displaced people. Take Australia, for example. In the 2016–2017 financial year, the Australian government spent more than US$700 million keeping 1,140 refugees and asylum seekers in offshore detention on Manus Island and

[69]The Editorial Board, "America Closes Its Doors on the World," *Boston Globe*, June 26, 2020.
[70]Margaret Taylor, "Declaring an Emergency to Build a Border Wall: The Statutory Arguments," *Lawfare* (blog), January 7, 2019.
[71]Figures can be found at the U.S. Customs and Border Protection website, www.cbp.gov/newsroom/stats/sw-border-migration.
[72]Caitlin Dickerson, "Border at 'Breaking Point' as More Than 76,000 Unauthorized Migrants Cross in a Month," *New York Times*, March 5, 2019.

Nauru. That's more than half a million dollars per person. Meanwhile, in the Asia Pacific region, where Australia is situated, UNHCR was engaged in caring for the needs of 5.8 million displaced people. It budgeted a mere US$599 million for its work. It received only US$290 million from the global community. Australia contributed less than US$20 million.[73]

As Western countries focus on keeping displaced people at a distance, the costs of doing so and the risks that asylum seekers endure in order to seek safety keep spiraling upwards. Refugee scholars Anne McNevin and Antje Missbach put it well:

> At present, the diversion of resources [away from UNHCR and humanitarian actors] to non-entrée strategies contributes to the "crisis" those strategies are designed to address by driving demand for irregular passage. When licit means of transit are increasingly unavailable to those who are displaced or otherwise in need of mobility, a market is sustained for illegal border crossings. The costs of this circular pattern are high in financial and human terms.[74]

How lamentable it is that the right to seek asylum, which was the foundation of the global refugee regime established in the wake of the Holocaust, is now being undermined by those with greatest capacity to provide home, as wealthy states erect ever more complex and costly legal and material structures to keep vulnerable people at a distance, to turn them back from their borders, and to detain for longer and longer periods those who manage to cross those borders.

Certainly, countries need to carefully assess the cases of those who apply for asylum. They should limit the entry of predatory or ill-intentioned applicants to preserve the safety and security of existing members of society. Impoverished or unstable countries and countries overwhelmed with massive numbers of applications may need to appeal for other countries to help share the responsibility and opportunity to extend kinship to the vulnerable. But no country should be in the business of containing desperate people in

---

[73]Australian Government Department of Foreign Affairs and Trade, "United Nations High Commissioner for Refugees (UNHCR)," *Humanitarian Policy and Partnerships*, accessed January 28, 2019, https://dfat.gov.au/aid/topics/investment-priorities/building-resilience/humanitarian-policy -and-partnerships/Pages/un-high-commissioner-refugees.aspx; Paul Karp, "Australia's 'Border Protection' Policies Cost Taxpayers $4bn Last Year," *Guardian*, January 4, 2018; UNHCR, *Global Trends: Forced Displacement in 2017*, 68; and UNHCR, "Asia and the Pacific," *Global Focus: UNHCR Operations Worldwide*, accessed January 28, 2019, http://reporting.unhcr.org/node/29.

[74]Anne McNevin and Antje Missbach, "Hospitality as a Horizon of Aspiration (or, What the International Refugee Regime Can Learn from Acehnese Fishermen)," *JRefS* 31, no. 3 (2018): 292-313, at 306-7.

distant regions, deterring them from seeking safety, or detaining them for lengthy periods in the hope that they give up, go home, or seek welcome elsewhere. The provision of pathways and opportunities for desperate, displaced people to continue to move in search of more permanent safety and sustenance needs to be a part of any comprehensive response to our global crisis of displacement.

Addressing Root Causes of Displacement

In addition to sharing the opportunity to respond to displacement—by contributing to the care of the temporarily displaced, the facilitation of safe return, the provision of resettlement, and the provision of opportunities to seek asylum—countries should also share the opportunity to tackle root causes of displacement in their regions and around the world. There is much that countries can do, individually and collectively, to help other countries thrive and their people flourish. There is urgent need for greater investment from the global community in local peace building: remediating conditions known to be conducive to conflict and displacement, such as the presence of political, social, and economic grievances and entrenched gender inequality; assisting countries to develop effective, legitimate, and inclusive governance; helping to establish electoral and judicial institutions; promoting the full and equal participation of women in societies; and providing expertise and capacity for human rights monitoring, dispute resolution, law enforcement, and peacekeeping. There is also urgent need for greater international efforts to alleviate poverty, to assist with development, to address local impacts of global climate change, and to reduce the risks of natural disasters within at-risk countries.

Such displacement-prevention strategies, in addition to preventing suffering, represent value for money. Migration scholar Michael Clemens, for example, finds that, on average, a prevented homicide in the Northern Triangle of Central America leads to four fewer unaccompanied child migrants being apprehended in the United States. And yet the United States spends roughly ten times as much on managing the arrivals of unaccompanied child migrants, at a cost of $50,000 per apprehension, as it does on assisting with the prevention of violence in the Northern Triangle. Clemens concludes that greater funding of regional security measures would be "a bargain for U.S. taxpayers."[75]

---

[75]Michael Clemens, "Regional Security Means Border Security: New Data on Why Central American Children Flee to the United States," *War on the Rocks*, November 30, 2017.

These country-specific displacement-prevention strategies, however, need to be accompanied by more fundamental changes in how countries relate to each other. The deeper roots of displacement, after all, are the structural global injustices that wealthy countries have long sustained and from which they continue to benefit. If we in the West are serious about loving our displaced neighbors, we can't be content with merely responding to individual cases of threatened or actual mass displacement. We need to grapple with our role in their recurrent production.

Consider Martin Luther King Jr.'s reflections on the parable of the good Samaritan in his powerful Riverside Church speech against the Vietnam War:

> A true revolution of values will soon cause us to question the fairness and justice of many of our past and present policies. On the one hand we are called to play the good Samaritan on life's roadside; but that will be only an initial act. One day we must come to see that the whole Jericho road must be transformed so that men and women will not be constantly beaten and robbed as they make their journey on life's highway. True compassion is more than flinging a coin to a beggar; it is not haphazard and superficial. It comes to see that an edifice which produces beggars needs restructuring.[76]

We in the West need to grapple with the global structures and practices that repeatedly facilitate and even generate mass displacement. We need to confess our historical and ongoing role in their construction and implementation, and embrace the opportunity to work humbly toward renewal. It is tiresome, perhaps, to again catalogue our sins. But we need urgently to reckon with them. We must stop waging foolish wars in distant countries (think of Iraq in 2003 and threats issued against North Korea, Venezuela, and Iran since 2017); stop fueling horrific civil wars with arms and finances (think of Syria since 2011); stop trading arms to abusive regimes (think of Saudi Arabia and its war crimes carried out with Western arms in Yemen since 2015); stop constructing and enforcing global economic rules that increase the vulnerabilities of the already vulnerable (think of wealthy countries subsidizing and cheaply exporting produce to poor countries in the name of free trade, ruining local economies, exacerbating instability, and triggering displacement); and stop destroying the global climate (think of its contribution to the violence and displacement that has followed the Arab Spring since 2011).[77] So much displacement of our global

---

[76]Martin Luther King Jr., *A Call to Conscience: The Landmark Speeches of Dr. Martin Luther King, Jr.*, ed. Clayborne Carson and Kris Shepard (New York: Warner Books, 2001), 158.

[77]Guy J. Abel, Michael Brottrager, Jesus Crespo Cuaresma, and Raya Muttarak, "Climate, Conflict and Forced Migration," *Global Environmental Change* 54 (January 2019): 239-49.

kin could be avoided if the world's most powerful, wealthy countries were to cease harming strangers for their own benefit.

The church has a profound opportunity to encourage a radical shift in how the global community deals with the present crisis of forced displacement. The task is far from easy, particularly in an age of resurgent nationalism and international antagonism. Yet about a third of the global population presently confesses Jesus Christ as Lord. If Christ followers lived out faithfully the biblical ethic of kinship with displaced people, global politics could change overnight.

There are some signs that the global community understands the need for renewed engagement with the plight of displaced people. In December 2018, an overwhelming majority of countries voted at the United Nations in favor of a *Global Compact on Refugees*.[78] The compact recognizes "an urgent need for more equitable sharing of the burden and responsibility for hosting and supporting the world's refugees, while taking account of existing contributions and the differing capacities and resources among States." With this in mind, the compact "intends to provide a basis for predictable and equitable burden- and responsibility-sharing among all United Nations Member States, together with other relevant stakeholders." To this end, countries have committed themselves to ease pressures on host countries via humanitarian assistance and development cooperation, to support conditions in countries of origin for safe and dignified return, and to expand access to resettlement in third countries.[79] In the compact countries have also recognized the need to address the root causes of displacement, including, significantly, climate change.[80]

The compact reveals a clear recognition that countries need to do significantly more for the sake of displaced people and also an understanding that countries are unwilling for now to commit to anything concrete. It purports to represent "the political will and ambition of the international community as a whole." But it acknowledges that it is not legally binding and refrains from offering any tangible, measurable targets for countries to meet, either individually or collectively. Rather, it is to be "operationalized through voluntary contributions" from countries.[81]

With respect to resettlement, the compact lays down that "UNHCR—in cooperation with States and relevant stakeholders—will devise a three-year

---

[78]UNHCR, *Global Compact on Refugees, A/73/12 (Part II)*, September 13, 2018, www.unhcr.org/gcr/GCR _English.pdf.

[79]UNHCR, *Global Compact on Refugees*, 3, 4.

[80]UNHCR, *Global Compact on Refugees*, 2.

[81]UNHCR, *Global Compact on Refugees*, 3.

strategy (2019–2021) to increase the pool of resettlement places, including countries not already participating in global resettlement efforts." It adds that "pledges will be sought, as appropriate, to establish or strengthen good practices in resettlement programs," including, for example, prioritizing the resettlement of people in situations of protracted displacement and dedicating resettlement places for emergency or urgent cases identified by UNHCR.[82] A draft of a 2016 agreement that formed the basis for the 2018 compact included a provision calling on states to resettle 10 percent of the global refugee population each year. This provision, which would have required more than a tenfold increase in global resettlement, was unfortunately removed from the final version of the 2016 declaration and not included in the 2018 compact.[83]

Voting in favor of the compact were 181 countries. Only two countries voted against it. Sadly, one no vote came from the United States. The other was Hungary.[84] The US representative present at the vote justified the negative vote on the grounds that the compact "contains elements that run directly counter to my government's sovereign interests." While correctly noting that the compact is not legally binding, she insisted that the "global approach" taken in the document "is simply not compatible with U.S. sovereignty."[85]

This is regrettable. The compact is far from perfect; however, it errs not in its failure to protect the interest of Western nations but in its failure to do more for displaced people. It says little, for example, about the harms produced by the containment, deterrence, and detainment practices of Western countries or about the need for these countries to open up pathways to asylum. But it voices an agreement that countries need urgently to cooperate and make use of their capacities for the sake of vulnerable people. In this, it is not unlike the agreement reached by great powers at the Congress of Vienna in 1815, calling for the abolition of the slave trade. Such international agreements, even when nonbinding, can make a real difference. They are commitments to which countries and their leaders can be called to account.[86]

---

[82]UNHCR, *Global Compact on Refugees*, 18.

[83]Rebecca Dowd and Jane McAdam, "International Cooperation and Responsibility-Sharing to Protect Refugees: What, Why, and How?," *International Criminal Law Quarterly* 66, no. 4 (2017): 863-92, at 892.

[84]The Dominican Republic, Eritrea, and Libya were the only three countries that abstained from voting.

[85]Kelley Currie, "Explanation of Vote in a Meeting of the Third Committee on a UNHCR Omnibus Resolution," United States Mission to the United Nations, November 13, 2018.

[86]Kenneth W. Abbott and Duncan Snidal, "Hard and Soft Law in International Governance," *International Organization* 54, no. 3 (2000): 421-56.

The agreement, while strong, would be even stronger with the support of the United States.

But even in the absence of US government support for this *Global Compact for Refugees*, we can hope that the church will join with other like-minded transnational advocacy groups and political leaders to remind countries of the commitments they have made, both in this compact and in earlier declarations and conventions. We can hope that the church will model the cultivation of contagions of compassion and the joyful creation of new kin relationships, encouraging countries to break free from the relentless pursuit of their own selfish strategic and economic interests, persuading them to embrace and institutionalize new habits of love for the vulnerable, and to cooperate and accept risks and costs for the sake of our displaced global kin.

Conclusion

KINSHIP CREATIVITY

EMILY PARSONS DICKAU is director of programs at Kinbrace Community Society. Emily comments on the resistance some of us in Western democracies may feel toward those "others" who have come seeking refuge:

> We often forget that people are not coming to Canada just because it's a wonderful country. People are being forced to come here because they are fleeing conflict, persecution, or possible death. We need to be humble. While Canada is a great place, refugees aren't coming to steal our jobs or healthcare. Almost every person at Kinbrace would go back to their home country in a heart-beat if they could be safe there.

In this book, we have considered the interpersonal realities of global displacement, reflected in Emily's poignant comments, through the lens of kinship. The refugee knows well the agony of kinship lost but may yet hope to recover some of that sense of belonging in a new land. The person who offers welcome may well do so from a sense of felt kinship—even with someone whose home was once far away and whose customs may seem strange. Between the newcomer and the welcomer a new relationship may grow on this fragile lattice of hope for a new home, hope for new ties of kinship, hope for the human family.

The biblical call to extend kinship to displaced people that we have unfolded in this book is a voice responding to the present dilemma regarding how to respond to massive global displacement. Scripture invites us to reject the prevailing rhetoric of suspicion and hostility, to discipline our creativity and our will for a better purpose, and to take risks for the sake of people on the move by nurturing creative kinship.

RETRACING OUR STEPS

Let us take a bird's eye view of how our argument has unfolded in this book. Part one revealed the biblical call to enfold displaced people as kin, offering kinship protection and belonging. Chapter two showed how, in Old Testament times, Deuteronomy called God's people to adopt as kin the stranger seeking a home. Chapter three offered a mosaic of portraits of inclusion from the Old Testament, including that of God as a maternal protector of outsiders in the book of Ruth. We explored Jesus' creative kinship in chapter four, seeing how Jesus embraced as family those who have been denied community.

Part two unfolded in a single chapter how this biblical ethic of kinship might shape the mission of the church. It provided a transition point for the book, building upon the ethic of kinship retrieved in part one in order to show how the church's mission includes a responsibility to both model and advocate for compassionate and mutually transformative responses to forced displacement.

Part three applied these insights to nations. Chapter six argued that nations should seek to regulate their borders and preserve their identities only insofar as this serves Scripture's call to human flourishing, including the flourishing of vulnerable foreigners in need of a home. Chapter seven showed that while sovereign states have a responsibility to care for their own citizens, they also have a responsibility to care for displaced people, and this especially as Western nations are so often implicated in their displacement. Chapter eight then offered practical ways in which national communities can reimagine themselves, letting go of entrenched fears and nurturing compassion for vulnerable strangers.

Part four demonstrated the opportunity for a collaborative global response to forced displacement. Chapter nine rejected the fear-based ethic of Christian realism and argued instead for a renewed vision for international relations, grounded in a biblical ethic of global kinship with the vulnerable. Finally, chapter ten outlined what a comprehensive global response might look like, recommending, among other things, that countries collectively increase global resettlement numbers tenfold as soon as possible.

Given this biblical ethic of creative kinship, what are the next steps? What's next for you, as you near the end of this book?

CHRIST WHO WELCOMES, CHRIST WHO IS IN NEED OF WELCOME

The challenge before us is, above all, a spiritual one.[1] Scripture's call to enfold the stranger is an invitation into a knowledge of God—a theological process. And it is an invitation to know God—a spiritual process. A painting by the Italian master Caravaggio, *Madonna di Loreto*, provides us with a creative starting point for this spiritual journey. Caravaggio depicts Christ as a baby, held by his mother Mary, welcoming pilgrims who come to the door— and presumably the door represents the door of the cathedral for which the painting was commissioned. The pilgrims, who appear to be aging and impoverished, kneel before Jesus, drawing close to Christ, their host. Christ is both one who welcomes and one who is in need of welcome here, for the child himself was on the move, first to Bethlehem and then as a fugitive to Egypt. Caravaggio's painting is an evocative lens for the spiritual challenge before us: Christ as a host, Christ as a stranger.

Our journey through this book has unfolded the character of God as the divine kin-keeper who welcomes us and hosts us. Many human families have a kin-keeper, someone who works tirelessly to keep the family connected, to knit it together (in the Glanville family, our sister Sarah fills this role). God is the divine kin-keeper who adopts those who are in Christ as daughters and sons (Rom 4:1-7; 8:12-17) and who makes a covenant of kinship with the saints and with all those who are displaced (Deut 10:18-19).[2] Christ followers are those who share a Father (Mt 5:9). None of us are independent; rather, we are both dependent and interdependent. Like a child with her mother,[3] we are beloved, upheld, welcomed, comforted, forgiven, lamented, and celebrated. Everything is a gift. Everything. Even our very breath. This is true uniquely for the church, and yet it is also true for all of humanity, for God has made a covenant with every person and every people group (Gen 9:8-11). But how far we have strayed from our identity as created ones: we act so often toward displaced people as if *we* created the world or, just as foolishly, as if we are the *only* ones who are beloved. May it not be!

---

[1]We gratefully acknowledge our conversations with Anika Barlow as formative for this section, including her pointing us to Caravaggio's *Madonna di Loreto*.

[2]See the discussion of Deuteronomy 10:18-19 in chap. 2.

[3]Recall in the book of Ruth the maternal image of God as a mother bird who protects her chicks under her wings (chap. 3).

May we who are befriended by God, hosted by God, adopted by God, gratefully extend God's radical welcome to others.

God's adoptive kinship is also trinitarian. Those who are in Christ participate in the kinship-communion of the Godhead: Father, Son, and Holy Spirit (Rom 6:5). I (Mark) still remember when I was eighteen years of age, realizing that for all eternity the Godhead is in relationship, in community with one another. I remember realizing through this that at the heart of reality is loving relationship: this is the love of God, the desire of the three divine persons for one another, the movement of the three divine persons toward one another, for all eternity. As Henri Nouwen puts it: "The movement from the Father towards the Son, and the movement of both the Son and the Spirit toward the Father, become a movement in which the one who prays is lifted up and held secure."[4]

In a human family, the movement of two parents toward one another holds the children secure so that the children feel safe. The children participate in the parents' love for one another. So too, we participate as children of the Father in the divine love. We are invited to "choose this house of love as our home," as Nouwen reflects.[5] As we are awakened to the reality that we are adopted by the divine Kinsperson who is our source and protector, we are slowly and tenderly awakened to our responsibility to nourish kinship with others. We have been welcomed into a "house of love" in Christ, and so we offer a land, a hearth, a food system, a place, a workplace, a home, a community for those who are displaced.

And yet, our welcome is profoundly mutual, for in the stranger we meet Christ, as we have already seen in the parable of the sheep and the goats— Christ is not only our welcomer but also one in need of welcome.[6] In some early monasteries, when there was a knock at the door, the porter would call out: "I'm coming, Lord!"[7] Christ comes to us as a pilgrim, as the other who is strange to us beyond description. Christ is other to us in his glory as the Son of God. And Christ is other to us as we grasp after privilege, for Christ

---

[4]Henri J. M. Nouwen, *Behold the Beauty of the Lord: Praying with Icons* (Notre Dame, IN: Ave Maria Press, 1987), 32. Nouwen is here reflecting upon Andrei Rublev's depiction of the Holy Trinity.
[5]Nouwen, *Behold the Beauty of the Lord*, 31.
[6]Matthew 25:31-46; see the discussion of the parable of the sheep and the goats in chap. 4.
[7]One example of this practice is a seventeenth-century Jesuit lay brother, a porter named St. Alphonsus Rodriguez ("The Light at the Door: Celebrating St Alphonsus Rodriguez," Jesuits in Britain, October 30, 2017, www.jesuit.org.uk/blog/light-door-celebrating-st-alphonsus-rodriguez. This principle is expressed in the Benedictine Rule §53, and summarized in the Latin phrase *Hospes venit, Christus venit* ("Christ comes, the stranger comes").

came not as a divine being but as human, not as a prince but as a peasant, not as an adult but as a newborn, not as one with honor but as one who embraced shame, not as one who rose to the top but as one who was crucified. Christ desires to dwell within us as a stranger, as our God of grace. So, in the "stranger," we meet Christ through this person who is *like* Christ. In one who is in need of welcome, we are reminded of our own dependence, vulnerability, brokenness, and strangeness. When Christ meets us as one who is in need of welcome, we are jolted out of merely offering charity and invited into something mutual and transforming. In this vein, Anika Barlow reflects on her work at Kinbrace: "I may have this role of welcomer, but Christ is the welcomer. Someone living next door may be a refugee claimant, but Christ comes as one in need of welcome." Amen.

The task before us, then, is both theological and spiritual. We come to know God more deeply through studying Scripture, through prayer, and also through praxis—through personally encountering Christ in the stranger. We have spent much time in this book exploring Scripture and praxis. Yet, our need for prayer, dependent and childlike, cannot be emphasized enough. In prayer, we realize that things are not up to us and that if they were we would muck them up. It is all up to God. In prayer we remember that no matter what the crisis, nothing will stop God being God, and this should arise in us a silent awe.[8] Of great value is what is known as the Jesus Prayer, a short prayer that is meant to be repeated over and over: "Lord Jesus Christ, Son of God, have mercy (on me, a sinner)."[9] One way to pray this prayer is to take a deep slow breath, filling your lungs, then slowly exhale, uttering the prayer: "Lord Jesus Christ, Son of God, have mercy (on me, a sinner)." You can pray the Jesus Prayer until one of the five names of Jesus uttered stands out for you and Christ meets you in the way that is revealed by that particular name. The Jesus Prayer becomes habitual, taking little cognitive energy so that it can be prayed while we are in deep grief, in physical pain, or in exhaustion. Of course, there are many different ways in which to pray, and yet however we pray, as Bernard of Clairvaux taught his disciples, we should always approach the Lord in the posture of someone in need of healing. In this way, prayer reminds us of our vulnerability and humanity, forming in us a posture of solidarity with displaced people.

---

[8]Rowan Williams, "The Problem of Prayer," Nomad podcast #146, www.nomadpodcast.co.uk/nomad-129-rowan-williams-problem-prayer/.

[9]The words "on me, a sinner" are included in some traditions.

Worshiping Communities of Creative Kinship

How, then, may a worshiping community embody in its shared life this communion with God, especially in light of global displacement? We suggest, perhaps surprisingly, that *your* faithful response to the biblical call to kinship with displaced people may not necessarily have anything to do with refugees—or not in first instance, anyway. The starting place may be simply living well in your own neighborhood, as a sign to Christ's love, experiencing the creative kinship of the kingdom of God locally, up close and personal, sacrificially, and for the long run. Hopefully, this can be done by a whole worshiping community though often an individual person or individual household will shape their lives around the gospel in this way. Either way, seek to find companions on the journey. We offer four steps for you to consider as you lean into the creative kinship of the kingdom of God.

A first step toward creative kinship is knowing God, as we have already reflected in this chapter. A second step is to cultivate tenderness (Mk 1:40-41). Some of us live close to refugees, and some of us don't. Yet, all of us live nearby to struggling single parents, aging seniors, people who are lonely, mentally ill, addicted, anxious, hungry, or depressed. Indeed, are we not all broken in some of these ways? Is Christ inviting you into a time of discernment around ways in which you might express the tenderness of Christ? For example, are you being called into your local school to assist children who need help in reading? Is your church being called to start a program to offer meaningful work for underemployed people in your neighborhood? Is Christ leading you to be a companion to lonely people in your church, lonely people like you? Are you being called to care for the creation, our common home? Pope Francis is right to call for a "revolution of tenderness," for our tenderness is a sign that the Spirit of Christ is moving among us (Phil 2:1).[10]

A third step toward creative kinship is sharing life in diversity, as we explored in chapter five. Both as households and as churches we need to remodel our kinship circles around the example of Christ. How can your worshiping community begin to reflect the diversity of your neighborhood? Do you need to sing in other languages? Do you need to prioritize those with little as you set your table, as Christ did? Do you need to contemplate a broader range of issues than your preaching and Bible studies tend to address? Your worshiping community may have the privilege of sharing your life with newcomers to your country. Perhaps your church is able to step into

---

[10]Laurel Wamsley, "In Surprise TED Talk, Pope Francis Asks the Powerful for a 'Revolution of Tenderness,'" *NPR*, April 26, 2017.

a supportive role for people who have been forcibly displaced. If you do have this opportunity, enter into these relationships humbly, anticipating that you will transform and enrich each other just like two friends would.

A fourth step toward creative kinship is seeking the kingdom of God not only in our personal lives and the lives of our worshiping communities but also in the lives of our nations and even the global community. Christ's mission infuses each of these dimensions: the personal, the corporate, and the systemic. First, the Spirit works in us personally, bringing us to the likeness of Christ (Rom 8:29). Second, the Spirit transforms our corporate lives so that as churches we live as a foretaste of the renewed creation. In our shared life, we embody the love and creativity of the kingdom of God (1 Pet 2:1-12). Kinbrace began when a few faithful Christians took a small step toward supporting refugee claimants. Is there an invitation here for *your* church? Third, the Spirit sends us into the world to address systemic issues at the local and national level, and even at the global level, seeking the flourishing of every person, especially those who are marginalized. We are to integrate the personal, communal, and systemic in our response to God's grace. As individual Christians and communities of worship, we have a wonderful opportunity to invite national and global communities to reimagine themselves, to move from fear to trust, antagonism to welcome, and to accept costs, take risks, and find profound joy in enfolding refugees as kin.

For those of us who are already convicted by the Scripture's call to welcome displaced people as kindred, dialoguing with people who disagree with this ethic, even people who passionately disagree, will be par for the course. And it is natural for us to feel both grief and anger when we encounter strong resistance to Christ's call to tenderness. Yet we must ourselves be able to demonstrate the tenderness of Christ even to those who disagree with this biblical call. Ours must be a life that bears the fruit of the Spirit to animate the pursuit of biblical justice, for without "love, joy, peace, patience, kindness, goodness, faithfulness, gentleness, and self-control," we are no more than a clanging gong (Gal 5:22-23, 1 Cor 13:1). How can we call people to welcome others if we ourselves are not able to welcome those who disagree with the Scriptures' call to welcome? Our pursuing kinship for people on the move must begin with our own prayer, our own repentance.

You might recall the story of Lava and her family and their successful refugee hearing. Over community dinner at Kinbrace, following the positive determination, we celebrated. After eating, we gathered around a cake lit up with candles, and together we sang the Canadian national anthem,

"O Canada," to celebrate our friends' new place of belonging. You may not be surprised to learn that I (Mark) don't generally feel comfortable during national anthems. But this evening brought me to tears. I was overcome by the family's own tears of joy. And I was proud of Canada, that we had rightly accepted these wonderful people, these friends of mine. I was overcome as well because this father had broken down with tears of gratitude the day before, as he thought of his children growing up and thriving in a safe place.

"Borders don't make people safe; crossing borders makes people safe," Loren Balisky says in an interview.[11] And as *we* cross borders, as we soften the borders of our lives to welcome in others who bear the image of God, we welcome Christ into our lives. The most hopeful sign of the kingdom of God in the West today, in our experience, is Christ's birthing and renewal of worshiping communities that are seeking out this way. These communities, many of them small, are striving to be a foretaste of the kingdom of God by their shared life of worship and kinship. Many of these churches are encountering Christ anew as they welcome and support refugees and other newcomers. And some of these churches express the kinship of Christ in other creative and Spirit-led ways.

We sit and ponder how to conclude our book amidst the COVID-19 pandemic. Within worshiping communities, national communities, and the international community, attention and resources are being reoriented away from the plight of refugees and other forcibly displaced people and toward matters of domestic and global health. This is certainly understandable. But meanwhile displaced people remain displaced. And, living in cramped conditions in densely populated refugee camps, or in impoverished and precarious conditions in urban centers within transit countries, or in overcrowded detention centers with limited access to sanitation or health care, many are at heightened risk of contracting the virus. The responses of some governments to the pandemic, moreover, has further amplified the vulnerability of many displaced people. While UNHCR has sought to explain to governments how they might minimize health risks while still resettling refugees and upholding the right to seek asylum, borders have been shut tight, resettlement offerings have been substantially reduced, and asylum seekers have been turned away from points of entry and even summarily deported from within states.[12]

---

[11]For more on the Worn Words media project this interview was part of see www.eringoheenglanville .com.

[12]Jeff Crisp, "The End of Asylum?" *United Against Inhumanity*, July 15, 2020; Mark Akkerman, "COVID-19 and Border Politics," *Border Wars Briefing*, July 2020.

In contrast to such reflexively exclusionary practices, churches, nations, and international bodies are in many ways showing remarkable flexibility in their response to the pandemic. Many are displaying significant capacities to reimagine themselves and their purposes, policies, and procedures. Churches have been forced to reimagine how they meet together, how they care for vulnerable members, and how they love their neighbors. Nations are rapidly reorienting their health and social security systems, with many finding the money for enormous stimulus packages aimed at preserving livelihoods and securing the well-being of citizens. International organizations are striving to offer possibilities of coordination and cooperation among states to stop the spread of the virus, to reduce its terrible impact, and to help communities recover.[13]

Our prayer is that we may use this enormous imaginative capacity to reimagine refuge too. For most of us, our lives have been shaken by the COVID-19 pandemic, unmoored from the stability and security to which we have grown accustomed. The constant feeling of having the rug pulled from under us, as regulations change, hotspots emerge, and news reports filter in, is surely a small window into the chronic uncertainty and vulnerability of those who are displaced. And perhaps it can function as another prompt to reimagine refuge—to reimagine how, in a time when we all feel a heightened degree of vulnerability, we may offer safety, community, and kinship to those who are displaced and especially in need.

Mark's nine-year-old daughter is speaking on the phone to one of her best friends, the daughter of Sahel (whose refugee experience appeared in chapter six). A parcel just arrived at the door: face masks to protect us from contracting the virus—a gift from Sahel. This moment is a living reminder that Christ's invitation to kinship is a gift to be received with joy. And what a joy it is, to reimagine refuge! What a joy, to bring biblical kinship into global politics!

---

[13]See for example Editorial Board, "The Pandemic Has Made Europe Stronger," *Washington Post*, July 29, 2020.

DISCUSSION QUESTIONS

THE BIBLE

- What is the significance, for you, that God has a covenant relationship with displaced people? (Remember the use of the word *love* in Deut 10:17-19 discussed in chapter one.)

- How would you describe the "Way of Christ"? (Recall our discussion of Jesus' kinship in chapter four.)

THE CHURCH

- What does a missional church (a church that is on the move) have in common with refugees? (See "Human Movement and God's Mission," in chapter five.)

- As you read this book, is there an invitation for your own worshiping community or for your own life?

THE NATION

- What is the self-conception of the nation-state in which you reside and how might this national identity be reimagined so that it is more oriented toward justice? (Recall our discussion of national identity in chapter six.)

- For whom are our nation-states responsible? (Recall our discussion of sovereignty, citizenship, proximity, and culpability in chapter seven.)

THE WORLD

- How might existing approaches to international relations be reshaped by an ethic of global kinship? (See our discussion of hope for global kinship in chapter nine.)

- How might your country work with others to better care for and provide welcome to forcibly displaced people? (See our discussion of global cooperation in chapter ten.)

FURTHER READING

BIBLICAL ETHICS AND THEOLOGY

Annan, Kent. *You Welcomed Me: Loving Refugees and Immigrants Because God First Loved Us.* Downers Grove, IL: InterVarsity Press, 2018.

Bauman, Stephan, Matthew Soerens, and Issam Smeir. *Seeking Refuge: On the Shores of the Global Refugee Crisis.* Chicago: Moody Publishers, 2016.

Brett, Mark G. *Political Trauma and Healing: Biblical Ethics for a Postcolonial World.* Grand Rapids, MI: Eerdmans, 2016.

Carroll R. (Rodas), M. Daniel. *The Bible and Borders: Hearing God's Word on Immigration.* Grand Rapids, MI: Brazos Press, 2020.

Glanville, Mark R. *Adopting the Stranger as Kindred in Deuteronomy.* AIL 33. Atlanta: SBL Press, 2018.

Heimburger, Robert W. *God and the Illegal Alien: United States Immigration Law and a Theology of Politics.* Cambridge: Cambridge University Press, 2018.

Heyer, Kristin E. *Kinship Across Borders: A Christian Ethic of Immigration.* Washington, DC: Georgetown University Press, 2012.

Hollenbach, David, SJ. *Humanity in Crisis: Ethical and Religious Response to Refugees.* Washington, DC: Georgetown University Press, 2019.

Houston, Fleur S. *You Shall Love the Stranger as Yourself: The Bible, Refugees, and Asylum.* London: Routledge, 2015.

Kaemingk, Matthew. *Christian Hospitality and Muslim Immigration in an Age of Fear.* Grand Rapids, MI: Eerdmans, 2018.

Pope Francis. *A Stranger and You Welcomed Me: A Call to Mercy and Solidarity with Migrants and Refugees.* Maryknoll, NY: Orbis, 2018.

Rajendra, Tisha M. *Migrants and Citizens: Justice and Responsibility in the Ethics of Immigration.* Grand Rapids, MI: Eerdmans, 2017.

Snyder, Susanna. *Asylum Seeking, Migration and Church.* Surrey, UK: Ashgate, 2012.

Soerens, Matthew, and Jenny Yang. *Welcoming the Stranger: Justice, Compassion & Truth in the Immigration Debate*, rev. ed. Downers Grove, IL: InterVarsity Press, 2018.

REFUGEE STUDIES

Espiritu, Yen Le. *Body Counts: The Vietnam War and Militarized Refugees.* Oakland: University of California Press, 2014.

Fiddian-Qasmiyeh, Elena, Gil Loescher, Katy Long, and Nando Sigona, eds. *The Oxford Handbook of Refugee and Forced Migration Studies.* Oxford: Oxford University Press, 2014.

Glanville, Erin G. "Creatures in a Small Place: Postcolonial Literature, Globalization and Stories of Refugees." In *The Gospel and Globalization*, edited by Michael W. Goheen and Erin G. Glanville, 269–282. Vancouver: Regent College Publishing, 2009.

Nguyen, Viet Thanh, ed. *The Displaced: Refugee Writers on Refugee Lives*. New York: Abrams, 2018.

HISTORY

El-Enany, Nadine. *(B)ordering Britain: Law, Race and Empire*. Manchester: Manchester University Press, 2020.

Gatrell, Peter. *The Making of the Modern Refugee*. Oxford: Oxford University Press, 2013.

Orchard, Phil. *A Right to Flee: Refugees, States, and the Construction of International Co-operation*. Cambridge: Cambridge University Press, 2014.

POLITICAL THEORY

Bauman, Zygmunt. *Strangers at Our Door*. Cambridge: Polity, 2016.

Carens, Joseph H. *The Ethics of Immigration*. Oxford: Oxford University Press, 2013.

Fine, Sarah, and Lea Ypi, eds. *Migration in Political Theory: The Ethics of Movement and Membership*. Oxford: Oxford University Press, 2016.

INTERNATIONAL RELATIONS

Aleinikoff, T. Alexander, and Leah Zamore. *The Arc of Protection: Reforming the International Refugee Regime*. Stanford: Stanford University Press, 2019.

Fitzgerald, David Scott. *Refuge Beyond Reach: How Rich Democracies Repel Asylum Seekers*. Oxford: Oxford University Press, 2019.

Mehta, Suketu. *This Land Is Our Land: An Immigrant's Manifesto*. London: Penguin, 2019.

REFUGEE FICTION

Hill, Lawrence. *The Illegal: A Novel*. New York: W. W. Norton, 2015.

Hosseini, Khaled. *Sea Prayer*. London: Bloomsbury, 2018.

Thien, Madeleine. *Dogs at the Perimeter*. New York: W. W. Norton, 2011.

CHILDREN'S BOOKS

K'Naan. *When I Get Older: The Story Behind "Wavin' Flag."* New York: Tundra Books, 2012.

Roberts, Ceri, and Hanane Kai. *Children in Our World: Refugees and Migrants*. New York: B.E.S., 2017.

Trottier, Maxine, and Isabelle Arsenault. *Migrant*. Toronto: Groundwood, 2011.

DOCUMENTARIES

Boochani, Behrouz, and Arash Kamali Sarvestani. *Chauka, Please Tell Us the Time*. Sarven Productions, 2017.

Goheen Glanville, Erin. *Borderstory* and *Listening.* Worn Words, 2020. https://www.erin
    goheenglanville.com/borderstory.
Orner, Eva. *Chasing Asylum.* 2016.

Memoirs

Boochani, Behrouz. *No Friend but the Mountains.* London: Picador, 2018.
Bui, Thi. *The Best We Could Do.* New York: Abrams Comic Arts, 2017.
Do, Anh. *The Happiest Refugee.* Crows Nest, NSW: Allen & Unwin, 2010.
Leddy, Mary Jo. *At the Border Called Hope: Where Refugees Are Neighbours.* New York:
    HarperCollins, 1997.
Kurdi, Tima. *The Boy on the Beach: My Family's Escape from Syria and Our Hope for a New
    Home.* New York: Simon & Schuster, 2019.
Scholtens, Martina, MD. *Your Heart Is the Size of Your Fist: A Doctor Reflects on Ten Years
    at a Refugee Clinic.* Victoria, BC: Brindle & Glass, 2017.

AUTHOR INDEX

SUBJECT INDEX

SCRIPTURE INDEX